MW01285931

THE SECOND PEARL HARBOR

THE SECOND PEARL HARBOR
The West Loch Disaster, May 21, 1944

GENE ERIC SALECKER

UNIVERSITY OF OKLAHOMA PRESS : NORMAN

Also by Gene Eric Salecker
Disaster on the Mississippi: The Sultana Explosion, April 27, 1865
 (Annapolis, 1996)
Fortress Against the Sun: The B-17 Flying Fortress in the Pacific
 (Cambridge, MA, 2001).
*Rolling Thunder against the Rising Sun: The Combat History of U.S. Army
 Tank Battalions in the Pacific in World War II* (Mechanicsburg, PA,
 2008)
*Blossoming Silk against the Rising Sun: U.S. and Japanese Paratroopers at
 War in the Pacific in World War II* (Mechanicsburg, PA, 2010)

Library of Congress Cataloging-in-Publication Data
Salecker, Gene Eric, 1957–
 The Second Pearl Harbor : the West Loch Disaster, May 21, 1944 / Gene
Eric Salecker.
    pages cm
 Includes bibliographical references and index.
 ISBN 978-0-8061-4476-4 (hardcover : alk. paper) 1. World War,
1939–1945—Hawaii—Pearl Harbor. 2. Marine accidents—Hawaii—Pearl
Harbor—History—20th century. 3. Explosions—Hawaii—Pearl Harbor—
History—20th century. I. Title.
 D767.92.S33 2014
 940.54'26693—dc23
                    2013046738

1 2 3 4 5 6 7 8 9 10

To my nieces, Casey and Elise,
May you grow up to be strong, beautiful, independent women

Contents

Illustrations

Photographs

Diagrams

Maps

Introduction

In mid-May 1944, the Americans in the Pacific were knocking on the outer defensive ring of the Japanese. GEN Douglas MacArthur was continuing his leapfrog tactics along the northern coast of New Guinea, striking at Sarmi on the northwest coast on 17 May and at the nearby island of Wakde on 18 May. In the Central Pacific, ADM Chester Nimitz was getting ready to attack and seize the Mariana Islands. With Saipan, the northernmost island in the chain, only 1,270 miles from Tokyo, seizure of that important island would place Japanese cities well within range of the newly developed B-29 Superfortresses.

In order to transport the Marine and Army invaders to the beaches of Saipan, the Navy had assembled a vast array of transports, including forty-nine landing ship, tanks (LSTs). Near 3 P.M. on Sunday, 21 May 1944, during the loading of thirty-two of those ships in an area of Pearl Harbor known as West Loch, something went terribly wrong. Without warning, an explosion and fire on the top deck of one of the ships soon spread to several others. Dark clouds of black smoke billowed into the sky as subsequent explosions threw flaming debris in all directions. Crews on ships anchored nearby fought valiantly to save their vessels as their skippers tried to get away from the growing conflagration. When it was all over, six of the precious LSTs had been lost and over five hundred sailors, Marines, and Army personnel had been killed or injured.

What follows is the story of that terrible afternoon that threatened to disrupt and delay one of the largest and most important amphibious invasions in U.S. history. Only the valor and heroism of the Navy and Coast Guard officers and crews and the Marine and Army passengers prevented the disaster from having more of an impact than it did. The LSTs, supplemented with a few replacement ships, left Hawaii only one day behind schedule. They caught up to fleet en route, and the invasion of Saipan took place right on schedule.

Abbreviations

Ships and Landing Craft

amtrac	Amphibious Tractor (see LVT)
APD	High-Speed Destroyer Transports
ARS	Salvage Vessel
AVP	Small Seaplane Tender
CM	Minelayer
DUKW	Amphibious Truck
LCI	Landing Craft, Infantry
LCI (G)	Landing Craft, Infantry (Gunboat)
LCI (L)	Landing Craft, Infantry (Large)
LCM	Landing Craft, Mechanized
LCT	Landing Craft, Tank
LCVP	Landing Craft, Vehicle, Personnel (Higgins Boat)
LCP	Landing Craft, Personnel
LSD	Landing Ship, Dock
LST	Landing Ship, Tank
LVT	Landing Vehicle, Tracked (aka amtrac)
LVT (A)	Landing Vehicle, Tracked (Armored)
PT Boat	Motor Torpedo Boat
YNT	Yard Net Tender, Tug
YTB	District Harbor Tug Large
YTL	District Harbor Tug Small
YTM	Yard Motor Tug

Army and Marine Corps Ranks

CPL	Corporal
PLN SGT	Platoon Sergeant
PFC	Private First Class
SGT	Sergeant

Naval Ratings—Officers

ADM	Admiral
CAPT	Captain
ENS	Ensign
LCDR	Lieutenant Commander
LT	Lieutenant
LT(jg)	Lieutenant (junior grade)
RADM	Rear Admiral
VADM	Vice Admiral
XO	Executive Officer

Naval Ratings—Enlisted Men

Asst. Eng. Off.	Assistant Engineering Officer
BKR	Baker
BM	Boatswain's Mate
CE	Chief Engineer
Ck	Cook
CM	Carpenter's Mate
COX	Coxswain
CQM	Chief Quartermaster
E	Electrician
EM	Electrician's Mate
F	Fireman
GM	Gunner's Mate
MM	Machinist's Mate
MoMM	Motor Machinist's Mate
PhM	Pharmacist's Mate
RM	Radioman

S   Seaman
SC   Ship's Cook
SF   Shipfitter
SK   Storekeeper
SM   Signalman
XO   Executive Officer
Y   Yeoman

THE SECOND PEARL HARBOR

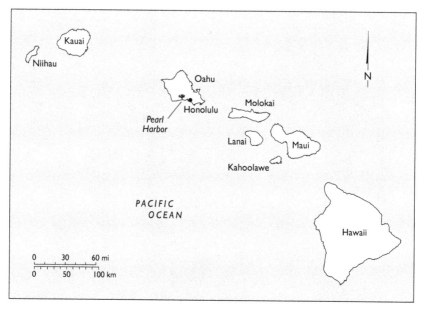

The Hawaiian Islands, the United States Territory of Hawaii. Drawn by Gene Eric Salecker, redrawn by Bill Nelson. Copyright © 2014 by the University of Oklahoma Press.

CHAPTER 1 | # Operation Forager

VADM Richmond Kelly Turner, the commander of 5th Fleet Amphibious Force, wanted his men to be well trained for the upcoming invasion of the Mariana island of Saipan. Accordingly, he scheduled five days of full-blown rehearsals to take place around Hawaii in mid-May 1944, "the biggest and longest held to date in the Pacific Campaigns."[1]

The seizure of Saipan, along with the islands of Tinian and Guam, all within the Mariana Islands, only 1,270 miles from Japan, would put hundreds of Japanese cities, including the capital of Tokyo, within range of the B-29 bombers. Additionally, by capturing the Mariana Islands, the Americans would drive a wedge between Japan and its forward naval base at Truk, south of the Marianas, which would be left to wither on the vine.[2]

The idea of invading the Mariana Islands had been suggested in 1943. ADM Ernest J. King, chief of naval operations in Washington, had wanted to win the Pacific war by driving straight through the Central Pacific toward Japan proper. GEN Douglas MacArthur, commander of the Southwest Pacific Theater, had wanted the Army to attack westward along the northern coast of New Guinea and then northward through the Philippines. Historian Charles R. Anderson reported, "A series of Allied planning conferences in 1943 failed to resolve the issue. The strong identification of each strategy with a different military service—Central Pacific with the

U.S. Navy and Southwest Pacific with the U.S. Army—tended to undermine an unbiased appraisal of either course of action and to encourage the potentially dangerous pursuit of both with inadequate resources."[3]

By the end of 1943, however, the development of the B-29 airplane made the choice for the drive through the Central Pacific the most plausible. In December 1943, the American commanders finally decided that the major thrust toward Japan would go through the Central Pacific, using captured islands as bases for the advancing B-29s. At the same time, General MacArthur would continue his drive toward the Philippines, thereby dividing the attention and resources of the Japanese. The date for the invasion of the Marianas was set for November 1944.[4]

In November 1943, the 2nd Marine Division (2nd MarDiv) and the Twenty-seventh Infantry Division (27th IDiv) invaded the Gilbert Islands. Although the landing went well for the soldiers attacking Makin Atoll, the Marine Corps landing on Tarawa Atoll was almost turned back by the Japanese. Trouble with a shortage of amphibious tractors or amtracs (officially, Landing Vehicle, Tracked or LVTs), tides, a coral reef, and a dozen other things almost cost the Marines the capture of Tarawa. These problems, however, had taught the planners that better training, more rehearsals, and more cooperation between the Navy and the invading forces were necessary to pull off a more successful invasion the next time around.[5]

In January 1944, the Americans invaded the Marshall Islands, making sure that they had enough LVTs to get them over any outlying reefs—a definite problem at Tarawa.[6] By the time Admiral Turner was ready for the invasion of Saipan, new LVT-4 troop carriers, with a ramp at the rear that allowed the occupants to exit without having to expose themselves by climbing over the sides, were beginning to replace the old LVT-2s, which did not have ramps. Since almost seven hundred LVTs would be needed for the invasion of Saipan, Turner had to use both the old and the new LVTs. He hoped that extensive training and rehearsals would get his men out of the vehicles and onto the beach no matter what type of amtrac carried them to shore.[7]

The speed with which the Americans captured the Marshall Islands—by mid-February instead of May—presented the

Americans with a golden opportunity. Realizing that the war could be shortened by advancing the Marianas timetable, the invasion date for Saipan was moved up to 15 June.[8] An unfortunate outcome of the success in the Gilberts and Marshalls, however, was the fact that Admiral Turner now had to rush to assemble his equipment and men and get them ready to invade Saipan, Tinian, and Guam.

All of the ships involved in the invasion of the Marianas, code-named Operation Forager, would come from the 5th Fleet (Task Force 50), commanded by ADM Raymond Spruance. Subordinate to Spruance was Vice Admiral Turner, a foul-mouthed, short-tempered man who had taken command of the Amphibious Force in August 1943 and had gained valuable experience in amphibious landings in the Gilberts and Marshalls.[9]

Task Force 56, the invading force, was broken into two sub-groups. Saipan and Tinian would be invaded by the Northern Troops and Landing Force (NTLF), consisting of the 2nd and 4th MarDivs, the XXIV Army Corps Artillery, and the Saipan and Tinian Garrison Force, a total of 71,000 men. The Southern Troops and Landing Force (STLF), made up of the 3rd MarDiv, the 77th IDiv, and the III Army Corps Artillery, 56,500 men, was assembled to capture Guam. Held in reserve was the 27th IDiv.[10]

With the seizure of Saipan as the first objective of Operation Forager, Admiral Turner elected to take personal command of the men, ships, and transports of the northern attack force. However, realizing that the weight of joint control of both the entire operation and the NTLF would be too much for even himself, Turner parceled out some of his duties to his second in command, RADM Harry W. Hill, making Hill responsible for the ships and amtracs that would transport the Marines and soldiers to Saipan.[11]

For the arduous task of transporting the men, equipment, and supplies of the NTLF 3,200 miles from Hawaii to Saipan, the Navy assembled 110 transport vessels including 10 high-speed destroyer transports (APDs) and 47 Landing Ship, Tanks (LSTs).[12] "Since the preferred beaches on Saipan were fringed by a reef and since it would be impossible to negotiate a crossing of the reef in conventional landing craft," wrote Marine Corps historian MAJ Carl W. Hoffman, "the landing plan contemplated the use of LVTs . . . as the principal assault vehicles." In all, Admiral Hill collected 579 troop-carrying amtracs, plus 140 armored amphibian tanks, for the invasion of Saipan. As historian Gordon L. Rottman noted, the 719 LVTs "would be the largest use of amtracs to date and would set the standard for future operations."[13]

All of the amtracs would be carried to Saipan inside LSTs. Since the long, slim LSTs had enough room to carry the assault troops assigned to the amtracs, there would be no need for the men to climb down rope nets and into waiting watercraft. Instead, the troops would simply climb into the amtracs inside the bellies of the LSTs and ride out the gaping bow doors toward the enemy beaches.[14]

The large 105mm howitzers of some of the artillery units would be transported to the beaches in DUKWs (pronounced "ducks"), the amphibious version of the 2.5-ton truck. Because of their weight, the howitzers would be loaded aboard the DUKWs in Hawaii, and the amphibious trucks would then be carried to Saipan inside the big LSTs.[15]

After the bloody battle of Tarawa, the ranks of the 2nd MarDiv had been refilled with fresh recruits from the states who had never seen combat, while most of the men of the 4th MarDiv were still considered "green," since they had captured the Marshall Islands in only two days. Likewise, most of the LVT and DUKW crews, and even the LST crews, had never before seen combat. In order to ensure coordination between the various units, Turner and Hill wanted the two Marine divisions to rehearse together, along with the LVT and DUKW crews and especially the LST crews. According to historian A. Alan Oliver, "The crews of the LSTs were . . . largely fresh and untried. While most of these vessels had participated in previous invasions, the rapid expansion of the amphibious fleet saw all too many crews unfortunately thinned by the many transfers of experienced hands to newly commissioned ships. Wartime casualties, leaves, and normal crew rotations necessitated that youngsters fresh out of boot camp or specialist training be assigned to these veteran ships. [The rehearsal] was the attempt to weld these new crewmen into tight knit teams." The five-day rehearsal was set for 15–19 May at Maalaea Bay on Maui and at Kahoolawe Island, Territory of Hawaii.[16]

In preparation for the rehearsal, the LVTs and DUKWs were loaded aboard the various LSTs at Pearl Harbor, Kahului Harbor on Maui, or from the beaches of Maalaea Bay. ENS Carl V. Smith

(LST #224) described the loading of the LVTs onto their ship. "Much of the cargo was placed by the Army quartermasters on the tank deck [lowest deck], piled about 3 feet deep. They then covered all their cargo with 1 by 6 inch rough lumber called dunnage. It was crisscrossed so that the [LVTs] could be parked on [top of] it securely."[17] Once the lumber was in place, the LVTs or DUKWs were backed into the mouth of the LSTs and parked atop the wooden supports. Each LST could carry seventeen LVTs or LVT(A)s (amphibious tanks) or eleven DUKWs.[18]

While the LVTs and DUKWs were being loaded at Pearl Harbor, some of the LSTs were getting an LCT (Landing Craft, Tank) hoisted up onto their main deck. According to MoMM2/c John H. Dougherty, "An LCT was over 120 feet long and was wide enough to just fit on the deck of an LST. They weighed more than one hundred fifty tons and were similar to a large powered barge, with an open cargo carrying area capable of carrying several tanks, a large bow ramp that lowered to open, and a navigation bridge, crew's quarters, and engine room at the stern. They were powered by three diesel engines and carried a crew of around twelve men and one officer."[19]

To get the massive craft onto the open main deck of the LST, shipyard crews used large cranes or floating crane barges. Ensign Smith described the process of loading the massive LCT onto an LST: "[The LCT was] placed on our main deck with a huge crane, mounted in a massive wooden cradle, and placed on huge wooden skids with large quantities of lubricant between the cradle and the skids. They were securely attached to the deck and equipped with a restraining cable, so that when the time came to launch the craft, it could be done in a most efficient manner." Added George Gross of LCT-794, "Whoever had the idea to put an LCT on an LST had it all thought out. . . . The LCT is not resting on the deck, but on a series of wooden skids about 10" square and longer than the beam [width] of the LCT. Both the skids and the LCT are lashed down with cables and turnbuckles."[20] In other words, the LCTs were carried to the warzone piggybacked on wooden skids on the top or main deck of the LSTs.

E3/c Kenneth Tidwell from LCT-982, which was placed aboard LST #274, recalled, "Before we went on maneuvers to Maui there was a big old crane at Pearl Harbor there that picked us up and put us on the deck of an LST. The way they did that is they had some big timbers about a foot square. They put three of them down on the deck of the LST and then put axle grease on each one of those three, and then put another two by four big timber. And then this crane lifted the LCT up and put it on the deck on those two timbers."[21]

Once in the invasion zone, the LST no longer had the convenience of a huge crane to lift the LCT off the top deck and place it neatly in the water. Ensign Smith remembered the unloading process. "All restraining chains were removed at the time of launching. Water was pumped from the port ballast tanks [of the LST] over to the starboard side, causing the [LST] to list to starboard eleven degrees. On a given signal the restraining cable was cut with a fire axe, and the LCT slipped gracefully into the water." George Gross, however, recalled: "You release all cables except one which has a special hook on it. (I don't remember the name of the hook, but it is hinged and held closed with a ring.) You take a sledge hammer to bang off the ring, stand back to avoid the flying cable, and away she goes! When she hits the water she creates a huge splash between the LCT and the LST. This serves as a cushion to prevent any damage."[22]

While the ballast tanks on one side of the LST were being filled (usually the starboard or right side), the LCT crew members were getting their own craft ready. "It takes a while to fill the tanks on the LST to put a list on her," said S1/c Walt Slater, from LCT-982. "On the LCT, they'd fill the void tanks, so that when it slid off into the water, the weight in the ballast would bring it back up against the side of the LST after it slid into the water." None of the crew was on board during the launching, since no one was sure if the craft had been ballasted right and would stabilize itself in the water. "Some of them did turtle [flip over]," Slater continued. "If you didn't have the void tanks filled, it would not come back up. If done right, it went off on the side, and the weight of the void tanks would bring the landing craft back to an even keel, and even bump up against the fenders of the LST."[23]

To add a little extra punch to the invasion, Admiral Hill had turned three LCTs into floating gunships, equipping each with eight 4.2" mortars. VADM George C. Dyer noted, "These were desired primarily to protect the left flank of our Landing Force against Japanese reserves moving down the coastal road from Garapan [a city on Saipan's west coast just above the landing beaches]. By having the [mortar-laden] LCTs steam parallel to the beaches, they would also be able to cover the landing beaches with a blanket of heavy mortar fire while the assault waves were being formed."[24]

As the big, flat-bottomed LSTs set out for the rendezvous point south of Maui on the night of May 14/15, they were fully combat loaded for the upcoming rehearsal, especially the new "LCT gunboats." Recalled ENS C. E. Gubellini, the commanding officer of LCT-963, a converted gunboat aboard LST #353, "Our LCT was loaded with approximately 5,000 to 5,500 rounds of 20mm ammunition, various .30 caliber, .45 caliber, and .22 caliber ammunition, and 700 cases of 4.2" mortar shells [two shells to a case], mostly high explosive and some white phosphorus." Loaded up and ready to go, with the LVTs and DUKWs tucked safely inside their bellies and the larger LCTs chained to their decks, the LSTs set off for the rehearsal beach, never suspecting that trouble was just around the bend.[25]

CHAPTER 2 | # Rehearsal for Disaster

Unfortunately, the weather on the night of 14/15 May was "very rough." Marine Robert L. George, aboard one of the 2nd MarDiv LSTs, felt that the weather was akin to a "hurricane." "The ocean waves kept rolling back and forth across our decks and we kept waiting for [the LST] to capsize, but it seemed to stop short just in time," he wrote. "We were down below decks for a long time while the storm raged."[1] Undaunted, the LSTs continued through the darkness and rough seas toward the rehearsal area off Lahaina Roads.

At 2:19 A.M. on 15 May, while the LSTs were about fifty air-miles south of the Hawaiian island of Lanai, the heavy seas suddenly became killing seas. Marine Corps historian Carl Hoffman reported, "Aboard LST #485, which was transporting a portion of the 2d [MarDiv], men were sleeping in a Landing Craft, Tank (LCT-988), which was secured on the deck of the LST. The weather was rough and the strain on the cables was too great . . . the craft was pitched overboard with the sleeping men aboard. Nineteen men were either missing or killed, and five were injured as the craft was rammed and sunk by the next LST in column."[2]

Marine Eldon Ballinger was asleep aboard LCT-988 when she went over the side. He wrote, "Around 2330 the sea began to get rough and within a two-hour period the sea became very turbulent with high waves. The flat-bottomed LST rocked back and forth so violently that the straps broke on the stacks of ammunition, falling on the sleeping men. Then the steel cables snapped, releasing the LCT, ripping the large skid beams loose, and the waves washed everything off the deck of the LST's starboard [*sic*] side. The LCT hit the water right-side up, except the ramp was down. I remember a crewman and I were trying to start the engine so that the ramp could be raised. It was then that the trailing LST [#29] hit us broadside, flipping the LCT completely upside down. The LCT sank within minutes with those that were still alive going down with the ship."[3]

The officer of the deck on LST #485 at the time of the incident made the following notation in the ship's log:

0219 [2:19 A.M.] Straps on LCT 988 carried on foredeck parted allowing the boat to slide over port side carrying away all port life lines, two 20 millimeter guns and mounts, ships gangway, destroying the LCT skids, damaging a third 20 millimeter gun. Six men were injured. . . . Missing are as follows: (41) forty-one enlisted E Co. 8th Marines, 7 enlisted Naval Medical hdqtrs. 2nd Batt., 8th Marines, 12 enlisted of crew LCT 988 and officer in charge.

0220 All engines stopped. Twelve life rafts launched. All hands to general quarters. 0231 lowered ships boats. 0340 Ships boats carried away by heavy seas and all equipment lost.[4]

William L. C. Johnson explained further what had transpired:

On the night of 14–15 May while en route to the rehearsal area several of the LSTs encountered bad weather. Because of the heat and crowded conditions, some members of the 8th Marines, Second Marine Division were sleeping topside on LST #485. Some were sleeping in the LCT, which was being carried on the main deck.

This LCT came loose from the #485 and rolled into the sea. The next LST in the column [#29] rammed this LCT, and sank it with a total of nineteen dead or missing and five injured.

Johnson, a pharmacist's mate and veteran of the Maui rehears-als on LST #69, was critical of the captain of LST #485. He wrote, "LT H. F. Breimeyer, USNR, commanded the crew of the #485, and their seamanship left something to be desired in the way the ship had been prepared for inclement weather."[5]

After LST #485 returned to Pearl Harbor, Breimeyer tallied his losses more accurately. Two Marines were dead, eleven Marines and four LCT-988 crewmen were injured, and twelve Marines and three LCT crewmen were missing.[6] The missing men, who had gone into the heavy seas without life jackets, were as good as dead. Likewise, LCT-988 was lost for good. The lost vessel was one of Admiral Hill's heavily loaded, mortar-equipped LCT gunboats.

As the high seas continued to play havoc with the flat-bottomed LSTs, another landing craft, LCT-999, was tossed off the main deck of LCDR Frank E. Miner's Coast Guard–manned LST #71. At 2:45 A.M., LCT-999, loaded with sleeping Marines, broke its mooring chains and slid overboard. The officer of the deck re-ported that "0245 lines securing L.C.T. to deck broke, L.C.T. slid overboard; rang general alarm. Began clearing wreckage. Maneu-vered to stay close to L.C.T."[7]

Since LCT-999 had its bow ramp closed, the vessel remained upright and "suffered little damage." However, "several lives . . . were lost when the LCT went over the side and was quickly swamped in the stormy seas," reported S1/c Karl F. Koehler (LST #242). Although LCT-999 was waterlogged, LST #71 took the craft in tow and dragged it into calmer waters off Maui. At 6:30 A.M., a salvage ship showed up to bring the prelaunched craft back to Pearl Harbor.[8]

Unfortunately, another mortar-equipped gunboat, LCT-984, was also prematurely launched by the heavy seas on the night of 14/15 May. Unprepared for the accident, LCT-984, chained to the deck of LST #390, commanded by LT J. M. Edinburg, USNR, had its engine room doors open and its front ramp came down when it hit the water. The open ramp and doors caused the craft to become "so badly waterlogged that it capsized." As the craft bobbed upside-down in the center of the rehearsal assembly area, it became a "marine hazard." Consequently, a submarine chaser sank the LCT with some well placed gunfire.[9]

F1/c Dale Moore on LST #242 remembered the accident: "We got GQ [general quarters] and we went and ran topside and then

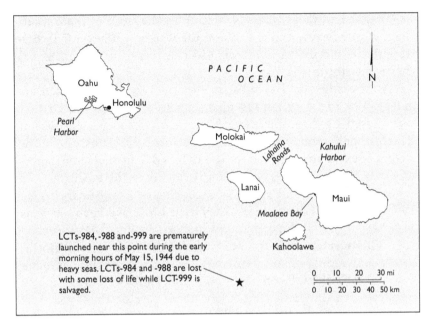

PACIFIC
OCEAN

N

Oahu

Honolulu

Pearl
Harbor

Molokai

Lahaina
Roads

Kahului
Harbor

Lanai

Maui

Maalaea Bay

LCTs-984, -988 and -999 are prematurely
launched near this point during the early
morning hours of May 15, 1944 due to
heavy seas. LCTs-984 and -988 are lost
with some loss of life while LCT-999 is
salvaged.

Kahoolawe

0   10   20   30 mi

0 10 20 30 40 50 km

The Saipan invasion rehearsal area, May 15–19, 1944. Drawn by Gene Eric Salecker, redrawn by Bill Nelson. Copyright © 2014 by the University of Oklahoma Press.

somehow or another they got permission to turn on searchlights. I know it was kinda risky there because [Japanese] submarines could have been in that area. We were up for hours, I know, and kept searching back and forth there and we never found anybody. From what I understand, the ramp was open on this LCT when they hit the water and of course any of the troops that might have been sleeping in there, man, they may not have even known what the heck hit them."[10] Throughout the night, the many ships in the area continued to search the "heavy seas" for survivors from all three LCTs.[11]

When morning light came and the ocean waves died down, the searchers "found most of the men floating in the water, but no survivors," recalled Robert George. "They either died in the water or were crushed by the LCTs when they went over the side."[12]

As the ships began gathering in the assembly area, word of the accidents was kept quiet. "Now, of course, we didn't know it until we got back to Pearl Harbor and then we heard the story through the grapevine," Electrician Tidwell of LCT-982 explained. "These

LCTs that had these mortars welded on the deck of them made them a little heavy, and they claim the weight of these LCTs that were made into mortar craft were so heavy that in the rough seas they went off the side."[13]

An investigation was subsequently held to look into each accident. The investigation revealed that the loss of all three LCTs was caused by "insufficient and perhaps improper securing." It was further reasoned that for the two lost LCT gunships, "The weight of extra ammunition for the LCT's 4.2-inch chemical mortars may also have been contributory factors to the mishaps."[14] In other words, the chains and cables securing the two heavily loaded LCT gunships to the main decks of their LSTs had been too weak to hold such heavily loaded vessels in place during "heavy seas."

"This accident brought orders to the other LSTs in the flotilla to affix emergency chains to their LCTs in one big hurry," remembered S1/c Koehler. Strangely enough, the LCTs were never meant to be used in the maneuvers. "Once you were on there you were never launched," said Seaman Slater. "Once you were aboard, you were aboard until you got to where you were going [i.e., Saipan]." When the LSTs eventually returned to Pearl Harbor on Saturday, 20 May, all of the LSTs except the unlucky three still had their LCTs piggybacked to their decks. The additional chains had held.[15]

When daylight came on 15 May, the weather continued to be a factor. "The first day rehearsal was further marred by the non-arrival of one LST Group due to the very rough weather," reported Admiral Dyer. In spite of these setbacks, the two Marine divisions managed to pull off "preliminary exercises" in "debarkation, launching of assault elements and artillery from LSTs and tanks from LSDs." Throughout the day "LVTs and amphibious craft were launched; the assault battalions practiced ship-to-shore movements; shore party personnel and beach parties were landed with their communications equipment; [and] artillery was beached and dragged ashore."[16]

On 16 May, the second day of the rehearsal, both the 2nd and 4th MarDiv landed their troops on the shores of Maalaea Bay, Maui, with the assault troops riding in on their LVTs and the artillery coming in on the DUKWs. Recalled PLN SGT Arthur W. Wells with Second Amphibian Truck (DUKW) Company, "[We were] aboard LST 354. After her huge bow doors opened and the ramp lowered beneath the water, the drivers backed the DUKWs down it for a last practice landing." Medium M4 Sherman tanks came out of their LSDs (Landing Ship, Dock) and rumbled ashore while the reserve troops practiced transshipping from LCVPs (Higgins boats) to LVTs. "Battle conditions were simulated as far as was practicable," reported one Marine Corps historian.[17]

As the DUKWs of Second Platoon were leaving LST #354, the bobbing seas caused two DUKWs to sink. Sergeant Wells remembered that one DUKW sank when "a huge wave hurled it into a corner, punching a massive hole in the vehicle's side. It headed for the bottom very quickly but the men aboard were saved." The second DUKW sank because "someone had failed to replace the gas cap after gassing it, allowing water to surge into the gas tank when the DUKW backed out of the LST. With no motor to operate the automatic bilge pumps, the emergency hand pump couldn't handle the volume of water shipping over the sides and the DUKW sank; all hands were rescued." Sergeant Wells admitted, "It had been a costly day for 2nd DUKW."[18]

On the third day of rehearsal, Wednesday, 17 May, the assault troops hit the beaches around 9:30 A.M.[19] Once again the rough seas and heavy weather caused unforeseen problems for some of the LST crews. When LST #121 under LT J. P. Devaney, USNR, attempted to disembark its load of eighteen DUKWs, "Heavy seas caused undue strain on [the] ramp breaking [the] port ramp chain." Additionally, "a short in the degauzing coil" set off a small fire which was quickly put out. Still, the last DUKW did not leave the ship until nearly 4:00 P.M.[20]

Simulating the two divisional front invasions planned for Saipan, the dual landing took all day. That night, most of the assault troops and their assault craft spent the night on the beach. Although the rehearsal landings had gone well, command personnel were not satisfied. The limited area of the practice beach prevented the Marines from spreading out once brought ashore. "As an exercise in ship-to-shore movement the rehearsal was useful," wrote historian Philip A. Crowl, "but it failed to give the troops an adequate foretaste of the problems involved in consolidating a beachhead once they had landed."[21]

The next morning, 18 May, the fourth day of the rehearsal, the jumble of troops and equipment on the beach began to reembark so that they could do it all over again for the last day of training. By noon, in spite of still "rough water," almost everyone and everything was back aboard their assigned ships, and a critique was held on board one of the attack transports. The next day, the troops would invade Kahoolawe Island, an unpopulated island southwest of Maui. This time, the practice would be a complete ship-to-shore assault.[22]

Well before 9:00 A.M. on 19 May, the big LST transports began belching forth their LVTs carrying the assault waves from the two Marine divisions. At the appointed hour, the amtracs "approached the shore under actual cover of naval and aerial fire," but did not land. Instead, after reaching a line 300 yards from the beach, they suddenly turned back. "But in every other respect this was a full-dress rehearsal," wrote Crowl, "with units, positions, intervals, distances, and other details as prescribed in the operation plans." The invasion was staged twice, once with naval and air support, and the second without. By 1:00 P.M. the entire exercise was over, and the LVTs began returning to their mother ships.[23]

Perhaps because of the continuous rough running seas, the crowded conditions in the pick-up areas, and the inexperience of many of the LST captains and crews, the threat of collision or sometimes actual collision was unavoidable. On 16 May, LST #34, skippered by LT James John Davis, Jr., USNR, and carrying a set of pontoons, collided with LST #484, putting a big dent in her starboard side, while LST #226, under LT T. A. Perkins, USNR, managed to avoid a collision with drifting ships on both 17 May and 19 May. While anchored off the rehearsal beach reloading its LVTs on 19 May, LST #275, skippered by LT J. P. Dunlavey, USNR, drifted to the left and struck LST #225, "doing minor damage."[24]

In addition to minor collisions, many LSTs suffered both minor and major breakdowns. On 15 May, the bow door on LST #34, which had collided with LST #484, suddenly broke and swung open. Although the crew worked diligently, it took all night to assemble an "emergency rig" and get the door closed. Never skipping a beat, LST #34 was at its assigned position the next morning unloading its contingent of LVTs with the rest of the ships.[25]

On 16 May, LST #275 had the chains holding the bow ramp part, which took two and a half hours to repair. Three days later, when the rehearsals were over, LST #226 snapped both of her bow ramp chains during the reembarkation of her LVTs. For three hours, while the ship moved at one-third speed in reverse back toward Pearl Harbor, the crew worked hard to rig emergency hoisting gear. Once the ramp was up and the bow doors were closed, LST #226 did an immediate about-face and raced full speed back to Pearl Harbor.[26]

On LST #222, skippered by LT A. Thompson, USNR, the trouble was so severe that the ship was forced to head for "calm waters" with its bow doors wide open and its bow ramp down. For the next few hours, Thompson fought to get his ship into shallow waters without swamping her, even calling for a tow from LST #129 under LT M. J. Prince, USNR. When tow cable after tow cable snapped under the heavy strain, Prince left LST #222 to fend for herself and headed back toward Pearl Harbor. Finished for the night, Thompson dropped anchor in about 300 feet of water to await the first rays of morning.[27]

A few miles away, LT R. J. Figaro's LST #39 went back to the invasion beaches to retrieve a broken-down LVT. The lieutenant noted, "Arrived at point [but] while lowering [the bow] ramp a heavy wave caught it and broke both ramp chains." The crew built a 4 foot high barrier on the forward end of the cavernous tank deck "to hold out water" and then #39 moved into calmer waters to begin "repairs to ramp handling gear and chains." Around 3:30 A.M. on Saturday, 20 May, Figaro reported, "Completed repairs, raised ramp." After retrieving the crew of the broken-down amtrac, LST #39 started back to Pearl Harbor.[28]

Very early Saturday morning, Lieutenant Thompson tried again to repair the broken bow ramp on LST #222. Nothing his crew did seemed to work. By mid-afternoon, as "the sea [became] too heavy," the crew built "an emergency 4 ft. bulkhead in [the] bow as a sea wall." Around 4:00 P.M., Thompson slowly began moving toward Lahaina Roads. Six hours later, #222 finally anchored in Lahaina Roads, and the crew went to work on the stubborn doors and ramp. Shortly after midnight, the officer of the deck finally reported, "Ramp up and bow doors closed and dogged." With his ship finally sealed, Lieutenant Thompson headed #222 back toward Pearl Harbor. He was more than twenty-four hours behind everyone else.[29]

CHAPTER 3 | # The LST

After the five days of rehearsals, Admiral Hill and others made an assessment. Hill deemed the activity "very ragged and poorly conducted." Unfortunately, the weather had played a big part. Still, other officers felt that the rehearsals "proved to be immensely beneficial in providing much needed supervised drill for [the] Commanding Officers of the LSTs in the expeditious launch of tractors [amtracs] at the right time and right place." Vice Admiral Dyer added, "In other words, the rehearsal served its essential purpose."[1]

Slowly but surely the LSTs headed back to Pearl Harbor on Saturday, 20 May, to replenish their supplies and diesel fuel oil, take on fresh water, or make whatever repairs were necessary. Although nobody yet knew which Japanese island was going to be invaded, everybody knew that an invasion was in the works. It was only a matter of time. The LST captains and crews had to be ready whenever they received the word "Go."

The LST, or Landing Ship, Tank, was actually the brainchild of Winston Churchill, the wartime prime minister of Great Britain. During the Allied retreat from Dunkirk, France, in May and June 1940, when thousands of soldiers had to wade out to hundreds of ships to evacuate mainland Europe in the face of the German blitzkrieg, Churchill had recognized the need for a flat-bottomed ship capable of going all the way onto the beach.[2]

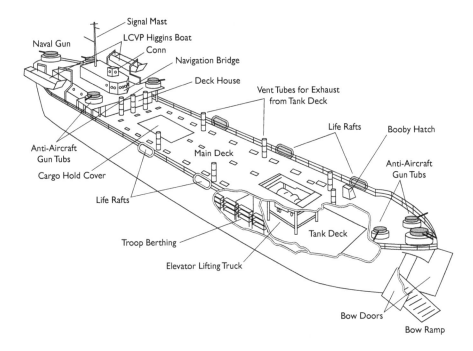

Parts of a Landing Ship, Tank. Drawn by Gene Eric Salecker, redrawn by Bill Nelson. Copyright © 2014 by the University of Oklahoma Press.

Although the Allies already had small landing craft with drop-down ramps, nobody had ever built a large oceangoing vessel capable of beaching itself. While British designers were trying to solve the problem, three shallow-draft, English-built Venezuelan oil tankers were modified to have a "blunt design" bow with a "drawbridge gate and two 68 foot sliding ramps." In order to get themselves off the shore once they beached themselves, the three ships were given a stern anchor that was dropped behind the ship well before it reached shore. Once everything was unloaded, the cable was winched back in and the ship was dragged back into deeper water. Unfortunately, these ships left much to be desired when they were used for the first, and only, time during the Allied invasion of French Morocco in November 1942.[3]

A year earlier, however, even before America entered the war, the British had asked the U.S. Navy's Bureau of Ships to design

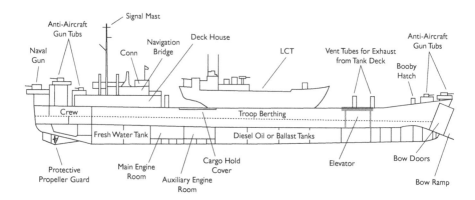

Cross-section of a Landing Ship, Tank carrying a landing craft, tank. Drawn by Gene Eric Salecker, redrawn by Bill Nelson. Copyright © 2014 by the University of Oklahoma Press.

a large landing ship for purchase through Lend Lease. John Niedermair eventually came up with the basic design. To enable the flat-bottomed ship to be light enough to beach its bow but heavy enough to withstand an ocean voyage, Niedermair ran a series of ballast tanks on either side of the hull. When the ballast tanks were full, the ship floated low in the water and was seaworthy. When the ballast tanks were empty, the ship was high and light and ready to be beached. Designed with a sloping keel or bottom, the LST, when fully loaded, would have an 8-foot maximum draft forward, and a 14.5 foot maximum draft aft. It was a simple but brilliant design.[4]

Eventually the LST was standardized with dimensions of 328 by 50 feet. Construction began in June 1942, and by the end of the year, twenty-three ships had been commissioned. As the ships continued to steam out of the shipyards, construction became more streamlined and workers became more adept at their jobs. Production increased dramatically. In early 1943, it took the shipbuilders four months to complete an LST. By 1945, the process was cut to only two months. And later, by using prefabricated sections built at other facilities, a few LSTs came off the blocks in only three and a half days.[5]

Unlike the sleek, fast ships of the "fighting Navy," the LSTs were considered the ugly ducklings of the fleet. The standard design was fairly simple. At the very bottom was a hold, divided into "over forty different compartments, tanks, and voids" containing, for the most part, ballast water or diesel fuel. About two-thirds back from the bow was an auxiliary engine room, containing three small engines that ran the lights, pumps, winches, etc. Behind that was the main engine room with its two large diesel engines. The long propeller shafts from the two engines ran aft through a narrow "shaft alley" on either side of the ship.[6]

The heart and soul of the LST was the main engine room. "Naturally," wrote MoMM2/c John Dougherty (LST #481), "the first noticeable thing in both [the main and auxiliary] engine rooms was the noise, which was loud enough that you had to yell to be heard by the person standing next to you. Next was the heat." Although the equipment might vary slightly from ship to ship, most LSTs had two main engines, usually General Motors V12 900 horsepower 12-567A diesel engines. LT Jules Fern (USCG) of LST #169 wrote, "The engine room is hot, full of valves and gauges, and sweating machinist's mates that seem in love with pistons, oil lines, and pumps. They are happy below decks—ascend now and then for coffee or a look at the sea, then back to the bowels and the copper colonic system of a power plant."[7]

Two ladders mounted inside vertical trunks or shafts, one on the forward right side and one on the forward left, were the only exits and entrances into the engine room. In case of an emergency, the engine room was a tough place to escape.[8]

Attached to the business end of each of the two propeller shafts as a four-blade propeller (usually called a screw) 7 feet in diameter. To protect the blades during beaching, a "runner-like guard" was welded beneath them. A rudder was placed behind each screw. At normal speed the ship moved at close to 9 knots [10.3 mph], but under emergency conditions it could make a maximum speed of 11.5 knots [13.2 mph]. "We were the dogs of the battle fleet," admitted SF Francis T. Hillibush (LST #127). "When we went out with a convoy we slowed everyone else down, and they'd kid us about that. But we knew we were the workhorses of the Navy, and we felt personally responsible for winning the war."[9]

The next deck up, the tank deck, was 288 feet long and 29.5 feet wide. Long and cavernous, the tank deck was the work center of any LST and where they stored the LVTs, tanks, DUKWs, trucks, jeeps, and everything else. However, only 262 feet of the tank deck could be used for storage because of a "hump" built behind the bow ramp to hold back any water that seeped in through the bow doors. Running down either side of the deck and across the back were a number of compartments used as storerooms, workrooms, and shops.[10]

Since the LST was the only "enclosed landing ship" (meaning it had a closed roof) that allowed drivers and crews of the various landing craft and vehicles to start their engines inside the ship, the tank deck needed an adequate ventilation system. Twelve high-speed exhaust fans in the "ceiling" sucked the noxious gasoline exhaust fumes up and out of the enclosed tank deck through funnels 40 inches in diameter that extended 8 feet above the main (top) deck.[11]

Built above the tank deck compartments, but still inside the cavernous deck, was a second level of compartments, known as the "wing deck." While the lower tank deck compartments contained all of the ship's stores and storage areas, the wing deck compartments were mainly for crew and troop berthing. Typically, the crew compartments were at the very aft end of the wing deck while the troop compartments ran forward along each side.[12]

Both the tank and wing decks narrowed at the bow into what Gordon L. Rottman described as a "throat" measuring 14 feet wide. Ten feet forward of this "throat" were the two massive bow doors and the bow ramp. When the doors were open and the ramp was down, the opening was 13 feet, 3 inches wide and 13 feet, 7 inches high. The twin doors that made up the bow each measured 24 feet high and 14 feet, 11 inches wide. When closed, the doors were secured with a clamp and turnbuckles and reinforced with horizontal I-beams.[13]

The ramp itself was a drawbridge affair measuring 15 feet, 4 inches wide by 23 feet, 3.5 inches long. It was raised and lowered on chains connected to a 10 horsepower engine. A brake could stop the ramp at any angle, but when lowered all of the way, the ramp rested 2 feet below the "lip" of the open bow.[14]

Above the tank deck was the wide, flat main deck, which ran from the very tip of the ship, or forecastle, all the way back to the deck house, which took up the aft one-quarter of the deck. On an LST, the main deck was about 15 feet above the waterline, although

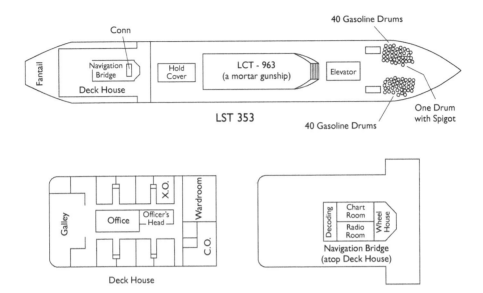

LST# 353. Drawn by Gene Eric Salecker, redrawn by Bill Nelson. Copyright © 2014 by the University of Oklahoma Press.

the front curved upward to about 20 feet to help the ship "confront the open sea." Protruding up on the aft part of the main deck were four square hatch covers with mushroom-shaped tops. As an LST historian explained, "Two of these hatches serve as escape trunks from the main engine room, while the other two serve the auxiliary engine room. Their distinctive shape does serve a specific purpose. They serve to provide the fresh air necessary for the main and auxiliary engines. The mushroom shape forms an overhang. The overhang is open allowing air to pass under the overhang, over a half-wall and down the trunk into the engine room."[15]

The main deck contained all of the armament used to protect the ship. Although armament varied on each LST, depending upon certain weapons and accoutrements that were available during its outfitting, most LSTs carried at least five 40mm dual or single Bofors antiaircraft guns, six 20mm single Oerlikon antiaircraft guns, two .50 caliber Browning air-cooled or water-cooled machine guns, and four .30 caliber Browning air-cooled machine guns, usually concentrated on the forecastle and fantail.[16]

At the very front of the forecastle was the forward armament grouping. While LSTs varied in the size and number of protective guns, the typical setup started with a large, round gun tub, or steel bulwark, at the very tip or point of the bow, usually holding a single or dual antiaircraft gun and its ready ammunition. Directly behind, and on either side of the big gun tub, were two slightly smaller gun tubs. Further back, and off to either side, were raised gun tubs equipped with antiaircraft guns with steel ready racks holding loaded magazines.

On the stern, the aft armament group usually had a 3-inch, .50 caliber dual-purpose gun in an elevated gun tub on the fantail, or very aft end of the ship, which could be used against enemy planes or ships. With shells weighing 27 pounds each, the 3-inch .50 was the heaviest gun on an LST. Back and to the sides were more raised gun tubs holding smaller antiaircraft guns.[17]

Directly behind the forecastle gun tubs, on either side of the main deck, were "booby hatches," or covered hatchways that looked like small outhouses. These hatchways, with the entry doors facing aft, led down to the tank deck. Just aft of the booby hatches, in the center of the deck, was the LST's elevator, which allowed for the storage of military vehicles atop the open deck. With an opening of 13.5 feet by 23.5 feet, the elevator could support a 10-ton vehicle and was raised and lowered by four steel cables worked by a 20 horsepower winch. Steel guideposts were placed upright from the tank deck just outside of the four corners to give support and guidance while the elevator was in use. The process of erecting or removing these guideposts took about an hour and a half. In order to allow passage back and forth inside the tank deck, however, the guideposts had to be removed. Once the guideposts were in place, the elevator could lift a vehicle in about 56 seconds and lower one in 52. As Rottman explained, "It required 2½–3 minutes to drive a vehicle on, raise it, drive it off, and lower [the elevator] for the next."[18]

Although the center portion of the main deck was wide open for the stowage of cargo, vehicles, or an LCT, a cargo hatch, measuring 16 feet by 29 feet, 9 inches, was located near the far aft end, just in front of the deckhouse. This hatch opening allowed large items of cargo to be loaded by crane down into the tank deck, where the items were usually stored behind the parked vehicles. Once the loading was completed, the crew laid four I-beams over the wide opening and then placed 2-inch-thick rectangular wooden panels atop the beams. A heavy tarpaulin was then secured over the covered opening to weatherproof the hatch for high seas.[19]

A deckhouse, the home and sanctuary of the ship's officers, occupied the rear one-quarter of the main deck. Measuring approximately 35 by 65 feet, the deckhouse contained the captain's cabin, officers' cabins, officers' wardroom (dining room), pantry, galley (kitchen), and lavatory. Although nothing fancy, "Officer's country" was still better than the accommodations allotted the enlisted men.[20]

Immediately behind the deckhouse was the fantail. The aft gun tubs took up most of the space, but there was still room enough for the all-important stern capstan. Connected to a 3,000-pound Danforth kedge anchor with 900 feet of 1-5/8-inch steel cable, the stern capstan was the main device used to get an LST off the beach.[21] LST veteran Joseph Panicello explained how the stern anchor was used in his novel *A Slow Moving Target: The LST of World War II.*

> In the back of the [deckhouse] . . . there is a huge motor powered capstan that is used to reel in the rear anchor. The cable for the rear anchor is a 900-foot galvanized wire [cable] that has a mark every 100 feet. . . . Before an LST is to be beached during an invasion, [the] rear anchor will be dropped off the stern of the ship at a specific time as it approaches the beach. The object of this anchor is to help pull the LST back out and off the beach by reeling it in with a capstan, and with the support of the main engines running at full speed astern and its screws in reverse. This is the only way an LST can pull itself off of the beach and out into the open sea. It's quite an operation but it does become much easier after the ship is unloaded of its heavy cargo making the bow lighter and not wedged into the sand.[22]

Atop the deckhouse stood the navigation bridge. Although small, the bridge contained the wheelhouse, radio room, chartroom, degaussing room (where the magnetic field of the ship was neutralized), and the captain's sea cabin. When underway, the captain rarely slept in his quarters but instead spent his time in the sea cabin, near at hand and ready to give an order or make a decision in a hurry.[23]

Erected atop the bridge was a rectangular conning station, or conn, open at the top except for a canvas covering to keep the sun off. From this location, the captain or officer of the deck would oversee the maneuvering of the ship and pass down orders to the bridge. Dougherty recalled, "The speed and direction of travel of the ship was controlled from the conning tower by the Officer of the Deck, who would instruct a man stationed in the wheelhouse area of the bridge to ring up the correct speed on the engine room annunciators. This method was used for major changes in speed, from stop, to slow, to half, to full, or to flank speed and either ahead or astern. This speed and direction would be indicated on the annunciators in the engine room, and the man on the electric throttles would adjust the throttles accordingly."[24]

The elevated height of the conn was supposed to give the officer a full view of where the ship was going. However, because the LST was so long, it was difficult even from the elevated conn to see what was immediately in front of the bow. To correct this, another officer had to stand on the forecastle and use a headset and telephone to "relay steering instructions and closure rate [to the conn] when beaching or docking." Because of the importance of both the conn and the bridge, they were the only two sections of the ship, other than the gun tubs, to be reinforced with steel for protection against splinter fragments. Finally, rounding out the LST were two 1,000-watt incandescent signal searchlights on either side of the conn, the ships' radio antenna/flag mast behind the conn, several Carley float life rafts positioned along the side railings, and at least one pair of lifeboat davits, each usually holding an LCVP (Landing Craft, Vehicle, Personnel) on opposite sides of the deckhouse.[25]

Some of the LSTs fitted out for the invasion of Saipan also carried floating pontoons attached to either side of the hull. Since many invasion beaches were too shallow even for the flat-bottomed LSTs to get in close enough, floating pontoons had been designed to fill in the gap between the dry sand and the end of the LST's ramp. Ensign Carl Smith, from LST #224, wrote about the pontoon his ship carried and launched during a previous invasion:

"Pontoons were made up of steel cubes measuring 6' × 6' × 6'. The steel was about ⅛" thick. These cubes were joined together by 6' steel angle irons, and the pontoon could be as long as the need dictated. . . . We carried two of these double wide pontoons, mounted on each side of the ship, hanging out over the water. . . . Cables lashed it into place. When it came time to launch, the cables were released and the pontoon fell into the water."[26]

Dougherty recalled how the pontoons were attached: "Pontoon mounting brackets were welded along both sides of the hull near the waterline. After the pontoon brackets were added, four big pontoons were mounted, two on each side of the ship. A crane lifted the pontoons on their sides and lowered them so the bottom of the pontoon rested in the mounting brackets. They were held tight to the side of the ship by chains fastened to the deck. We were to drop them at some future location by removing the chains and allowing the pontoons to fall into the water alongside the ship."[27]

In order to operate a ship with the size and capabilities of an LST, the Navy needed 8–10 officers and 100–115 men. The commanding officer, or CO, usually had the rank of lieutenant or lieutenant, junior grade. Other officers included the executive officer, the second in command, called the XO, and first lieutenant, both typically with a rank of lieutenant (jg), the engineering officer, communications officer, gunnery officer, supply or stores officer, operations officer, assistant first lieutenant, and a watch officer, all usually, but not always, with the rank of ensign.[28]

Among the enlisted men were radiomen, electricians, motor machinist's mates (responsible for running the diesel engines), gunner's mates (tasked with firing the various guns and defending the ship), pharmacist's mates (a sort of medic), a cook, a baker, and dozens of other trained men. Typically, two or three men were trained to perform the same task.[29] When all of the officers and men were on board, and the decks, compartments, engines, cables, wires, etc., were put together, the LST proved to be a remarkable, durable military vessel.

During World War II, the United States built 1,051 LSTs in sixteen shipyards, some even in "cornfield yards" established along the Illinois and Ohio Rivers. Capable of carrying a half dozen kinds of fighting vehicles inside its tank deck or atop its flat exposed main deck, the LST would see use in both Europe and the Pacific and gain a reputation as a versatile, reliable workhorse. Nicknamed the "Large Slow Target" because of its sluggish speed, the LST proved to be a very rugged ship. Throughout the course of the war, only twenty-six LSTs were lost to enemy action, while another thirteen were lost to accidents or rough seas.[30] Unfortunately, six were lost on 21 May 1944, in the calm, shallow waters of West Loch, Pearl Harbor, Territory of Hawaii.

Typical LST underway. Photo by LT Hal Bleyhl, CO USS LST #1080.

LST with open bow doors and lowered ramp beached at Normandy, June 12, 1944. Courtesy of the U.S. National Archives.

LST piggybacking an LCT to the battlefront. Courtesy of Real War Photos Galleries.

LST piggybacking an LCT. Note the LCT is carrying a Higgins boat (LCVP) (left) and a small patrol boat. Courtesy of Real War Photos Galleries.

LST underway with a pontoon section strapped to her side. Courtesy of Real War Photos Galleries.

A typical deck load for an LST involved in an invasion. Courtesy of Real War Photos Galleries.

LSTs loaded for the invasion of Italy. The LSTs in West Loch were similarly
crowded and berthed next to each other. Courtesy of Real War Photos
Galleries.

CHAPTER 4 | West Loch, Pearl Harbor

Most of the LSTs that had participated in the Maui rehearsals returned to Pearl Harbor on the island of Oahu. Some had incurred minor damage and needed to repair the dents, dinks, and scrapes before setting out for the invasion beaches. Almost all were returning to replenish the ammunition and high-octane aviation gasoline that the LVTs and DUKWs had used up in the rehearsals. For the crews and invading troops, however, all were returning for a well needed rest. "We returned to Pearl Harbor on 20 May 1944 with our Marines on board," recalled PhM2/c William Johnson. "All were glad to return to Pearl Harbor, as we expected to be there for a few days. Maybe we would enjoy some liberty."[1]

In 1778, when English captain James Cook first stumbled upon the Hawaiian Islands, then known as the Sandwich Islands, the basin on the southern shore of Oahu, eventually called Pearl Harbor, was unsuitable as a port for large ships because of a coral bar obstructing the entrance. The first American ship visited the islands in 1826, and by 1893 American businessmen, in order to gain favorable trading rights, had persuaded the Hawaiian people to overthrow their monarch and declare Hawaii to be under U.S. control.[2]

In 1900, after the Spanish-American War showed the strategic importance of the Hawaiian Islands as a coaling station halfway between the West Coast of the United States and the Philippines,

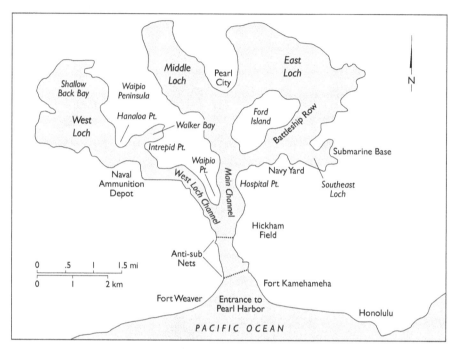

Pearl Harbor, May 1944. Drawn by Gene Eric Salecker, redrawn by Bill Nelson. Copyright © 2014 by the University of Oklahoma Press.

Hawaii became a U.S. territory. Two years later, and continuing for the next several years, steam-powered floating dredges began tearing into the coral bar that blocked the entryway into Pearl Harbor. Deepened, straightened, and widened, the entrance eventually measured about 50 feet deep and 600 feet wide. In 1910, the first deep-draft vessel finally entered Pearl Harbor.[3]

In physical description, Pearl Harbor looks like a three leaf clover. There are three main areas or "lochs," East, Middle, and West, and a long stem leading up to them from the Pacific Ocean. By May 1944, any ship entering Pearl Harbor first had to go past two Army fortifications guarding either side of the entrance, and a steel antisubmarine net that was stretched across the mouth of the channel each night.[4]

A little beyond the main entrance, past another antisubmarine net, the channel split off to the left at Waipio Point, the tip of a peninsula that separated West and Middle Lochs.[5] Built on the peninsula was the Waipio Amphibious Operating Base, where, among other things, the LCTs were lifted atop the big LSTs. "We were at a place around Waipio," recalled Seaman Slater of LCT-982. "I think that's where we were at the time before we went on top of the LST."[6]

At Waipio Point, if a ship goes to port (left), it enters the narrows leading to West Loch but if it stays to starboard, it heads toward Middle and East Lochs. On 7 December 1941, when the Japanese made their surprise attack on Pearl Harbor, they concentrated their efforts on the ships and facilities in East Loch. By May 1944, ADM Chester Nimitz, commander in chief of the Pacific Fleet, had his headquarters set up in the Pearl Harbor Submarine Base, located at a small manmade inlet off East Loch known as Southeast Loch.[7]

Making the turn to port at Waipio Point, ships enter a narrow channel leading into West Loch. "Pearl Harbor has a section named West Loch," wrote S1/c Karl Koehler. "It is a baylike area that is relatively shallow and cannot accommodate the front line ships such as battleships, aircraft carriers, cruisers, or other deep-draft vessels. Thus shallow-draft vessels such as amphibious ships and craft mostly utilized this area for loading and assembly. West Loch also was the site of a large ammunition depot."[8]

Turning into the narrow channel, a ship would have Waipio Point, Waipio Peninsula, and the sprawling Waipio Amphibious Operating Base on the starboard side. On the port was the Navy Advance Base, Reshipment Depot, where sailors who had lost their ships or wanted reassignment waited until they were given a new home.[9]

On the port side of the channel was a ferry boat slip, where ferry boats shuttled civilian workers to their job assignments around the bay. North of the twisting, turning channel was Powder Point, and just beyond that, still on the port side, was the all-important naval ammunition depot.[10]

Built on the southern shore of West Loch, on the outcrop of land behind Powder Point, the sprawling ammunition depot eventually became the main ammunition storage facility for ships at Pearl Harbor and quite possibly the entire Pacific. Originally built on less than 200 acres of land, by May 1944, the area had been expanded to cover some 537 acres.[11] In describing the area, one naval historian wrote: "New construction included twelve 25-by-50-foot, high-explosive magazines, fifteen 50-by-86-foot assembled-mine magazines, five 10-by-14-foot and three 20-by-25-foot magazines for fuses and detonators, and 11 magazines for dispersed torpedo storage. In addition, 12 other buildings were constructed to store pyrotechnics, inert material, mine anchors, fixed ammunition, and projectiles. Work on the waterfront included extension of an old wharf and the construction of a new 1,000-foot wharf. Also constructed were 9 miles of railroad and personnel structures for 600."[12]

Although civilian stevedores loaded and unloaded most of the ships at the ammunition facility, Navy Seabees also helped out. ENS James Hoyt Strimple, a member of the Thirty-fifth Special Naval Construction Battalion, recalled, "We had men down there working the docks, sure, sixteen-inch shells, two thousand pounds each. They have nose rings in them and you pick up five at a time. Pick them up, bang them against the ship, and put them down the hold, perfectly safe. It's not until they put in the fuse that you have problems."[13]

Opposite Powder Point and the huge naval ammunition depot was Intrepid Point, which jutted out to a very slender tip on the starboard shore and hid Walker Bay, a small inlet of water. The land behind Intrepid Point formed the southern side of Walker Bay, while sugar cane fields along Waipio Peninsula formed the northern shore. To the east, jutting back out into the main channel, was Hanaloa Point, just above the ammunition depot. Then, further ahead, past Hanaloa Point, was a cauliflower-shaped cove of upper West Loch. Inside this wide, shallow cove were a couple dozen small berthing spots listed as WL-1, WL-2, etc.[14]

Although West Loch was big and sprawling, most of the naval activity took place around the ammunition depot and the shores near Walker Bay. In fact, a number of docking spots, known as tares, lined Waipio Peninsula, opposite the depot. Starting in the narrow channel that led to the depot were Tares 1 through 3. Almost directly east of the depot, on the opposite shore, were Tares 4 through 7, with Tare 7 being just around the tip of Intrepid Point. Any ship berthing at Tare 7 was actually moored at the very mouth of Walker Bay. Across the mouth of Walker Bay were Tares 8 through 10. Each tare consisted of a few dolphins or pilings of wooden beams that resembled telephone poles, wrapped with iron bands and sunk upright into the bottom of the harbor a few yards from shore. When a ship docked at a tare, it simply moved up alongside the dolphins and tied up sideways, bow and stern. Loading and unloading were accomplished via small boat or landing barge. If another ship docked at the same tare, the additional ship simply moved alongside the first ship and the two ships fastened themselves to each other with hawsers, or thick lines. Both ships relied on the anchorage of the first ship to the dolphins to keep them from floating away. The distance between the different "nests" of ships was 100–150 yards.[15]

CE Lonnie Funderburg (LST #124) remembered the tares. "The pilings were multiple telephone poles pulled together, and if there was enough strength to them there might be two, three, four ships tied to one piling. There'd be a walkway or gangplank, so you could walk from one ship over to the next ship. You'd be close enough that only, what we called fenders, only the fenders would keep you from being against the other ship, and the fenders were just a big coil of fascicle rope, and it just kept the ships from crunching each other. Our ships were that close. You'd be a foot, or two, or three away from each other, so if you wanted to cross and weren't carrying equipment, you'd get up there and you'd just get across."[16]

While dozens of LSTs had participated in the invasion rehearsals, a few ships, for various reasons, had been left behind. The eight LSTs belonging to LT CDR John F. Dore's support artillery group, including his flagship, LST #272, had stayed behind to take on fuel oil and water and all kinds of ammunition and supplies needed by the two Marine Corps divisions.[17]

On the morning of 18 May, while the rehearsals were in midstride, Commander Dore's LST #272 moved from East Loch to West Loch after undergoing repairs to her ramp chains. After traversing the narrow channel into the loch, Dore moored his ship at Tare 6 to the starboard side of LST #20, a Coast Guard ship commanded by LT C. W. Smith. Already moored inboard of LST #20, and tied to the dolphins, was LST #334.[18]

The two vessels already at Tare 6, LSTs #20 and #334, had been moored together in West Loch since 12 May. After "much maneuvering," due to a problem with its port engine, #334 had tied up with its port side to the Tare 6 dolphins on 11 May, and although the skipper had been hoping to get a call to move to the big dry dock in East Loch as soon as possible, his ship was eventually deemed disabled for the upcoming invasion, so it would have to wait. Priority in the dry docks was being given to ships about to make the 3,200-mile journey to Saipan. On the morning of 20 May, #334 was still sitting beside the dolphins at Tare 6, awaiting orders to go to dry dock.[19]

The other vessel already at Tare 6 was Lieutenant Smith's LST #20. Sometime after midnight of 11/12 May, #20, which was also scheduled to miss the upcoming invasions because of bad engines, tied up on the starboard side of #334. On 13 May, while both ships sat idle, LT Robert S. Blieden, USNR, became the new skipper of #334, replacing LT(jg) Jack J. Reed, who was being transferred to the command of LST #127. The two disabled vessels had been at Tare 6 ever since.[20]

Another ship already in West Loch was LST #205, under LT Raymond J. Buchar, USCG. After tying up to the Tare 8 dolphins on the afternoon of 18 May, the crew had immediately set to work repairing a 15' × 1' gash that had been torn along the port bow when Buchar collided with an oil pier while backing out of an East Loch berth. "They were always doing that. They were always bumping into things," said Yeoman Ford Kaiser (LST #225). "The captains were so young . . . probably in their twenties." Worried about the damage done by the collision, the crew of #205 began inspecting and testing the bow doors and ramp. By Saturday morning, 20 May, as the rehearsal ships began returning to Pearl Harbor, #205 was still moored to the pilings of Tare 8 but with its bow doors and ramp in good condition for the upcoming invasion of some unknown Japanese-held island.[21]

One more vessel had arrived in West Loch on 18 May. At 6:35 P.M., LST #169, a Coast Guard ship skippered by Lt. Robert L. Kittredge, USCGR, had tied up at Tare 6 with its port side to the starboard side of Commander Dore's LST #272. On the main deck LST #169 carried LCT-1061, while inside it carried a full complement of LVTs, DUKWs, 105mm ammunition, sixty enlisted men, and two officers of the Army's 104th Field Artillery Battalion, 27th IDiv.[22] With the arrival of Kittredge's ship, there were four vessels moored at Tare 6: LSTs #334, #20, #272, and #169.

Another one of Commander Dore's Support Artillery Group ships that missed the Maui rehearsals was LST #480, commanded by LT H. William Johnson, USN. Affixed with a set of pontoons, the vessel was in East Loch taking on a load of supplies on Saturday morning, 20 May. "We [had been] tied up to a dock in Pearl Harbor for three days," recalled MoMM2/c Harold J. Knebel, "while being loaded with a variety of military vehicles loaded with nitroglycerin in ice boxes, dynamite, 155mm cannon shells, bazooka shells, mortar shells, hand grenades, and 100 barrels of 100-octane aviation gasoline lashed down on the bow of the main deck." Another crewman, RM2/c Arthur T. Freer, added, "Our ammunition was loaded about four foot high on the tank deck and on top of that was DUKWs. On topside was probably hundreds and hundreds of gasoline drums."[23]

In the early morning hours of 20 May, LST #480 moved from East Loch to West Loch and moored alongside the pilings of Tare 9. "We tied up to the center, inboard set of dolphins," Knebel wrote. He and the other crewmen then started preparing the ship for the upcoming invasion.[24]

Shortly after LST #480 tied up to the dolphins, LST #240 under the command of LT Kenneth P. Wells, USNR, pulled in on the port side. Like the other vessels moving into West Loch that morning, #240 belonged to the support artillery group and had been busy for the past few days taking on her complement of supplies, ammunition, vehicles, and men.[25]

While all of these LSTs were entering West Loch, USS *Terror* (CM-5), "the Navy's only minelayer built specifically for minelaying," under the command of CDR Horace W. Blakeslee, entered the loch and moored with her starboard side to a pier near the ammunition depot and across the channel from Tare 5. During the afternoon, the big 454' 10" long, 60' 2" wide *Terror* began taking on service ammunition for the ship's use. The activity would take all afternoon and part of the next day.[26]

By 7:20 A.M. on 20 May, the seven LSTs and various smaller vessels in West Loch were tied off and undergoing routine maintenance or emergency repairs when the first of the Maui rehearsal ships began filtering into the shallow water anchorage. Over the next few hours, West Loch became a busy, crowded place.

CHAPTER 5 | A Busy Saturday Morning

Twenty-five LSTs and seven LCIs (Landing Craft, Infantry) reached the entrance to the Pearl Harbor channel shortly after 5:00 A.M., but they had to wait for daylight before they would be allowed through the antisubmarine nets.[1] During the trip to Oahu, many of the amtrac crews aboard the LSTs took the opportunity to refill their vehicles. In most cases, up to one hundred 55-gallon drums of high-octane aviation gasoline had been strapped to the forecastle of the LSTs' top decks, crammed around the forward antiaircraft gun tubs to be used to refuel the amphibious tractors. Since the LVTs got less than 2 miles per gallon in the water, they drank up gasoline like a horse drank water and had to be refueled after every use. Instead of waiting to get back to Pearl Harbor, many of the crews refueled from the stored drums.

"I refueled my tractor and on that same day all seventeen tractors were refueled," remembered PFC Thomas J. Jacobs on LST #353. "My tractor holds 110 gallons of gasoline, and I think the day it was refilled it took about 40 gallons. When we refueled the tractors, we were still at sea, sometime after we completed our maneuvers." Of course, the refilling of so many amtracs left empty or half-empty drums of aviation gasoline tied to the forecastle of each ship, a very dangerous situation because the remaining fumes were highly combustible.[2]

Entry into the harbor began at 6:17 A.M. when LT Roy L. Guy's LST #42 passed into the harbor mouth.[3] Out of the twenty-five LSTs and seven LCIs returning from the Maui maneuvers, twenty-one LSTs and most of the LCIs made the turn to port at Waipio Point and headed toward West Loch. The first ship to enter West Loch and tie up was LST #225, the flagship of LT CDR Joseph B. Hoyt, USNR, commander of LST Unit Four, but skippered by LT Lawrence J. Goddard, USNR. As they entered the loch, they received instructions to dock at Tare 8 beside #205, which was awaiting work on the tear in her port bow. At 7:20 A.M., LST #225, with LCT-355 atop her main deck, pulled in gently beside #205.[4]

As the crew on LST #225 was securing the vessel, LST #274 under LT Russell Ellis Sard, Jr., USNR, moored on their starboard side. Near 8:00 A.M., the Coast Guard ship, LST #69, under LT Robert T. Leary, USCG, and carrying LCT-983, limped in next to Sard's vessel, extending the number of ships at Tare 8 to four.[5]

Throughout the entire Maui maneuvers, LST #69 had been having trouble with its engines. Twice during the rehearsals, the main engines had broken down, causing a quick loss of power in the rough seas. Only through quick actions had the following vessel avoided colliding with the suddenly stalled LST. Then, on the way back to Pearl Harbor, the engines had quit again. An oil line had broken on one main engine, and the compression test cocks were leaking on the other. "LST #69 returned to Pearl Harbor in a broken down condition," admitted Leary. Obtaining permission from a "higher authority," the lieutenant had his crew "secure the main engines immediately upon entering port [West Loch] so that repairs could be made prior to [the Saipan] sailing date."[6]

At 8:25 A.M., almost a half hour after the crew of LST #69 began breaking down their engines, LST #43 under LT William Henry Zuehlke, USNR, which carried a set of pontoons, sidled in on the starboard side of #69.[7] The next ship to arrive at Tare 8 was LST #179, commanded by LT William F. Mullis, USNR, carrying LCT-961. Like so many of the other ships on the Maui maneuvers, LST #179 had run into some trouble during the rehearsals. The heavy seas had swept most of the Marine Corps gear off the main deck, which would have to be reissued. In addition, recalled LT(jg)

King Richeson, "We had torn the propeller off the ship, and we were supposed to go in dry dock and get it fixed." The wait might take a day or two.[8]

The last ship to tie up beside the other six vessels at Tare 8 was LST #353, LT(jg) Chester A. Martin, USN. Resting securely atop #353, having survived all of the rough weather and heavy seas, LCT-93 was the only remaining LCT mortar gunboat. The seven ships now at Tare 8, LSTs #205, #225, #274, #69, #43, #179, and #353, were all facing roughly northeast, starboard side-to-port side, connected with heavy rope hawsers and wire lines, with the thick fo'c'sle rope fenders in between and gangplanks connecting one ship to the next.[9] It was the largest collection of ships at one tare in West Loch.

At Tare 9, directly behind Tare 8 and slightly to the southwest, several LSTs spent the time between 7:40 and 9:00 A.M. tying up to LST #480 and #240, both of which had missed the Maui maneuvers to take on supplies, ammunition, and, in the case of #480, a pair of pontoons. Both ships had moved into West Loch earlier that morning with LST #480 mooring to the dolphins and #240 hooking up on her starboard side.

At 7:40 A.M., LT Clyde Mack Pugh, USNR, brought the port side of his LST #224 up to the starboard side of LST #240. Atop Pugh's ship was LCT-964. The next to come up was LST #340 under LT L. Haskell, USNR. Having encountered some trouble with one of his engines during the rehearsal, as well as some damage to one of the bow doors, Haskell immediately requested permission to begin work on his ship to get it ready for the upcoming invasion. At 8:55, LT George A. Martin, USCGR, sidled his LST #23 next to #340. With the mooring of Martin's Coast Guard–manned ship, there were now five vessels tied up at Tare 9: LSTs #480, #240, #224, #340, and #23.[10]

Tare 10, the next anchorage southwest on Hanaloa Point, was empty when the LSTs began returning from Maui. At 8:45 A.M. Lieutenant Guy's LST #42, carrying an LCT on its main deck, tied up with its port side to the dolphins. Within the next hour and fifteen minutes, LST #267, skippered by LT E. O. Spring, USNR, and Lieutenant Dunlavey's LST #275 sidled in beside Lieutenant Guy's vessel. Near 10:15 A.M. LST #244, with LT L. W. Aderhold,

USNR, in charge and carrying a pair of pontoons, tied up on the port side of #275.[11]

Before the morning was over, one more LST attached itself to the four ships already anchored to Tare 10. At 11:06 A.M., Coast Guard–manned LST #166, LT Fred B. Bradley, USCGR, at the conn and carrying LCT-993 on her main deck, moored beside the pontoons hanging off the side of LST #244.[12] In only a few short hours, the empty Tare 10 had become as busy as all of the other berths around West Loch.

Scattered east of Tares 8, 9, and 10, beyond the mouth of Walker Bay, the rest of the LSTs tied up at Tares 5 and 6 near Intrepid Point. Like Tare 10, Tare 5 had been empty when the ships began returning from the rehearsal but just before 8:00 A.M. LST #242 with LT Justin W. Winney, USNR, in charge, pulled up beside the dolphins. Like so many of the other ships entering West Loch, LST #242 was having problems with its bow ramp. Almost immediately, the crew began repairs on a ship that the skipper deemed "not in condition to go to sea."[13]

Soon thereafter, LST #126 with LT H. C. Krueger, USNR, at the helm and LCT-926 on her main deck sidled in next to LST #242. Around 8:30 A.M., Lieutenant Devaney's LST #121, also with an LCT on her deck, moved in beside LST #242, and a half hour later LST #45 with LT George C. Gamble, USNR, in command, moved in beside the other ships. At 9:50 A.M., LST #34, carrying a pair of pontoons, commanded by Lieutenant Davis, "moored portside to USS LST #45" and near 10:30, Lieutenant Perkins's LST #226 arrived to complete the chain of ships tied to Tare 5. Six ships were now docked at Tare 5, facing roughly toward the southeast with their sterns pointing back toward the ships at Tares 8, 9, and 10.[14]

At 8:02 A.M., LST #273, under LT John F. James, USNR, slipped into Tare 6, which already had LSTs #334, #20, #272, and #169 tied together. The engine room crew immediately began breaking down the bad starboard engine in hopes of getting it repaired in time for the upcoming invasion. Less than an hour later, LST #129, skippered by Lieutenant Prince and carrying LCT-998, pulled in beside Lieutenant James's vessel. The seventh and final ship to dock at Tare 6 was LST #354 with LT

William A. Henry, USN, at the conn, which had suffered the loss of two sunken DUKWs and a rammed bow ramp during the Maui rehearsals.[15]

The last mooring station along Intrepid Point, built on the very point itself, was Tare 7. It soon became home to four APD high-speed transports, old World War I destroyers that had been converted into transports.

USS *Stringham* (APD-6), skippered by LCDR Ralph H. Moureau, USNR, arrived first and tied up with her starboard side to the dolphins. The next fast transport to arrive was USS *Waters* (APD-8) under LCDR C. J. McWinnie, USNR, which tied up on the port side of the *Stringham*. Near noon, USS *Overton* (APD-23) captained by LCDR D. K. O'Connor, USNR, extended the number of ships at Tare 7 to three, and two hours later USS *Manley* (APD-1) under LT R. T. Newell, Jr., USNR, increased the number to four.[16] After all four ships were in line, they faced roughly northwest with their bows facing toward Tares 8, 9, and 10.

Shortly after the various ships were tied up, the real work began. Many of the LVTs and DUKWs were driven onto land, most of them on Hanaloa Point just west of Tares 8, 9, and 10 "for servicing and other maintenance after the saltwater dousing off Maui." SGT Arthur W. Wells of the DUKWs wrote, "The first platoon was in a flat spot on Waipio Peninsula between a dirt road paralleling the Loch and the water's edge. It was only a few yards from LST 205, the first ship from shore in Tare 8 berth. The other company DUKWs were ashore on Hanaloa Point astern of the last nest of LSTs."[17]

Almost immediately after the LSTs had moored, most of the Marines on board were given liberty. Harry Pearce remembered, "We . . . went to Honolulu. We were going to have a couple of days there, give some of the men liberty. Not all, just a few of them." Those Marines who stayed behind were members of special work details, needed in the reloading of the LSTs after the Maui rehearsals.[18]

A few hours after most of the ships had been secured from sea duty, half of the crew were granted liberty. As would generally happen on a Navy ship, either the crewmen berthed on the starboard side of the ship or the crewmen berthed on the port side received liberty. Very rarely did both sides get liberty at the same time.[19]

Safe from the rough seas that had battered the dozens of LSTs during the Maui maneuvers, the ship's captains and crews must have finally felt that they were out of harm's way when they had entered West Loch. However, trouble was still lurking right around the corner.

At little after 8:00 P.M., LST #226, the outside ship at Tare 5, moved over to Tare 3, the fresh water dock, and moored with its port side to the dolphins to "top off" the fresh water tanks. A half hour later, LST #354, the outside vessel from Tare 6, hove into view, also having been ordered to take on fresh water. As LST #354 neared the tare, she failed to reduce speed. "[LST #354] Approached very close with headway unchecked," reported the duty officer on #226. "Sounded collision on General Alarm." Perhaps finally realizing the danger, LST #354 slowed and only bumped LST #226. The damage was reported as "negligible." Four minutes after 9:00 P.M., the #226 duty officer wrote, "Secured from collision quarters."[20] Major trouble had been averted.

CHAPTER 6 | # A Sunny Sunday Morning

It did not take long for the Marine passengers to make themselves at home aboard their LSTs. Although quarters for the amtrac crews and Marines were provided in the wing deck compartments, along both sides of the cavernous tank deck, many of the men opted to set up their bunks on the main deck, where it was cooler and less stuffy and did not smell of vehicle exhaust fumes. Although the deck was already crowded with jeeps, trucks, and trailers, the Marines did not seem to mind. LT(jg) Albert Norman Gott of LST #69 told the board of inquiry that the main deck was covered with camp cots and Marine bedding.[1]

One of the favorite places for the Marines was in the shade under the cradle holding the LCTs, which allowed a man to almost stand upright beneath it. Harry Pearce was one of the Marines on LST #69. "Sam and I, my buddy, we had moved our cots topside under the LCTs so we wouldn't have to be down in the hold where the body smell was. We'd have fresh air and sleep topside en route." Additionally, many Marines draped tarps and shelter halves between, around, and on the vehicles to help protect themselves from the burning rays of the sun.[2]

While some of the Marines set up their cots under the LCTs, many also placed their bunks inside the smaller landing crafts. S1/c Walter Slater from LCT-982 on LST #274 remembered, "We had cots on our deck and over the top of the whole thing there was a

tarpaulin stretched over and this is where the Marines were bil-
leted." His fellow crew member, Electrician Tidwell, added, "On
our craft we had about twenty or thirty cots out there for guys to
sleep on, and they had put up a metal support, like a pipe, and
stuff, with a tarp over the top."[3]

With the combat load that each LST was carrying, it was amaz-
ing that the Marines could find any space at all on the main deck.
"Like every other LST," Boatswain's Mate 2/c Bernard Hillman
from LST #126 wrote, "we were fully combat loaded with ammunition for ourselves and other ships such as 750 rounds of 5" 38
ammo for destroyers. The projectiles were stored in the open under
the LCT in 375 wooden boxes, two shells to a box." Likewise,
Electrician Tidwell on LST #274 recalled, "The space between
the bottom of the LCT and the deck of the LST was crowded with
5" and 8" powder cases for the guns. They were using all the space
they could to get armament and equipment over there."[4]

Although there were hundreds of military ships of all shapes
and sizes scheduled for the invasion of Saipan, there were only a
handful of actual ammunition ships, because most of them had
been sent to England for the 6 June D-Day invasion of Normandy.
"At this time there were only six ammunition ships available for the
whole Pacific Ocean Area," recalled Vice Admiral Dyer. "Because
of this, 16 LSTs had been designated to carry 750 rounds of 5-inch
38 caliber antiaircraft shells and the powder for them. Ten more
LSTs were designated each to carry 270 4.5-inch rockets, 6,000
rounds of 40-millimeter and 15,000 rounds of 20-millimeter machine gun ammunition."[5] In other words, in addition to their own
shells and fuel oil, twenty-six of the forty-seven LSTs scheduled to
take part in the invasion of Saipan would be loaded to the gills with
high explosives.

LT Robert T. Leary, the skipper of LST #69, a Coast Guard
ship, was not comfortable with the excess ammunition being
placed aboard his ship. Leary lodged a formal complaint with Harbor Command. "I objected to the way that they were loading our
ship and told them that this is not according to the book and highly
dangerous and it doesn't have to be this bad," he remembered.
"The way they were loaded, if they got on fire, there was potentially no way that you could exercise normal damage control and
contain it because it was all mixed up." The different vehicles, the

Marines, the shelter halves and tarps would hinder any use of a fire hose on the main deck. On the tank deck, the ship's magazines could be flooded with the flip of a switch, but there "was no means to flood the cargo ammunition and demolition outfits stored in the after end of the tank deck."[6]

In addition to the crates of ammunition, each LST was also carrying large numbers of 55-gallon drums of 100-octane gasoline on the forecastle. BM2/c Hillman remembered that "50 drums of aviation gas [were] stored above deck on the port bow. The gas was used in the ship's 18 LVTs. . . . The gas was stored above deck because there was no place to store it below decks." Marine Harry Pearce, assigned to LST #69, said, "On the bow of each ship were barrels of high-octane gasoline, somewhere between seventy and one hundred of these on the bow of every boat. They were tied so they wouldn't come off in high water, but there were fumes that were coming off of the 55-gallon drums. You could smell gasoline."[7]

On the morning of 21 May, CDR Joseph Hoyt, in charge of LST Unit Four and in command of LST #225, the second ship at Tare 8, made an inspection of some of the vessels tied alongside him. On LST #43, the fifth ship over, Hoyt had a conversation with LT William Zuehlke about "the danger of fire or explosions inherent in their loadings." On his way back, on LST #274, moored as ship number three, Hoyt spoke with LT Russell Sard about "the nature of the cargoes as well as the nature of the berthing." In fact, Sard told Hoyt that "if one LST caught fire due to the nature of the cargoes on board, probably all of the ships would be lost in one nest." Unfortunately, there was little Hoyt could do about it. With too few ammunition ships, the LSTs would have to transport the dangerous cargos to Saipan. As Seaman Milton H. Rhea wrote, "Literally each [LST] was a floating powder keg."[8]

In spite of the inherent dangers, the morning of Sunday, 21 May, dawned bright and sunny and promised to be a wonderful day. Activity aboard LST #267, the second ship in line at Tare 10, actually started long before dawn when at 4:45 A.M. the ship began jockeying around in order to get out of position between the other ships to head over to East Loch. An hour later, #267 was on its way, and the other ships simply slipped to their left, making the number three ship the number two ship, the number four ship the number three ship, and so on.[9]

At Tare 7, where the four converted high-speed transports were tied up beside each other, a much simpler maneuver occurred. Early in the morning, the outermost ship, USS *Manley*, built up steam and simply detached itself from the others. By 8:30 A.M. she was on her way out of the crowded loch.[10]

While some ships were leaving West Loch, a few ships were entering. LST #461, skippered by LT Charles Paul Geis, USNR, and carrying LCT-987, had hit one of the submarine nets the day before while entering Pearl Harbor and had been sent to East Loch for repair. By 8:19 A.M., the ship was back in West Loch and moored with her port side to LST #23 at Tare 9. There were now six ships moored together at Tare 9.[11]

About twenty minutes later, LST #127, with its new commander, LT Jack Reed, at the conn, pulled in at Tare 10 alongside LST #166. Because of the need for numerous repairs, Reed's ship was not scheduled for the Saipan invasion and had missed the Maui maneuvers. Before the crew of LST #127 had completely secured their ship, another LST sidled in next to them.[12]

LST #128 with LT H. T. Walden, Jr., USNR, in command had been receiving a pair of pontoons in dry dock in East Loch. During the procedure, however, the front ramp "fell to the bottom of the dry dock when the ramp chains parted." With the chains repaired and a pair of pontoons attached to her sides, LST #128 entered West Loch on the morning of 21 May and moored beside Lieutenant Reed's LST #127 at Tare 10.[13] The number of vessels tied to Tare 10 at 8:30 A.M. stood at six.

At Tare 6, LT M. J. Prince's LST #129, with LCT-998 on deck, simply switched berths. After spending the night as the outboard ship, Prince detached his ship from the tare, moved into Walker Bay, and beached the ship along the southern shore.[14]

Early that morning, Lieutenant Thompson's LST #222 finally arrived off the mouth of the Pearl Harbor channel. After struggling almost twenty-four hours to repair his broken bow ramp and get his bow doors secure, the skipper had pushed LST #222 at top speed in order to reach Pearl Harbor by 9:14 A.M. An hour and a half later, LST #222 was securely moored with its port side up against LST #461 as the seventh vessel at Tare 9.[15] The crew could now begin more permanent repairs to the troublesome ramp.

The final big ship to enter West Loch was Lieutenant Figaro's LST #39, which had also experienced problems with its bow ramp and chains during the Maui maneuvers. Although Figaro's ship had arrived ahead of Thompson's, #39 had spent a few hours at the Seabee base at Iroquois Point getting its troublesome ramp and chains repaired. Finally, with the morning more than half gone, #39, with a pair of heavy pontoons still chained to her sides, traveled up the West Loch channel and at 10:30 A.M. tied up next to LST #353, the outermost ship at Tare 8.[16]

With the arrival of LST #39, there were now eight ships moored at Tare 8. It was the largest collection of ships at one tare in West Loch. The eight ships—LSTs #205, #225, #274, #69, #43, #179, #353, and #39—like the seven ships at Tare 9 and the six ships at Tare 10, were all moored port side to starboard facing roughly northeast into a slight wind.

By midmorning, the Marines with liberty were gone. Left behind were the men who had drawn special assignments such as guard duty, fire watch, gangplank duty, or work details. Some, however, had remained behind to catch up on their correspondence. "We were listening to Tokyo Rose," said Calvin Frawley, a sailor aboard LST #179 who was writing a letter home, "and she predicted, 'You boys of the Second Marine Division will have many casualties before you ever reach your destination.' And nobody took her seriously, nobody." Another Marine, CPL Bill Hoover, remembered, "I was aboard an LST docked at Pearl Harbor waiting for orders to combat. I was listening to the radio. A female voice said, 'This is Tokyo Rose broadcasting to the Marines in the Pacific who are going to die.' She played a little stateside music, then said, 'A lot of you young men sitting in Pearl Harbor will never leave Hawaii.'" Throughout the war, Tokyo Rose, the disembodied Japanese American voice on the radio, had often predicted cataclysmic disasters that did not occur or exaggerated losses for the Americans and gains for the Japanese. Now, as before, most of the men ignored her warning. They just wanted her to shut up and play more American music.[17]

While the sailor and Marine work crews were loading their ships at the various tares, civilian stevedores, mostly Japanese Americans, were unloading 3,000 tons of ammunition from the merchant cargo ship SS *Joseph B. Francis* docked at the long wharf at the naval ammunition depot. When the civilian workers were finished, they would begin unloading another 3,000 tons of explosives from two "wooden lighters" or barges, moored about 500 feet to the west, in the shallower upper cove of West Loch.[18]

By midmorning, the loch was crowded with ships of all shapes and sizes. All of the LSTs were loaded or being loaded with tons of combustible ammunition and gasoline. Some of the ships had LCT landing craft chained to their main decks, and some had massive pontoons strapped to their sides. Most had ammunition and projectiles stored wherever there was space available, and each ship had between eighty and one hundred 55-gallon drums of high-octane aviation gasoline on their forecastles. It would only take a careless accident to set off a terrible chain reaction among vessels that were tied side-to-side, in tares only 100–150 yards apart. One little spark. One dropped shell. One tossed cigarette. The situation was ripe for disaster.

CHAPTER 7 | # Prelude to Disaster

On the morning of Sunday, 21 May 1944, VADM Richmond Kelly Turner admitted that a mistake had been made. With the loss of two of the three converted LCT gunboats to "heavy weather," Turner decided to scrap the project and return the one remaining gunboat to its original design. At that time, LCT-963 was chained to the main deck of LST #353 and loaded with eight 4.2" mortars and 2,500 rounds of ammunition.[1]

The eight mortar bases had been welded to the deck of LCT-963, but as ENS C. E. Gubellini, USNR, the commanding officer of the craft, realized, "Before there could be any cutting with the torch, it was necessary to remove the ammunition from the LCT." With 1,250 boxes of ammunition on board, Gubellini did not expect the unloading to be finished until 5:00 P.M.[2]

To make sure that all of the other LCTs were securely chained to their LSTs, Admiral Turner sent civilian workers from the Navy Yard out to West Loch to replace any damaged chains or add a few more if needed. Starting at Tare 8, a handful of workers began working on LCT-983, chained to the deck of LST #69 in the middle of the tare, while others began working on the gunboat, LCT-963, on LST #353, the number seven ship.[3]

SGT James Iver Carlson (Hq Co, 6th MarReg, 2nd MarDiv) was on LST #179, on the port side of #353, watching the civilian crew, and he "noticed civilians working and at one time I saw them smoking cigarettes . . . although there was a sign there saying No Smoking." PFC Donald Davis (Hq Co, 6th MarReg, 2nd MarDiv) noticed the same danger. "I remember noticing that on our ship, the 179, the security precautions were pretty lax. There had been considerable smoking aboard . . . most of the men were smoking, which seemed to me to be somewhat dangerous considering that we had so much inflammable cargo aboard."[4] At least on LSTs #179 and 353, the No Smoking signs were being ignored by both military and civilian personnel alike.

Around 9:30 A.M., an LCM (Landing Craft, Mechanized) carrying about a dozen African American soldiers from the 29th Chemical Decontamination Company arrived in front of LST #353. They were there to unload the mortar shells from LCT-963. Upon arrival, the men found that the sailors were erecting a long, narrow slide inside the cavernous tank deck, from the end of the lowered elevator out to the end of the open bow ramp. LCT-963 was sitting atop its cradle on the open main deck, facing forward, with its bow ramp down. As envisioned by the skipper, Captain Martin, the work party would remove the crates of shells from the LCT, stack them on the raised elevator, then lower the elevator and slide the crates forward along the long slide and into the waiting LCM. Since LCT-963 was still chained in its cradle and resting about six feet above the main deck, the hardest part would be lifting the mortar crates down from the lowered ramp to the waiting elevator.[5]

Apparently, once work commenced, the soldiers were none too careful with the ammunition crates. Three or four boxes dropped from the slide while the men were pushing them toward the waiting LCM. S1/c P. J. Marquez of LST #353 said, "While I was on the bow, I . . . saw the top broken off a couple of these mortar shell boxes that were being unloaded." Marine PFC Bernard M. Lebanowski (6th MarReg, 2nd MarDiv), a passenger on the LST, stated, "I do remember, there were at least three broken boxes of ammunition at 10:30 in the morning on the elevator."[6]

It was discovered that the unloading was taking too long and required lifting the 1,250 ammunition crates four times—from the LCT to the elevator, from the lowered elevator to the slide, from the slide to the LCM, and finally from the LCM into a big ten-wheel GMC truck once the LCM reached land. To hasten the unloading and eliminate some of the lifting, the truck was brought out to LST #353 and lifted up on the elevator to the main deck. Leaving the truck on the raised elevator, slides were placed from the 6-foot-high lowered ramp of LCT-963 to the raised tailgate of the truck. With most of the men working inside the LCT and only a couple of men working inside the back of the truck, the soldiers began lifting the mortar round crates from the deck of the LCT and pushing them down the slides to the waiting truck.[7] All the while, the civilian crew from the Navy Yard was working at replacing the turnbuckles holding LCT-963 in place.[8]

After a while, it was determined that the slides leading from the LCT to the truck bed were not working, so the ammunition handlers decided to forgo the slides and load the boxes directly by hand. "There were about ten men in the LCT," remembered James B. Cleveland, a member of the 29th Chemical Decontamination Company. "They were standing close together, and there was no interval in between. They were passing the ammunition, one man to the next one." Still, even after adjusting the unloading to make it quicker and simpler, the work party refused to be cautious. "When I was forward around 1230," S2/c W. S. Lindsey from LST #353 recalled, "I noticed that the men were handling the ammunition in a pretty rough way."[9]

At the same time that the ammunition handlers were removing the mortar crates and the civilian workers were strengthening the turnbuckles holding down LCT-963, the crew of LST #353 was doing some work of their own. Sometime before 10:30, SF3/c James Madison Cross and S1/c Doyle Knox began doing some welding work near the starboard side of the main cargo hatch, far away from the unloading of the mortar crates and from the 55-gallon drums of gasoline stored on the bow. "We were cutting angle iron for racks for life rafts to be welded to the outboard cabin bulkhead just a little aft of officers' quarters on the starboard side of the superstructure," recalled Knox.[10] Fully aware that they would be traveling into enemy waters for the upcoming invasion, the officers of LST #353 were adding additional life rafts for their Marine Corps passengers.

Although the sailors of LST #353 were worried about the Marines, it seemed that the Marines were not too worried about themselves. "During the day I saw a Marine draining some high-octane gasoline in a gallon size peach can [from the 55-gallon drums on the bow]," recalled S2/c Frank Scriva. "I noticed that these cans of gasoline were used all the time by the Marines to clean their guns." Indeed, on LST #179, on the port side of LST #353, at that very moment PhM2/c James J. Morrissey, assigned to the 2nd MarDiv for the invasion of Saipan, was sitting on the forward part of the main deck with two other pharmacist's mates and a Marine rifleman cleaning rifles using gasoline from a small tin.[11]

Very early on, many of the Marines had discovered that gasoline would leave a protective layer on the metal parts of a rifle, thereby protecting it from the highly corrosive sea air. It was not unusual for at least one 55-gallon drum to be equipped with a spigot so that the Marines could siphon off a bit of gasoline to coat their weapons. On LST #353, the drum with the spigot was located on the port side of the bow, among the eighty 55-gallon drums securely lashed behind the forward gun tubs.[12]

In spite of the inherent danger, with high-octane gasoline drums only 15 feet away, some of the Army ammunition handlers continued to smoke. "Two of the colored ordnancemen began to smoke, but Ames, the sentry on the tank deck below, made them stop," Marine Carl A. Kuscavage remembered. Despite the warning, however, some of the handlers continued to light up their cigarettes. "I observed that the men handling the ammunition were smoking, both above, within the LCT, and below in the LST," noted W. L. Stovall, a boatswain from Waipio Amphibious Operating Base, who was doing some work inside LCT-963.[13] Apparently, the ammunition workers were paying no attention to the No Smoking signs or the orders of the Marine sentries.

The civilian working party finished changing and adding turnbuckles to LCT-963 and left the ship at approximately 2:00 P.M. Before they left, however, Asst. Eng. Off. Ernest H. Lockwood II ordered two of the men to put out their cigarettes because the "no smoking" order was still in effect. On LST #69, three ships to the left, the civilian work party that had been working on the turnbuckles for LCT-983 also finished the job at about this time. Both groups had been working for about five hours. On LST #353, LT(jg) Raymond W. Thomas, the executive officer, went to check on the work being done by the soldiers from the 29th Chemical Decontamination Company. He was pleased to note that the unloading would be done in about two hours.[14] Still, the work of cutting away the bases of the eight mortars from the deck of LCT-963 with an acetylene torch would probably have to wait until tomorrow.

Near 2:30 P.M., the truck that was being loaded was declared full, and the elevator took it down to the tank deck. An empty truck was raised up to the main deck and placed in front of the LCT. Once again the ammunition handlers formed two lines and began passing the remaining boxes to two or three men who had climbed inside the canvas-covered bed of the new truck. It was now about 2:45 P.M. Down below, the loaded truck waited for an LCM to take it to shore.[15]

Around the same time, Shipfitter Cross and Seaman Knox finished their welding of the life raft frames. "I started to weld at 1030 and finished at 1430," recalled Cross. Knox added, "About fifteen or twenty minutes before [3:00 P.M.] we secured the equipment and I remember turning off the switch to the motor."[16] Having completed their welding, the two sailors left the main deck and went below.

About 2:55 P.M., Lieutenant Zuehlke, the skipper of LST #43, the fifth ship in line at Tare 8, climbed into the raised conn of his ship to see if he could find LST #226, the flagship for his group. He had to attend a meeting on the flagship but did not know where it was docked among the many ships tied up to the many tares in West Loch. Zuehlke was hoping that by getting a view from the conn tower, he might be able to spot the big white numbers 226 painted on the bow of the flagship.[17]

On LST #274, the third ship at Tare 8, a few Marines who had missed out on liberty had helped unload canned goods from an LCVP into the tank deck. For Albert G. Sutcliffe (Co. F, 25th MarReg, 4th MarDiv) and his Marine friends, the extra work had paid off. When nobody was looking, they had "short stopped" a case of pineapple juice. Now, at a little past 3:00 P.M., Sutcliffe and the others retired to a secluded spot in the cavernous tank deck and opened a few pilfered cans. It was time for their just rewards.[18]

Up above, in the ship's galley, S1/c Walt Slater, E3/c Kenneth Tidwell, and five other crewmen of LCT-982, chained to the main deck of LST #274, were playing poker. As Seaman Slater recalled, "LCT-982 was riding backwards. That was unusual because most of the LCTs put on were faced toward the bow, toward the front, but at that time they were putting them on with the ramp facing toward the conning tower of the LST. Our ramp was down, and it was facing the entrance into the galley of the LST. This was how we got on and off the LCT. We just walked down the ramp, which was at a slant." Although about half of the LCT crewmen were on liberty, the rest were playing a rousing game of poker. By 3:00 P.M., Electrician Tidwell was down to only one dollar.[19]

On the shore beside Tares 8, 9, and 10 sat the beached LVT alligators and DUKW amphibious trucks. "The DUKW men were restricted to the area," recalled PTN SGT Arthur Wells of 2nd DUKW. "Several first platoon men expressed wishes for a cold drink, water, or whatever, because the afternoon was hot and humid. So I decided to check with Lieutenant Blackburn for permission to take a DUKW to a small, nearby store to buy cases of Coca-Cola for the men. He reminded me of the restriction order but gave me permission when I suggested that, if stopped, I could use the excuse that we had been working on the DUKW's motor and were taking it for a test run." At a little after 3:00 P.M., Wells and a couple of other men set off in a DUKW down a "dirt road, just wide enough for a single vehicle, [which] was atop the levee separating the bordering cane fields and Walker Bay."[20]

Up on the main deck of LST #353, the second truck was filling up fast. Private Raymond Smith, one of the ammunition handlers, believed that the truck was "better than half full" by 3:00 P.M. while another handler, James Cleveland, believed that it was "about two-thirds full."[21] The men moving the crates from inside LCT-963 to the back of the truck took a break while the men inside the truck tried to get an accurate count of how many crates had already been loaded. Lieutenant Thomas had stipulated that no more than 110 crates should be loaded aboard each truck, lest the elevator give way and crash down to the tank deck.[22]

While the crates were being counted, Thomas and the skipper of LST #353, Captain Martin, were standing in the open top conning tower. "LST 179 [to the immediate left] had orders to move at 1700 [5:00 P.M.]," recalled Thomas, "and Captain Martin and I were deciding on the maneuver to be made in order to let LST 179 out of the nest." Inside LCT-963, crewmen MoMM1/c Vernon David Nichols and EM2/c Fred Connor, Jr., had been sitting on a

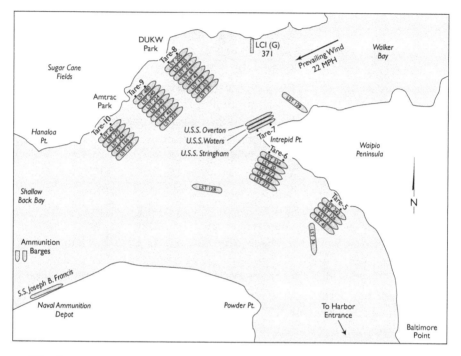

West Loch, Pearl Harbor, 3:08 P.M., May 21, 1944. Drawn by Gene Eric
Salecker, redrawn by Bill Nelson. Copyright © 2014 by the University of
Oklahoma Press.

midship ammunition ready rack watching the soldiers unloading
their ship. While Nichols noticed that there were still about 125
boxes of mortar shells, or about 250 rounds, remaining inside the
LCT, Connor's attention was drawn to the fact that the ammunition handlers were once again ignoring the "no smoking" orders.
"The Army boys were smoking when they did lay off for a while to
rest," he stated.[23]

Unfortunately, the laxity in obeying the smoking rules was not
confined to the men of the 29th Chemical Decontamination Company. Forward on the left side of the bow, just in front of the eighty
drums of high-octane aviation gasoline, one crewman and one officer were smoking. "I had . . . come up from below deck and was
sitting on the port side of the bow . . . talking with [ENS Dean Del-
bert] Urich," S2/c James Henry Kane remembered. "I had been
smoking a cigarette, and I believe other people were smoking on
the forecastle."[24] Indeed, others were.

"When I went up to the bow to get [a] line," recalled RM3/c Robert Richard Gillian, "there were two white enlisted Army or Marine boys smoking, and they were on the tip of the bow." Being a crewman on LST #353, Gillian surely would have recognized Ensign Urich, and he surely knew the difference between the dark blue trousers and light blue work shirt of Seaman Kane and the green utility uniform of a soldier or Marine. As Gillian stated, the two men he saw smoking on the bow were enlisted men. They most definitely were not Urich and Kane.

Gillian continued, "The boys who were smoking were about fifteen yards forward of the gasoline drums, almost dead center of the ship on the rail, and facing aft." Ensign Urich and Seaman Kane were along the port rail. Another crewman, COX William Donald Austin, said, "I saw . . . fellows smoking up in the bow." Like Gillian, he failed to identify any of the "fellows" as Ensign Urich, thus leaving one to believe that there were at least two groups of smokers on the bow. Obviously, several people were smoking on the forecastle in spite of the "no smoking" orders and the proximity of the aviation fuel.[25]

Shortly after 3:00 P.M. on Sunday, 21 May, while S2/c Kane and others were smoking cigarettes on the bow of LST #353, while the ammunition handlers were taking a break from unloading the mortar ammunition from LCT-963, while MoMM1/c Nichols and EM2/c Connor were relaxing inside LCT-963, and while hundreds of other men were working or relaxing upon the almost three dozen LSTs spread out around West Loch, the bow of LST #353 exploded.[26] In a split second, the peace of a beautiful Sunday afternoon was shattered.

CHAPTER 8 | # Explosion

Nobody was exactly sure when or where the initial explosion occurred. Some eyewitnesses claimed it came as early as 1:00 P.M.,
while others claimed it came as late as 3:30. The official military
investigation that followed fixed the time at 1508 hours, or 3:08
P.M. It is more than likely that the investigative board was not exactly sure either but took the 1508 time as an average.[1]

The earliest "official" reporting of the explosion was in the log
book of LST #273, moored as the number five ship at Tare 6,
which reported the explosion occurring at "1445" or 2:45 P.M.[2]
The latest reporting, coming from LST #354, which was docked
next to the dolphins at the fresh water dock (Tare 3), stated that
the explosion came at 3:25 P.M.[3] The disparity in times, as well as
an occasional misidentification of the exploding ship, proved how
sudden and shocking the explosion was. Nobody was expecting
the huge blast that came somewhere around 1508 hours on 21 May
1944. The explosion took everyone by surprise.

In addition to various times, some people were not even sure
where the blast originated. The very first communication to the
signal tower at Pearl Harbor came in at 1508 hours (3:08 P.M.) and
reported a "fire in LST #39." Since LST #39 was moored directly
outboard of LST #353, many people mistakenly believed that the
explosion and resulting fire had originated on the bow of #39.[4]

It has been established, however, that the explosion came from LST #353. Still, nobody knows just where on the ship the blast occurred. Lieutenant Martin, the skipper, believed that it came from in front of LCT-963, somewhere in the vicinity of the stored aviation fuel drums. He stated, "I am absolutely positive the explosion occurred aboard my ship. I was in the 'con' tower facing forward when I saw the explosion forward of the LCT or else just forward of the LCT." PFC Gale W. Hindman, a Marine in Co. B, 2nd Amphibious Truck Company, who was aboard LST #353, agreed. "As near as I could tell, the blast came from the extreme bow of the ship up near where the gasoline drums were stored. I am quite sure it was not from the ammunition, as I was close to that and the explosion was quite a distance from there."[5]

Another eyewitness was S2/c James Kane, who was on the bow smoking. "I was facing the starboard side, and the explosion seemed to come from in back of me about 25 or 30 feet along the port side of our ship, I am sure, and between the LCT and me. It seemed to come from the deck and was not below deck."[6]

However, ENS Dean Urich, who was with Kane, believed the explosion came from within LCT-963. "I do not exactly know where the explosion was, but it is my impression that it was on the port side of the LST but up in the LCT," he said. "It seemed to be contained in the LCT." Still, Urich had to admit, "I was facing to the port side but was looking out over the bow of the ship toward the water talking with Kane."[7]

It does appear that Ensign Urich, who by his own admission was "looking out over the bow . . . toward the water," was mistaken about the explosion occurring inside LCT-963. EM2/c Fred Connor and MoMM1/c Vernon Nichols, both crewmen on LCT-963 and both inside the LCT when the blast went off, survived to disagree with Urich. "The explosion was forward of the LCT," stated Connor. "The LCT was lifted under me, and I was thrown in the air a little." Nichols said, "It was a concussion of air and seemed to come from the starboard side and forward of the LCT where the gasoline drums were secured."[8] Had the explosion occurred inside LCT-963, both men probably would have lost their lives.

PFC Louis A. Garcia (Co. E, 23rd MarReg, 4th MarDiv) witnessed the explosion from the deck of LST #43, which was two ships to the left of LST #353. Garcia recalled, "This explosion was quite forward of where the Negro soldiers were unloading the ammunition from the LCT. The blast came from the bow of the ship, and the men were working amidships."[9]

Another Marine witness onboard LST #43, PFC Dick Shannon Crerar (Co. E, 23rd MarReg, 4th MarDiv), provided excellent information regarding the ship and location of the blast. "I was watching the Negro soldiers unloading ammunition from the LCT as I was standing on the starboard rail of LST 43," Crerar stated. "I saw the explosion, although I was too far away to see what caused it. The first explosion came from the bow of the 353 a little ahead of where they were working on the ammunition. The ammunition was being unloaded from amidships, and the explosion came from ahead of that location."[10]

At the same time that the investigative board was working hard to determine the exact time and location of the explosion, it was also trying to come up with the definitive cause of the blast. After taking hours of testimony, the investigation concluded that the "probable cause . . . was the explosion or detonation of a 4.2" H.E. [high explosive] mortar shell as it was being loaded onto the GMC truck on the elevator amidships of LST #353."[11] That was the official explanation. Others disagreed.

Actually, no one was quite certain about the cause of the first explosion, not even the investigative board. In the end, there were at least four possible causes bandied about by the board and eyewitnesses. At least a few people believed that the explosion was the result of an attack by an unseen Japanese submarine. Another possible cause was sabotage by one of the civilian workers who had been aboard the ship that morning. A third supposition, which was cited by the investigative board, involved a dropped mortar shell. The final possible cause, which is the most feasible and has the most evidence, was the ignition of gasoline or gasoline vapors from one of the aviation fuel drums stored on the bow of LST #353.

A few people, such as S2/c Chet Carbaugh, "thought the Japanese had come back" to attack Pearl Harbor. Many years later, even after all of the information gathered by the investigative board and the court of inquiry had been released to the public, MM Warren L. Boch, a Navy Seabee, still thought that perhaps "a Jap submarine had sneaked through the submarine nets that guarded the entrance to Pearl Harbor and torpedoed the first LST, which started a chain reaction with several others."[12]

According to the sabotage theorists, one or more of the Japanese American dockworkers who had been aboard LST #353 to tighten the turnbuckles on LCT-963 had planted an explosive device among the stored aviation fuel drums on the bow. After the workmen left, the device went off, either by a timed fuse or by an electrical signal from shore. ENS David L. Mincey, USS *Terror*, wrote, "I suspected it was sabotage, although I had no special knowledge of this. Many Japanese persons, U.S. citizens, worked at West Loch Ammo Depot." Marine military police officer Bob Arieta said, "It was sabotage. It was too well planned. And Tokyo Rose warned 'em right on the radio."[13]

Marine Elster Clements, on LST #39 on the right side of LST #353, said that he had seen "an LCVP loaded with civilian workers leave the #353." Clements believed that "members of that work party could very easily have planted an explosive charge in the 40mm ready room below the gun above, as that was where the first explosion occurred."[14]

In spite of all of the rumors, sabotage was never proven. Knowing that such a rumor was prevalent, however, the Navy investigative board spent some time looking into the matter. On July 24, it wrote: "As a result of the investigation conducted from 22 May 1944 through 27 May 1944, at which time the Board of Inquiry established by CinCPac [Commander in Chief, Pacific Command, i.e., Admiral Nimitz] instructed the District Intelligence Officer to cease any further investigation, there was no evidence or indication that the fires and explosions of the LSTs in West Loch, Oahu, T.H. [Territory of Hawaii], were the result of an act or acts of sabotage."[15]

Many more people, including the official Navy board of inquiry, believed that the explosion was the result of a dropped mortar shell during the unloading of LCT-963. The officer of the deck on board LST #353 at the time of the explosion, Asst. Eng. Off. Ernest H. Lockwood II, was called before the court of inquiry, and although he was not sure, he felt that "the most probable cause" was "the ammunition that was being off loaded from the LCT to the waiting truck on the elevator."[16]

Several people present at the time of the explosion agreed with Lockwood, claiming that the blast came from a dropped mortar shell. PhM2/c Morrissey, who was cleaning his carbine with a group of friends seated on the bow of LST #179, right next to #353, said the sound of the explosion "was very loud as if half the ship was being blown away." He remembered, "There was no smoke at all accompanying the explosion. There was just a flash and the sound. It was as if a shell had gone off, a shell on the middle of the deck." Almost immediately he thought that "somebody aboard the #353, while removing the shells, had dropped one," but he was not sure whether an unarmed shell "could explode by being dropped or not."[17]

PhM William Johnson, from LST #69, who would study the disaster in West Loch and write a book about it, questioned the "dropped shell theory." Said Johnson, "I've done quite a bit of research on this. . . . There was a court of inquiry that came up with their own conclusions, and they said that a mortar shell was dropped, actually about a 4.2-inch mortar shell, and that exploded and set off the conflagration. I don't agree with it. . . . I've seen a lot of mortar shells dropped, and unless they're armed, they don't go off. They have to be armed ahead of time."[18]

Carlton Drake, a radioman assigned to LST #353, agreed with Johnson. "Well, those 4-inch shells aren't detonated until they're ready to fire, unless somebody stuck a detonator in it, you know."[19] None of the shells aboard LCT-963 were "armed ahead of time," and in fact, some had been dropped earlier in the day, and none had exploded.

In February 1946, the Navy published a two-page "Report of Explosion at West Loch, Pearl Harbor, T.H., 21 May 1944," which concluded that "the most probable cause of this disaster was the explosion or detonation of a 4.2" H.E. [high explosive] mortar shell as it was being loaded onto a GMC truck on the elevator amidships of LST #353. All of the 4.2" H.E. shells had been removed from the boxes and made ready for firing and then replaced in the boxes without covers being nailed down." This statement, however, makes no sense. Since none of the LCTs were supposed to be launched during the Maui rehearsals, the crew of LCT-963, a mortar gunship, would not have readied their shells for detonation. There were no plans to fire the mortars from the ship while it was strapped to the main deck of LST #353. Likewise, it would have been dangerous to ready the projectiles for firing prior to launching the LCT over the side of the LST. Launching an LCT was a very tricky maneuver and always rocked the launched craft from side to side when it hit the water. The crew never would have readied the ammunition prior to a launch.[20] The dropped shell theory, although chosen as the cause by the court of inquiry, does not hold up under scrutiny.

The most feasible cause, believed by many, including this author, is that the explosion occurred when one of the gasoline drums stored on the bow of LST #353 ignited. The Navy court of inquiry had numerous eyewitnesses who claimed that the blast came from among the gasoline drums, but for some unknown reason they settled on the dropped shell theory. Oddly enough, in its own summary of the investigation, the court stated, "It is likely that the origin of the fire and explosions was caused by the escape of fumes from . . . [the] drum equipped with the spigot or a leakage from the same drum or from an explosion occurring among some one or more of the eighty drums lashed to the bow of USS LST 353."[21]

A number of witnesses called before the court believed it was a gasoline explosion. S2/c Kane, who had been smoking on the bow of LST #353, firmly believed it was a gasoline explosion. "My first thought," he said, "was the gasoline had gone up and I still believe that is what caused it. There was a deep long, drawn-out boom. . . . The gasoline tanks were all stowed forward about 35 or 40 feet from the bow of the ship along [the] starboard and port sides. The explosion seemed to come from the port side ahead of the ramp of the LCT."[22]

MoMM1/c Nichols, inside LCT-963 on LST #353, felt that "the explosion was caused by gas." He went on to describe the blast as "a bright light . . . it was one great blast and went off with terrific power." Nichols had been sitting inside his LCT watching the Army soldiers unloading the mortar shells, and he categorically disagreed that the explosion was caused by a dropped shell. "As nearly as I can remember the explosion," he told the court of inquiry, "it did not seem to be a mortar shell going off because that would have made several explosions. . . . It was a rather sharp explosion, and I remember a lot of black smoke but not very much else."[23]

Moored to the port side of LST #353 was LT William Mullis's LST #179. CM2/c Henry Soren Bonne, with the 1035th Construction Battalion, was working on LST #179 when the explosion occurred. Because of his work in construction, Bonne knew the difference between a gasoline explosion and an ammunition explosion. "I have seen lots of gasoline fires and dynamite explosions, and I am sure it wasn't ammunition. . . . There was a dense black smoke with reddish-orange flame and looked to me like a couple of barrels of gasoline."[24]

Marine CPL Fred Weinberger, also on LST #179, was just as positive as Bonne that the initial explosion was from gasoline. Weinberger had a history of witnessing both ammunition and gasoline explosions. He testified:

> I am quite sure it was a gasoline explosion. To begin with it was right among the gasoline drums which were stored in the bow of the 353. Furthermore I have seen a number of gasoline explosions—minor ones, I'll admit—and this one not only looked but sounded like a gasoline blast. About the first thing I saw was dense black smoke, then flames shot up in the midst of it. The sound wasn't loud like it would be if it had been ammunition going up. It was more of a muffled sound, sort of a swoosh, and I have never seen ammunition explode with that sort of noise. However, gasoline does sound like that. No, the blast didn't seem to start where the [ammunition handler] soldiers were but ahead of them right among the gasoline drums.[25]

On board LST #39, moored on the right side of LST #353, was MM1/c Ishmael Worth Tumblson, another Seabee with the 1035th Construction Battalion. Tumblson's testimony was compelling. "The first thing I saw was a sheet of flame across the bow of our ship. It looked like gasoline to me. I worked in oil fields for years and that is what I believe it to be."[26]

Only two ships to the left of LST #353 was LST #43. Marine Private Garcia (4th MarDiv) was on deck and testified:

> When the explosions came, I was standing just forward of amidships on LST 43 and looking into the direction of the blast. The first explosion wasn't a particularly loud one and the sound it made is hard to describe but it sounded more like a whoosh, I think, than like a loud report. The first thing I noticed almost simultaneously with the explosion was a cloud of dark black smoke followed then by flames. It was

more of a gasoline explosion than anything else, although I wouldn't say I was an expert on such things. However, I have seen small gasoline explosions and this one resembled them more than I would think that would resemble any explosion of ammunition."[27]

Interestingly enough, another person to testify from LST #43 did not see the explosion but presented the court with hard physical evidence that the initial blast was from one of the gasoline drums. "The first thing I noticed was that something hit my foot," stated Marine Gerald Joseph Zito (Co. E, 23rd MarReg, 4th MarDiv). "I thought it was a stray bullet, but almost simultaneously there was a big explosion from off to our starboard, several ships away. I still have the piece of metal which struck me, penetrated my shoe, and had to be removed from my foot. It is a piece of a gasoline drum, which I am keeping as a souvenir."[28]

PhM2/c Johnson was on LST #69 at Tare 8 and only three ships to the left of LST #353. After studying the disaster for years, Johnson concluded, "I think it's more likely, in view of the type of explosion and knowing what was going on onboard the ships, that the high-octane gasoline that they had on board was ignited because it was more that kind of an explosion. And there was a lot of smoke and fire. And the theory that the gas drums blew, in my experience, is more feasible than just somebody dropped a mortar shell."[29]

If it was the ignition of the gasoline that set off the first explosion, the question then has to be asked, what set off the gasoline? Once again, there is no definitive answer.

Many people believe that sparks from a welder's torch set off the gas vapors in the gasoline drums stored on the bow of LST #353. PFC Stan Ellis, a Marine with Co. F, 25th MarReg, 4th MarDiv, on board LST #274, four ships to the left of #353, recalled, "They never found out for sure how it happened, but there were some sailors doing some welding near the bow where some high-octane gas was stored. They figure some sparks got to the gas."[30]

Marine Harry Pearce, on board LST #69, three ships to the left, also thought that an errant spark from a welding torch had ignited the fuel. "The flames shot several hundred feet right straight up in the air," he recalled. "Sam [a buddy] and I always figured that it was sparks off of the welding torch and the high octane fumes because the blast was immediate, it was on top, and it went straight up."[31]

However, as shown in chapter 7, SF3/c Cross and Seaman Knox, the two welders on LST #353, had finished their welding job by 2:45 P.M., well before the established time of the first explosion, and at no time had the two been anywhere near the stored gasoline drums. On LST #39, moored to the immediate right of LST #353, where welding was also taking place, the work was being done in the conning tower, far away from the bow of LST #353.

On LST #179, however, moored to the immediate left of LST #353, there was also welding going on, and this time it appeared to be near the bow. Marine Jack Claven (Co. I, 23rd MarReg, 4th MarDiv) on LST #69, two ships to the right of #179, recalled, "I thought at the time that it was very risky doing what they were doing, with the sparks flying all over with so many barrels of aviation gas carried on the main decks of each LST."[32] Although possible, it is highly unlikely that a spark from welding on the bow of LST #179 could have arced all the way over to the gasoline barrels on the bow of LST #353, setting off the initial explosion.

A more likely scenario for the ignition of the gasoline or gasoline fumes is a careless cigarette. Crewmen, civilians, Marines, and ammunition handlers were carelessly smoking around the high-octane gasoline drums stored on the bow of LST #353. At least one gasoline drum had a spigot in it so that the Marines could siphon off some of the fuel to clean and grease their weapons, and it was believed that more than a few of the drums were half empty. With any gasoline container, it is not the gas that one has to worry about but the fumes. Gasoline fumes will ignite faster than gas itself. Noted Marine machine gunner Robert L. George, "We were cautioned not to smoke near them as these drums were beat up from battle and had a lot of dents and tiny holes in the lids, so the escaping fumes could be very dangerous."[33] One careless cigarette, one careless drag, one careless spark, and the gas fumes could explode. This author believes that it was a careless cigarette that caused the explosion on the bow of LST #353 at 3:08 P.M. on the afternoon of 21 May.

In their own summary of the explosion, the court of inquiry wrote that "there was evidence indicating that eighty drums of filled, partially filled, and empty gasoline drums [were] lashed on the bow of USS LST 353; the presence of a partially filled drum equipped with a spigot, for use by the ship's complement in cleaning their carbines, machine guns, and other equipment; it is likely that the origin of the fire and explosion was caused by the escape of fumes from the same drum or from an explosion occurring among some one or more of the eighty drums lashed to the bow of USS LST 353."[34]

Although the court eventually settled on the "dropped shell theory," the above statement proves that even they were not fully convinced. For his own part, machine gunner George wrote, "One of the survivors said that one of the Marines had flipped a cigarette over the bow and a gust of wind had blown it back over their heads and it had landed on one of the gasoline barrels."[35] At least that was the scuttlebutt among many of the Marines.

What actually caused the initial explosion will never really be known. Nor will it be known whether it was a gasoline or ammunition explosion. People have speculated for years and will continue to speculate, but as LT(jg) Raymond W. Thomas, the executive officer on LST #353, put it so brilliantly at the Navy court of inquiry in 1944, "It was an instantaneous explosion, and I believe anyone near it would never survive to tell what really caused it."[36]

On board LST #179 at the time of the initial explosion was Marine Jim Carlson with the 2nd MarDiv. Years after the West Loch disaster he wrote, "As a retired fire and arson investigator with forty years in the fire business, I have taken more than the normal interest, as I was on [LST] #179. . . . I agree that the definitive cause can probably never be learned. Usually, there may be a difference in results from the ignition of high explosives and gasoline vapors to indicate the exact point of origin, but as the two fuels were in such close proximity, ignition of either would result in immediate ignition of the other and give no evidence of which specifically had been ignited first."[37] In other words, it did not matter what set off the initial explosion. The results would be the same. Hell.

CHAPTER 9 | # Hell

The initial explosion on the bow of LST #353 was described by one survivor as "a terrible loud explosion." Another described it as "tremendous." A third described it as "awesome." More than likely, the very first explosion was a single gasoline drum. Almost instantaneously, however, that small explosion was followed by the explosion of numerous gasoline drums surrounding the first drum. To a casual observer, the first blast and the split-second detonation of the surrounding drums all seemed like one big explosion.

The blast had enough force to send objects and people flying into the air and shake ships at least 500 feet away. The concussion shattered windows in barracks near the ammunition depot, over 3,000 feet away. The explosion was heard on the northeast shore of East Loch, more than 4 miles away. As SK Donald Q. Kinney on the Coast Guard–manned LST #69 said, "For a moment, I thought the world was coming to an end."[1]

The explosion sent flaming debris and shrapnel arching outward in all directions, landing on ships moored at Tares 7, 8, 9, and 10, on some of the vessels moored in Walker Bay, and on some of the parked LVTs and DUKWs lining the southeast shore of Hanaloa Point. Bright reddish-yellow flames and thick black smoke shot skyward. Immediately, the remaining stored aviation fuel drums on the bow of LST #353 began to burn and explode. At the same time, debris landed atop the stored gasoline drums

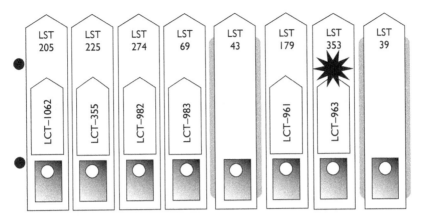

Tare 8: Explosion on LST #353. Drawn by Gene Eric Salecker, redrawn by Kristie Buckley. Copyright © 2014 by the University of Oklahoma Press.

on LSTs #179 and #39 moored port and starboard, respectively. Anyone near the center of the blast did not live to tell about it.

The first explosion occurred on the port (left) side bow of LST #353, among the eighty or so stored 55-gallon drums of high-octane aviation fuel. In a flash at least a dozen men from the 29th Chemical Decontamination Company, unloading the mortar shell crates from LCT-963 nearby, perished. Miraculously, some of the ammunition handlers survived because they had been taking a break and were inside the LCT when the blast went off.

Tech 5 James Caldwell recalled hearing a "deafening noise" and seeing a "bright yellow flame." Another handler, James Cleveland, said, "I went up in the air, and some rails, metal objects, went up in the air with me. I could see fire all around, just nothing but fire all around me. I thought I was dead." When Cleveland regained his senses, he rushed to the fantail of the ship and jumped overboard.[2]

Relaxing inside the LCT among the ammunition handlers were crewmen Connor and Nichols. When the explosion went off, both men were "blown into the air and returned to the deck in a sprawling position" as the front end of LCT-963 was lifted off its cradle atop the main deck of LST #353. Shaken but uninjured, Connor suggested that they "get off the boat," and the two scrambled over the side of their LCT and dashed to safety behind the LST deckhouse.[3]

The skipper of LST #353, Lieutenant Martin, and his executive officer, Lieutenant Thomas, were in the conning tower when the explosion occurred. "The explosion came as a complete surprise to Captain Martin and myself," said Thomas, whose left eardrum was ruptured by the concussion. After waiting until the material stopped falling, the two officers scrambled down to the main deck and tried to get their crew to "get water hoses operative on either side of the ship."[4]

Ensign Urich and Seaman Kane had been standing on the bow, smoking cigarettes. The blast blew Urich over the bow and onto the top of one of the big open bow doors. "I looked back," Urich stated, "and saw big flames and dark smoke." Kane was also pushed over the side by the explosion. "The first thing I knew," Kane testified, "it had sort of pushed me off and I was hanging on the LST bow doors over the ramp." Shoved over the gunwale of the ship and away from the explosion, both men were lucky to be alive to tell about their experiences.[5]

Because the first explosion was on the port side of LST #353, and because the prevailing wind was blowing from the northeast at 19 knots or almost 23 miles per hour, much of the debris blew onto the bow and amidships of LST #179, moored to the left of #353. Because of the spreading fires, it was only a matter of seconds before #179 and LCT-961, which was chained to her main deck, seemed in worse shape than #353.

Apparently, a large number of Marines were still on board LST #179, relaxing on the main deck, "playing cards, reading what was available, lying in the sun, or cutting each other's hair." Like most of the other LSTs moored in West Loch that day, the main deck of LST #179 was crowded with military vehicles and boxes of ammunition. Additionally, close to one hundred 55-gallon drums of aviation fuel were crowded on her bow.[6]

PFC Frank T. Thompson, a Navajo "code talker" with Hq Co., 6th MarReg, 2nd MarDiv, was on the main deck, heading toward a hatch to go below when he suddenly found himself down on his stomach, sliding "toward a gun mount on the LST." Once stopped, Thompson looked back and saw "a big fire coming from the gas barrels and ammunition" stored aboard LST #353. He also looked toward the raised elevator platform of his own ship, which just seconds before had been crowded with fellow Marines. "The platform which covered the main hole caved in," he recalled, "taking with it all the personnel that had been playing cards, reading, or sleeping. Screams and cries were heard all over the place, above and below, and the fire quickly spread to the other LSTs in the nest. Not a soul was moving in the area where the Army personnel had been handling the ammunition on #353." As flaming debris and shrapnel began to fall around him, Thompson ran to the safety of a nearby gun mount.[7]

Standing at a cargo hatch amidships was Carl Dearborn (Co. F, 25th MarReg, 4th MarDiv), who was passing cartons of canned goods to a Marine on a ladder who then passed them down to more Marines in a storeroom below. When the blast from the explosion hit LST #179, the concussion tore every "stitch of clothing" off Dearborn, pitched him completely over LST #43 to port, and dropped him into the water far below. Still, Dearborn considered himself one of the lucky ones. "Most of the Marines who were working in the [storage] compartment [below] were killed." While bobbing up and down in the water, Dearborn saw smoke and fire rise from the bows of several ships.[8]

PhM2/c James J. Morrissey and three other men were "on the main deck forward" cleaning their rifles with gasoline when there came "a blinding flash and explosion." Leaping to his feet, Morrissey raced forward a little before looking back. Instead of seeing the other men, he saw that everything was "all aglow, slightly aflame." Two of the other three men were gone, perhaps blown overboard, while the third was lying dead on the deck. A second later, Morrissey realized that his arms were on fire, probably from the gasoline that he had been using to clean his carbine. In panic, Morrissey jumped down the nearest hatchway, which somehow extinguished the flames.[9]

Not too far away was PhM3/c Orville Allen Sheppard, attached to Hq Co., 6th MarReg, 2nd MarDiv. Reading a book just "forward of the elevator platform of the #179," Sheppard glanced up in time to see a "large blot of flame" shoot across the deck. Blown down the elevator hatch opening, he landed heavily atop one of the LVTs parked inside the cavernous tank deck, injuring his left leg, right thigh, and buttocks. Unable to move his legs, Sheppard began pulling himself across the top of the amtrac to safety.[10]

Inside the tank deck, Carlyle Harmer was unloading cots for the contingent of Marines. "The blast knocked me up against a bulkhead and knocked me out cold," he recalled. Marine Calvin

Frawley, also inside the tank deck, was writing letters home. "When the first explosion came," he said, "it was the ship next to ours that blew up, and the concussion was so great that the lights on our LST went off and it was complete darkness down there in the hole of the ship where I was."[11]

LST #179 was scheduled to move to East Loch later that day for repairs. "That Sunday afternoon, we had torn the propeller off the ship and we were supposed to go in dry dock and get it fixed," recalled LT(jg) King Richeson. The skipper, Lieutenant Mullis, was off the ship, and Richeson was quietly censoring the crew's mail in the officers' wardroom when he felt and heard the explosion. Rushing outside, he instantly saw the devastation. "Almost immediately," he said, "the canvas we had on the trucks and things on the deck were on fire." Being the senior officer aboard, Richeson scrambled to get the crew to help the wounded and break out the fire hoses.[12]

Moored on the right side of LST #353 was Lieutenant Figaro's LST #39. Although carrying a pair of pontoons on her sides, which moored her just a few feet farther away from LST #353, and although upwind from the explosion, LST #39 suffered just as badly from the blast as did LST #179 on the left side. The detonation scattered flaming debris and red-hot shrapnel upon the forward half of LST #39, setting fire to most of the canvas coverings on the military vehicles on the main deck and on the jury-rigged shelter halves of the Marines. With fires breaking out all up and down the ship, the officers sounded the fire alarm and tried to get underway. Unfortunately, as Figaro reported, "Fire immediately spread to 88 drums of gasoline on [the] port and starboard side of [the] forecastle and set off 20mm ammunition in ready boxes and rolling equipment on top deck." Within minutes, the ammunition began to go off, endangering the lives of anyone fighting the fires on #39.[13]

Down below, S2/c Chet Carbaugh was in his "rack" reading letters from home when he heard the first explosion and thought that the Japanese were back. "I ran topside. It was a nightmare. There was smoke everywhere, shrapnel was falling down like rain, and the water was on fire from all the oil that had spilled. There was a fire on our fo'c'sle near the bridge where we had a lot of fuel stored." Knowing that the life of his ship depended on putting out the fire, Carbaugh gathered up some sailors, broke out the fire hoses, and started toward the blazing bow.[14]

LST #43, carrying a couple of pontoons, was the only ship to the left of LST #353. Lieutenant Zuehlke, the skipper, was in the conning tower when the first blast erupted. Immediately, general quarters was sounded and the crew rushed to man all available fire-fighting equipment. Although flaming debris and shrapnel rained down upon LST #43, within five minutes the crew had "all fire on board under control, [and] hoses played on fire on board LST 179 [to starboard]."[15] While the fires were being fought, the skipper made preparations to get his ship away from the three flaming ships off his starboard side.

Lieutenant Zuehlke, who had had a conversation with Lieutenant Commander Hoyt concerning the dangerous loading of the LSTs, felt that the first explosion came from a single gasoline drum. He said, "It was a minor explosion in which the flames shot into the air only about fifteen feet." As "a small amount of debris" rained down upon his ship, Zuehlke gave the order for general quarters, reasoning that "that was the fastest way to get the engine room manned and ready and also [get] all personnel on the topside." Although many of the canvas vehicle coverings on his main deck were in flames, he felt that the fires could be easily extinguished.

Only seconds after general quarters was sounded, however, Zuehlke saw a "terrible explosion" that shot across the decks of the moored ships in Tare 8. Rushing to the navigation bridge, he was trying to organize the rescue of his vessel when "all the gasoline went up" on #353. "This time," recalled Zuehlke, "the flames shot up maybe seventy-five or one hundred feet into the air." As he watched his crew coming topside to man their battle stations, he saw the first panic of evacuating Marines pouring across his deck from the burning ships to his right.[16]

CPL Jim Reed (Co. E, 23rd MarReg, 4th MarDiv) was asleep under one of the shady tarps on the main deck. "The explosion woke me up. I had no idea what it was. The whole canvas above me was on fire and it fell down and the cots started to burn." Sunning themselves inside one of the LST gun mounts were CPL Jesse Kirkes and a friend. "We jumped up when we heard the explosion," Kirkes recalled, "and then a second explosion followed and blew away the blanket we were lying on." Reed, Kirkes, and Kirkes's friend quickly fled with many other Marines across the decks of the inboard ships, heading toward the safety of shore.[17]

Crewman Joseph L. Wachter heard the public address system sound general quarters and rushed to his battle station. Once there, he recalled, "the order was changed to 'All hands man fire stations.'" As Lieutenant Zuehlke had hoped, his men had responded more quickly to a general quarters than any other alarm. "Hoses were unrolled, water was turned on, and water started to pour through the hoses," wrote Wachter.[18] In spite of the impediment of fleeing Marines from the outboard ships crossing over their deck, the crew of LST #43 worked hard to get things under control.

The crew of the U.S. Coast Guard–manned LST #69, which was piggybacking LCT-983, had the bow doors open and the ramp down and was unloading supplies from one of their LCVPs when the blast occurred. Fire and debris shot onto LST #69, setting fire to the tarpaulins and tents stretched all over the main deck. Although LST #69 was approximately 100 feet from LST #353, the explosion was felt as a mighty tremor throughout the ship. "I was going down to crew's quarters, and all of a sudden it seemed like the whole ship was picked up and out of the water and fell back again," remembered one crewman. "When I got back up on deck, there was fire and there was stuff flying all over the place."[19]

Harry Pearce and his Marine Corps buddy, Sam, were on their cots underneath LCT-983. "The blast just leveled everything. Sam and I were blown off our cots," recalled Pearce. "All we had was our skivvies and our shoes. We each grabbed a helmet and put it on." Looking around, they spotted SGT Paul Bass (Co. I, 23rd MarReg, 4th MarDiv), sprawled on the main deck, a victim of the concussive power of the initial explosion. "Blood was coming out of his eyes and ears and his nose and mouth," Pearce recalled. The two Marines rushed to his side.[20]

Marine Jack Claven (Co. I, 23rd MarReg, 4th MarDiv) was about to go down through a hatch to the tank deck when "a blast of air" came up through the open hatch and sent him flying backwards across the deck. In all likelihood, since the bow doors of LST #69 were wide open and the bow ramp was down, the blast of air was part of the concussion following the explosion on LST #353. A shaken Claven "did not wait long to decide to go over the side, in spite of the distance to the water."[21]

Inside the tank deck, PhM2/c Johnson was standing inside the open bow doors near the LCVP. "We had just completed [unloading the LCVP] when at 1508, a large explosion occurred in one of the LSTs moored outboard of my ship," he wrote. "I thought for a minute my head had blown off, the explosion was so terrific. . . . I was naturally upset and scared when the explosion occurred." Looking toward LST #353, Johnson saw "a man blown into the water from an outboard ship . . . covered with blood and [with] a large shrapnel wound in his back."

Since the LCVP had two first-aid kits aboard, Johnson, along with S2/c Robert W. Arbuckle and two other crewmen, climbed into the small craft and set out to pick up the wounded man. "But another boat reached him first and pulled the bleeding man, who had a large hole in his back, into the rescue craft." As Johnson looked up at the several burning LSTs at the far end of Tare 8, he saw men "jumping into the water from all the ships and the fires were spreading to all the ships like wildfire." He then ordered Arbuckle to take the LCVP around behind the burning vessels to start picking up survivors. Johnson admitted, "I knew that we were in for serious trouble."[22]

MoMM2/c James F. Casavant was inside the tank deck when he was "surprised by an explosion that rocked the ship." Rushing topside, he discovered that the outboard ships in Tare 8 were covered with fire. "Mooring stations were being piped," he remembered, "so I ran below to start engines and check the water pressure on the fire pumps." Although Casavant found the fire pumps working fine, he discovered that the "main engines could not be started because the compression test cocks had been removed and taken off the ship for repair." With the ship unable to move, Casavant headed back to the main deck to help fight the fires.[23]

Lieutenant Gott, the senior officer on board #69 since the skipper, Lieutenant Leary, and the executive officer were off ship, was up on the main deck when the first explosion occurred. He remembered that "the ship vibrated badly and debris and shrapnel started falling all over the ship." Gott told the engineering officer, LT(jg) Russell W. Anderson (USCGR), "Let's get the ship out of here!" Anderson responded, "We have no power."[24]

Hoping to find some way to save his vessel, Gott left LST #69 and rushed to LST #274, the number three ship on his left side, and asked an officer on the bridge if they could pull them free when

#274 started forward. Although the officer was willing, he said that Gott would have to sever the mooring lines to LST #43, the number five ship, before #69 could be pulled free. Satisfied with the answer, Gott rushed back aboard LST #69 to see about severing the lines.[25]

On LST #69, EM2/c Michael Angelich heard the officers calling for the crew to go to mooring stations, to try to get the ship away from those that were burning. Responding to the order, Angelich hurried down to the auxiliary engine room and started up two generators while MoMM2/c Robert H. Hanna fired up two of the three small auxiliary diesel engines. Within five minutes, they had all the fire and bilge pumps up and operating.[26]

On LST #274, four ships away from the erupting #353, general quarters was sounded less than one minute after the explosion. Shortly thereafter, all possible fire hoses were out in an attempt to fight the flaming debris on the decks of the burning LSTs to starboard. Within two minutes, LST #274 had her "main engines warmed up" and was getting ready to leave the burning ships behind. It was then that the fires spread to #274 and the crewmen changed from fighting the fires on the other ships to fighting the fires on their own.[27]

Two sailors, Electrician Tidwell and Seaman Slater, both crewmen aboard LCT-982 chained to the deck of LST #274, were inside the deckhouse of the LST when the explosion happened. "Seven of the LCT crew were playing cards in the galley when the first explosion occurred," Slater remembered. "We immediately went to the deck and had to go through this fire to get to the main deck of the LST. [The ramp on our LCT] was down, and it was facing the entrance into the galley of the LST." Tidwell added, "When the first explosion went off, of course, it vibrated the ship and all, and we jumped out of the galley into the open deck out there." Slater continued, "It was devastating. The explosion was more than a boom, it was a concussion. . . . We couldn't see through all the smoke, but we could hear shrapnel just raining down on us." While viewing the situation, Tidwell became worried. "Well, when I saw the smoke and felt the heat from that first explosion and saw the 100-octane gas in the drums on the bow of these craft, I thought, 'Boy, it's not gonna be long before the next one goes.'"[28]

Although most of the Marines from Co. F, 25th MarReg, 4th MarDiv, which had been assigned to LST #274, were on liberty at the time of the explosion, a few were still aboard. Private Sutcliffe was down in the tank deck, about to drink from his purloined can of pineapple juice, when he suddenly felt and heard the explosion. Looking forward, he was surprised to see "a Marine hanging on one of the ship's bow doors." As Sutcliffe recalled, "He had apparently been blown there from the deck. He hung there for a minute, then let go and landed on all fours on the ramp." A second later, the Marine scrambled into the LCVP that Sutcliffe and some other Marines had helped to unload and waited impatiently to be taken to shore.[29]

One of the ship's officers, LT Bob Broadwell, was on the tank deck supervising the unloading of the supplies when the first explosion hit. "We had the ramp down, the bow doors were wide open, and when the explosion occurred, I went up the port ladder to . . . the bridge because I knew that's where the 'Old Man' would be." As expected, Lieutenant Sard was there. "He was getting the engines and everything started at that point," Broadwell continued. "I sent one crewman. To this day I don't know who it was, but it was the bravest thing I've ever seen. I told him to go up on the bow because we had drums of high-octane gas for the amtracs and I told him to take a fire hose and go up into one of the gun tubs . . . and put a spray of water over those drums to cool them down in case anything hit them. He just looked at me, and I said, 'Now go.' And he went."[30]

Down in the main engine room, Chief MoMM Alvin Birch did not feel the ship shake. "I couldn't tell too much what was happening because I was in the engine room when it all started. I had the headphones on. That's the only way I could tell anything was going on. We could hear the explosion." Although the main engines were cold when the explosion occurred, Lieutenant Sard immediately gave the order to fire them up. Within two minutes Chief Birch had the engines up and ready. For the next few minutes, Birch listened to the noises through his headphones and waited for further orders from above.[31]

The officer of the deck on board LST #225, the number two ship, noted the extent of the spread of fire at Tare 8 in his logbook. "Explosion sent flaming debris atop all ships. Fires started on all ships in Tare 8. On LST 225 fire started in LCT-355, burning troop gear. Other fires on starboard life rafts, fantail refuse, canvas and crates on boat deck, and on water between LST 225 and LST 274 amidships." He added, "Fire alarm sounded immediately. Hoses brought out and most of fires put out plus one on fantail of LST 205 [to port]."[32]

A small number of Marines were still on LST #225. Marine rifleman James T. Cobb (Co. B, 25th MarReg, 4th MarDiv) was inside the cavernous tank deck when the blast erupted. Rushing topside, he looked toward the far end of the tare and saw smoke and flames rising above some of the LSTs. "It seemed like only a couple of minutes until the flames started jumping from ship to ship." Knowing that each ship was carrying numerous barrels of high-octane gasoline, Cobb realized that he was "in the midst of a very dangerous situation." As he recalled, "Extreme confusion existed, as wounded sailors and Marines retreated to [LST #225]."[33]

Unfortunately for the crew of LST #225, the flood of people from the outboard ships caused mass confusion aboard the flagship. As Yeoman Ford "Rusty" Kaiser remembered, "I was taking a shower when I suddenly felt the ship lurch and thought, 'What the hell?' So I put a towel around my waist and grabbed my wallet and watch and went topside." By the time Kaiser reached the main deck, dozens of refugees were streaming across LST #225 toward shore. "I saw the smoke and everybody was running from the other ships and somebody was yelling, 'Abandon ship,' so I went over to the side," he admitted. "I thought this towel isn't going to do me any good, so I threw that away and jumped into the water with my watch in one hand and my wallet in the other."[34]

Officially, the order to abandon ship was never given on LST #225, although Yeoman Kaiser and many others heard somebody shouting, "Abandon ship!" LCDR Joseph B. Hoyt emphatically testified before the court of inquiry that the order to abandon ship was never given. He testified that he believed that an officer on LST #205, inboard of #225 and tied up to the dolphins at Tare 8, had panicked and begun shouting for everyone to abandon ship, which was heard and followed by the men aboard #225.[35]

Shortly after the first explosion, Commander Hoyt had climbed into the conning tower to get a good look at what was going on around him. From his elevated position, Hoyt could see that LST

#353 was "heavily afire, forward." To Hoyt, the conflagration looked "like a gasoline fire from the type of smoke, and there was the detonations of small arms—nothing very heavy. A good deal of flaming debris was scattered all over the nest, and most of the inflammable stuff on the weather [main] decks of the LSTs had been ignited." As Hoyt noted, almost all of the "awnings, flag bags, halyards, and the trash" on most of the LSTs were aflame.

Alone in the conning tower, Hoyt noticed how badly his ship had been damaged by the blast. "The blinker, the 12" searchlight, and the lens had been smashed by some of the debris," he testified. "The radio antennae had been cut." With no way to communicate to any of the other LSTs, Hoyt tried to signal the ships in Tare 9 behind him by waving his arms. Although he could see "activity on the forecastles of the ships moored at Tare 9," he received no definite response to his frantic waving.

While Hoyt was in the conning tower, fire stations was sounded on LST #225 and the crew began breaking out the fire hoses and wetting down the decks. Hoyt went down to the main deck and crossed over toward the burning ships to see what he could do. Although he easily crossed over from #225 to #274, he was "knocked over by a stream of troops and Navy personnel from the outboard vessels" when he tried to go from #274 to #69. Infuriated, Hoyt rushed straight across #69 and onto the fifth ship, #43, stopping only when he reached the deckhouse. Speaking briefly with the executive officer, Hoyt told him to cast off his lines and move forward into the wind and away from all of the flaming debris blowing to the southwest. He then started toward LST #179, the number six ship, which was burning furiously. He hoped that he could still do something to control the raging fires.[36]

When the gasoline drums on LST #353 exploded, flaming debris rained down upon the Coast Guard–manned LST #205, which was carrying LCT-1062 on its main deck. Although tied to the dolphin pilings at Tare 8, six ships to the left of #353, the officer of the deck reported, "Small fires caused by hot debris in flag bag and aboard LCT." As the fires spread to other vessels and streams of refugees began pouring onto and across the deck of #205, the firefighting efforts of the crew were hampered. Pretty soon, panic began to grip some of the officers and crew of #205.[37]

CHAPTER 10 | # Hell from Afar

When LST #353 exploded in position number seven of Tare 8, debris and shrapnel also rained down upon some of the vessels moored in Tare 9, about 100 yards behind the ships in Tare 8. No matter where a vessel was tied up at Tare 9, almost everyone heard and felt the explosion.

Tare 9

Lieutenant Thompson's LST #222 crew had tied up at 10:45 A.M. They had spent the night racing back to Pearl Harbor after repairing her damaged bow doors and ramp. After debarking all of her LVTs onto the shore of Hanaloa Point, the crew was spending a quiet Sunday afternoon aboard ship when all hell broke loose.

"Explosion on LST 39 dead ahead of us," the officer of the deck mistakenly reported at 3:10 P.M. "Fire stations" was sounded, and within three minutes Lieutenant Thompson had his ship backing out of the berth, away from the exploding ships in front of him.[1]

On Lieutenant Geis's LST #461, with LCT-987 on her deck, one-third of the crew and most of the officers were ashore on liberty when the initial explosion occurred. However, within minutes, the officer of the deck reported, "Captain at conn. Executive officer on bridge. Both of ship's boats shoved off to rescue survivors."[2]

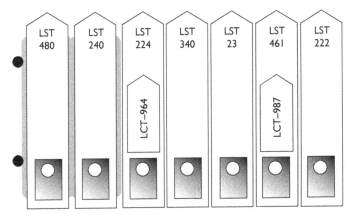

Tare 9. Drawn by Gene Eric Salecker, redrawn by Kristie Buckley. Copyright © 2014 by the University of Oklahoma Press.

"We were . . . one row remote when this happened," remembered XO Jack S. Futterman. "I gave orders to chop the lines. We were either the first or second out of there. I was the executive officer by this time, and we launched our life boats so we could help because there were men jumping in the water."[3]

Shipfitter Vincent Cavalier remembered the chaos. "Everything blew up in front of us and around us. . . . Half of the crew was on leave, they were on the shore, and there was only half the crew on the ship." As Cavalier recalled, the few crew members left behind broke out the fire hoses and axes. "Everything. We broke out everything we could."[4]

Down below in the engine room, MoMM3/c Dan Tanase "heard several loud bangs and the ship shivered." When Tanase went topside to see what was going on, he saw "the ships afire and blasts going off and fire and smoke. There was panic everywhere." With the fire stations alarm sounding, Tanase headed back down to the engine room to start the main engines. There he found CE Harry Fritts already on the job. Starting the two diesel engines, Fritts and Tanase had LST #461 ready to go in minutes. However, they still had to wait for the deck crew to cast off the lines to the ships on either side of them.[5]

Burning debris caused four small fires on LT George A. Martin's LST #23. As reported in the deck log, all fires were under control in less than two minutes as all hands responded to fire stations.[6]

"Debris from the '39' [sic] covered other LSTs," one crewman from #23 recalled. "Fire was breaking out on LSTs all around us. Our crew reacted quickly, and while some were throwing life jackets to men in the water, others were hosing down the decks to prevent fire from spreading to the '23'"[7]

As with every other vessel moored in the middle of a tare, Lieutenant Haskell, the skipper of LST #340, had to wait for the outboard ships to clear his starboard side before he could begin maneuvering out of harm's way.[8]

Since the wind was blowing toward the southwest, much of the flaming debris thrown up by the explosion on LST #353 was carried back toward LST #340. Marine Paul E. Cooper (Battery L, 14th MarReg, 4th MarDiv) remembered, "There was a terrific explosion on LST 69 [sic], which was directly ahead of ours. This explosion caused fires on several LSTs. The explosion sent men flying through the air and into the water. Other men started jumping overboard to get away from the fire."[9]

At the time of the explosion, LST #340 had only one of its main engines operational, and her "bow doors were open, as repairs were being done to one of the doors." Although half of the crew was on liberty, XO Anthony Tesori found enough men to man the fire hoses and play a stream of water across the forecastle "to keep the drums of gasoline on the main deck from catching on fire."[10]

The 23 mph wind from the northeast carried a large amount of debris onto Lieutenant Pugh's LST #224, which was carrying LCT-964. "Shells were bursting overhead, and flames were threatening to set fire to surrounding ships," ENS B. Rubin wrote. Within thirty seconds, #224 "sounded emergency fire alarm and passed word to extinguish all fires on top-side." While some crewmen began casting off the mooring lines, others soon had "All hoses in use to keep deck wet and extinguish any fires."[11]

A rain of exploding shells fell down upon the bow of LST #224. "Some of those shells were filled with phosphorous, and some of it landed on our gasoline barrels in the jettisoning racks," COX Eddie Farrow recalled. "Phosphorous and gasoline are a dangerous combination." Aware that burning phosphorous will reignite once it dries out, some firefighters were ordered to pour a continuous stream of water atop the stored drums.[12]

PhM George Gregory recalled another hazard of the phosphorous. "That day one of our crew was injured by a phosphorous shell that exploded. His arm was severely burned, and I could only pack it in petroleum jelly and send him to the hospital."[13] The injured sailor was MoMM3/c Ernest J. Garbitt, Jr. RM2/c Bernard Schofield witnessed the incident. "I was on the bridge. I saw . . . my friend, Ernie Garbitt, on the fo'c'sle become engulfed in flames from a phosphorous bomb. Ernie was evacuated to a hospital in Honolulu where he spent one year undergoing skin grafts." From his position in the radio room on the starboard side of the navigation bridge, Schofield had a bird's-eye view of what was going on around him. "There was thick black smoke and flames rising in the air. Oil was burning on the water and foreign matter was flying through the air and coming down on the ships and harbor."[14]

MoMM2/c Floyd "Dutch" Williams was on the fantail when the explosion came. "I was a crew chief. I headed for the engine room over the top of the guys trying to get topside. We started the engines, but because they had not had time to warm up, they kept dying when we tried to back down." While in the engine room, Williams wondered about what was going on topside. As he recalled, "I began to worry about all those fires on the main deck, all that ammunition stored in the tank deck, the gasoline on the main deck, and the fact that the engine room held us trapped below the water line."[15]

"The reason our ship was not burned . . . was because many of our crew responded to the emergency with complete disregard for their personal safety," wrote ENS Eugene Harter, the stores officer. "Immediately after the first explosion, we ordered 'general quarters' to be sounded, and the engineers got the engines running. . . . Meanwhile, our bow doors were open and our ramp was in the water and our crew was able to bring many sailors aboard who had jumped off the vessels that were exploding. This included quite a few injured men."[16] For the time being, LST #224 was safe.

Lieutenant Wells's LST #240 felt the blast as "a tremendous explosion." Instinctively, the crew immediately took fire and rescue stations and organized firefighting groups with complete equipment. Within minutes, the main engines were "lit off" and the crew was making "all preparations for getting underway." While Wells raced to the conning tower to move his ship out of the danger zone, the executive officer rushed forward to supervise the fire-fighting activities.[17]

Half of the crew of Lieutenant Johnson's LST #480 were on liberty, and none of the Marine or Army passengers were on board when the gas drums on #353 blew up. Moored to the dolphin pilings at Tare 9, #480 had to wait for all of the outboard ships to move before she could move herself, and because she was downwind of the explosion, #480 was struck with a large amount of debris and shrapnel. Devoid of an LCT, but saddled with a pair of pontoons, her main deck was crowded with trucks, jeeps, and trailers, all covered with canvas tops. The first rain of debris set many of the tops on fire.

Signalman James J. Gooley was blown off the bridge and had the signal light come down almost on top of him. "The compass was blown into the water. Everything started flying over to [our ship]. There were sacks of potatoes on the main deck, and they were blown into the air. . . . General quarters was sounded, and everyone went to his station."[18]

SF Art Sacco was on the tank deck when "a loud explosion knocked me down." Sacco "ran up the deck to topside fo'c'sle, [and] saw a ship on fire and exploding. Soon others were on fire and spewing fire and shrapnel on other ships." Remaining calm and collected, Sacco "manned a helmet and phone off a gun tub and told the engine room to build up pressure on the fire pump. I told a few seamen to grab the fire hose off the port booby hatch. I took the one off the starboard."[19]

MoMM2/c Harold Knebel was taking a shower after a busy work day when he suddenly "heard a loud boom followed by the fire alarm." As Knebel recalled, "I immediately got out of the shower, did not take time to dry off, put on my underwear shorts, then my pants and shoes, and proceeded to my fire station in the generator engine room and started the fire pumps and built up the pressure." Even over the noise of the engines, Knebel could hear the continuous explosions from the ships at Tare 8.[20]

Tare 10

The closest ship at Tare 10 was more than 1,000 feet away from LST #353. Although seemingly far away from the explosion, most

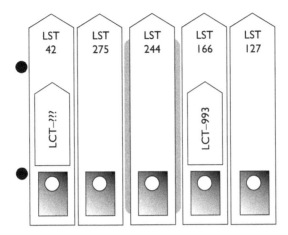

Tare 10. Drawn by Gene Eric Salecker, redrawn by Kristie Buckley. Copyright © 2014 by the University of Oklahoma Press.

of the ships in Tare 10 were touched by the rain of debris and shrapnel. Fortunately, because the number one ship in Tare 10, LST #42, was in the process of leaving the nest to get fresh water, most of the ships were already making "preparations for getting underway" when the first explosion came. Not surprisingly, the crews of all five ships in Tare 10 were quick to respond to the growing disaster.

Lieutenant Reed's LST #127, the outboard ship at Tare 10 and carrying her full crew and about 350 Marines, had been preparing to get underway since 2:38 P.M. but had been forced to wait for LST #128, then moored to her starboard side, to get out of the way. Only five minutes after the explosion, LST #127 was able to report, "Underway at various courses and speeds. Broke out fire fighting gear, wet down all topside."[21]

LT(jg) Seymour Tabin, a junior officer on #127, was inside the deckhouse at the time of the first blast. "In addition to the sound of the explosion, there was a big pillar of smoke and flame," he wrote. "Jack Reed, the skipper, was visiting on another LST in our tier. I ran to the bridge and ordered the ship to back full and the lines chopped. We were halfway backed out when Jack managed to jump aboard." As Lieutenant Reed raced up to the conn, the crew had their "fire hoses spraying as debris from explosions occasionally landed on our deck."[22]

The Coast Guard–manned LST #166, skippered by Lieutenant Bradley, was piggybacking LCT-993 to the battlefront. Two
minutes before the initial explosion, the crew of #166 was making
"preparations for getting underway as inboard LST [#42] prepared
to move out of [the] berth." Two minutes after the explosions, the
crew was manning the fire hoses as "ignited fragments from [the]
explosion land[ed] in various sections of ship and the LCT." At the
same time, the crew "commenced clearing the mooring lines from
LST 244 on [the] port side and LST 127 on [the] starboard side."
Seconds later, the ship began backing out of Tare 10.[23]

Although keeping a diary was strictly forbidden during wartime for fear that the book might fall into enemy hands and give
away vital secrets, Alfred E. Erickson, a sailor aboard LST #166,
managed to keep his diary hidden. For May 21, 1944, he wrote:
"Anchored in Westlock. LSTs tied in pods of four or five. Assigned
to boat duty. Left the ship at 1430 hrs. with a working party. About
75 yards from the LST 39. There was a tremendous explosion on
the bow of the 39. Looked like the 55-gallon drums of high octane
gas for the Marine amtracks blew. Men running toward the stern,
some jumping in the water. Boat picking up men out of the water.
In the meantime the LSTs . . . tied alongside the 39 caught fire and
ammo started to blow."[24]

Another crewman, MoMM1/c Richard MacNealy, was on
duty in the engine room when the first blast came. "I heard a loud
noise and was about to go on deck to see what was going on when
our general quarters alarm sounded and the signal came to start
engines. Once I got the engines running, the signal came to go
full speed astern." When other men assigned to the engine room
showed up, MacNealy went topside to see what was going on. He
wrote: "The air was filled with fire, smoke, flying debris, fifty gallon cans of gasoline, ammunition, bodies of both sailors and Marines, and shrapnel flying everywhere. . . . Our crew could not
untie the ships on either side of us because they were secured with
steel cables and the cables were secured on the ships next to us. . . .
We and the other ships that were tied together all had fires on our
decks from the debris that was all over the area."

Debris set fire to the loose deck material on LST #166 and the
canvas coverings on LCT-993. While the deck crew fought to extinguish the fires, the engine crew maintained power on the diesel

engines. "Boy," MacNealy wrote after returning to the engine room, "I thought I was gonna die because we were down in the engine room and the exhaust fans blow all the stuff down there and it was just smoke, smoke, smoke, and they wouldn't let us leave. So we'd go up into the passageway and then come back down with handkerchiefs." Eventually the thick smoke became too much. "We called up to the bridge and told them our situation and their answer was for us to stay at our duty stations. We took turns, one of us in the engine room with rags over our noses and the other three of us up on topside taking a break."[25]

Many of the Marines who had been assigned to LST #166 were topside when #353 blew. Although ordered to go below, William L. Maxam (Co. F, 10th MarReg, 2nd MarDiv) and a friend stayed on the main deck because they "didn't like the idea of being trapped inside the ship with all the ammunition aboard." As Maxam tried to stay out of sight, he noted that the sailors on LST #166 were "running like crazy to cut the hawsers" that tied them to the other ships. Looking over the side and into the water below, Maxam saw "parts of rifles, packs, and blankets" but no bodies.[26]

LST #244 was sporting floating pontoons on each side of her hull. Since LST #244 was getting ready to move to let LST #42 out from beside the dolphins, her main engines were "started and warming up" at the time of the first explosion. Within five minutes, the ship was backing out of the nest. Unfortunately, LSTs #166 and #127, both to starboard, had yet to completely cast off the hawsers and cables. As the officer of the deck, ENS M. J. McFarlane, reported, "LST 166 and 128 [sic] still had lines over to our starboard bow, and we pulled them out with us about 100 yards before they were completely cast off."[27] Subsequently, the crew of LST #244 felt that they had been the first ship to escape from Tare 10 and were responsible for saving LSTs #166 and #127, the two outboard ships.

Although LST #244 was almost 1,200 feet from the initial explosion, the blast had enough force to stagger crewman Henry D. Johnson. He saw "what looked like part of the deck going up in the air in a ball of fire accompanied by smoke." In all likelihood, what Johnson saw was LCT-963 on the deck of LST #353 rising up by the bow, since a half dozen eyewitnesses testified at the Navy court of inquiry to this occurrence. "After that," Johnson recalled, "everything was panic and confusion. Some of the LSTs started their engines and attempted to back off even before the lines holding them together were cast off."[28]

LST #275, commanded by Lieutenant Dunlavey, had her bow doors open and her ramp down. Perhaps being so far away from LST #353, Dunlavey's crew seemed to respond slowly to the building disaster. It took a full seven minutes after the initial explosion for the crew to cast off all lines to the ships on either side and for the engines to begin backing the ship full astern. To protect their own store of gasoline drums, Dunlavey ordered all fire hoses manned and a spray of water played across the bow. As they backed away from Tare 10, #275 had still not raised her ramp or closed her bow doors.[29]

LST #42 was hemmed in by all of the ships moored outboard of her. Fortunately, it had been about to move when the explosion occurred. The crew had been waiting for Lieutenant Guy to return from a meeting, and all of the ships outboard of her were getting ready to let her out and then shift over one spot. Almost immediately after the explosion, the remaining officers made the decision to move the ship without their skipper. Five minutes after the first explosion, as the outboard ships began to peel off, LST #42 began "backing down into [the] channel. . . . All fire hoses are broken out and topside is wet down."[30]

Earlier in the day, Captain's Talker Bill Warren had mistakenly called the crew to stations with a false special sea detail order. He was up in the conning tower worrying about what his skipper would say when, as he recalled, "Hell popped!" Looking out over the vast armada of moored LSTs, Warren had a grand view. "I saw a black cloud of smoke, two rows of ships ahead of my ship, which was followed by a roar." Instinctively, Warren put on his helmet and life jacket. "I then sheepishly glanced around the other LSTs to see if I was hearing things again, as I had 'heard' special sea detail sound." This time, however, the emergency was real, and every other crew was responding to the emergency.

With the skipper gone, ENS G. J. Duke climbed into the conning tower and took command. "Standing on top of the conn railings [because] he was a short man," wrote Warren, "we worked together; he gave what orders were necessary, such as casting off all lines from both pilings and the LST tied up to our starboard."

With flaming debris landing all over the main deck and the LCT, the crew asked permission to flood the main deck. As Warren remembered, "this was immediately done."[31]

Although LST #42 was almost one-quarter of a mile away from LST #353, the blast had enough power to knock Marine PFC Joe Drotovick (Co. F, 23rd MarReg, 4th MarDiv) out of his cot underneath the LCT. Drotovick rushed to the side rail and looked at the smoke and flames rising high into the air. As ships in Tares 9 and 10 began backing out of their nests, Drotovick had an unobstructed view of Tare 8. Later, he recalled seeing "many bodies in the water . . . [and] a few small craft rescuing men who were alive in the water."[32]

Another Marine from Drotovick's company was PFC Ray E. Fahnestock. "What a blast that was!" he wrote. Since LST #42 was moored next to the dolphins and only about 100 feet from shore, many of the Marines wanted to go over the side, but as Fahnestock remembered, "everyone held fast" and waited to see what was going to happen. As the Marines waited, the crew readied the ship to get underway. "This seemed like an eternity," Fahnestock admitted, "as the explosions continued to go off."[33]

Because of the close proximity to the exploding ships in Tare 8, all of the vessels in Tares 9 and 10 at West Loch that day were in immediate danger. Still, even vessels that were far away, moored on the other side of the basin at Tares 5, 6, and 7, or near the naval ammunition depot, were threatened. With the scope of the disaster unfolding in West Loch, no ship within a half-mile radius of Tare 8 seemed safe.

| # Nowhere Seemed Safe

No matter where a vessel was in West Loch on that Sunday afternoon, it was in danger. If a ship was not within range of the falling debris, it might have been in danger from the spreading gasoline and burning oil slick that leaked into the loch. Ships that had not been in close proximity might still end up in danger when some of the exploding ships began to drift. Even ships far away found themselves in danger, not so much from the burning vessels but from ships that were making a maddening, headlong, almost uncontrolled dash to get out of the area. No one was safe.

Tare 7

The high-speed transports *Overton, Waters,* and *Stringham* were moored at Tare 7 near the very tip of Intrepid Point, at the mouth of Walker Bay, facing northeast into the bay. Because of the placement of the dolphin pilings, they were the only major vessels in West Loch tied up with their starboard side to the dolphins. Also, because of the placement of the pilings, they were almost straight across from Tare 8 and the exploding LST #353.

Fortunately for the three ex-destroyers, most of the flaming debris was blown toward the southwest, away from them. However, even a strong wind could not stop the lethal, heavy shrapnel.

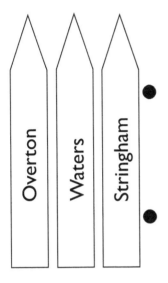

Tare 7. Drawn by Gene Eric Salecker, redrawn by Kristie Buckley. Copyright © 2014 by the University of Oklahoma Press.

USS *Overton* was tied up as the outermost ship at Tare 7 and was only 600 feet away when #353 exploded. The crew immediately sprang into action. Two of their four small boats were put over the side to pick up men in the water, the fires were started under the boilers in an attempt to raise immediate pressure to get underway, and the men hurried to man their fire stations.[1]

"The fire immediately gained fury, causing ships to be abandoned," noted the *Overton* quartermaster. "The LST on her port caught fire [#179]. . . . Hundreds of small explosions occurred; presumably it was ammunition." Within three minutes, LCDR D. K. O'Connor's crew was throwing all ready ammunition overboard and wetting down the decks.[2]

USS *Waters* was having repairs done to her main air pumps. The deck log of *Waters* described the initial blast on #353 as "a violent explosion . . . which started a raging fire followed by other explosions." While the crew rushed to their fire stations, the engineering officer estimated that it would take at least two hours to get the pumps back together and the ship operational. Stuck in a bad situation that was quickly getting worse, the men of *Waters* watched as the raging fires on #353 began "spreading to LST #39 and others inboard of #353."[3] Without any means of propulsion, LCDR C. J. McWinnie could only wait and hope that the engine room crew could put the disassembled air pumps back together in record time.

Within seconds of the initial explosion, general quarters was sounded on the high-speed transport *Stringham*. While a few men jumped into the small boats and went to the rescue of men pouring off the decks of the LSTs, most of the crew prepared the ship to get underway. Locked in against the dolphin pilings, however, Lieutenant Commander Ralph H. Moureau had to wait for both *Overton* and *Waters* to cast off from his port side before he could leave the area.[4]

Morris Folstad was aboard the old World War I destroyer and remembered, "An explosion occurred on an LST about 100 yards on our port quarter. Fire quickly spread to other LSTs. . . . We were lucky to be on the lee side and it didn't spread our way."[5] As the crew of *Stringham* waited for the two outboard ships to move, they could only wet down their decks, wait for their small boats to return with survivors, and hope for the best.

Tare 6

Tucked around the far side of Intrepid Point was Tare 6, with five LSTs. Since Tare 6 was on the northern bank of the winding channel that led into West Loch, the LSTs were moored with their fantails pointing almost directly toward Tare 8. Moored about 1,500 feet away from LST #353, the ships at Tare 6 had little to fear from the flaming debris but were still well within range of the spray of shrapnel.

Perhaps because of the distance from LST #353, Lieutenant James on LST #273 did not begin to make preparations for getting underway until five minutes after the first explosion.[6]

When LST #353 exploded, S1/c Bill Gourlay, who was below deck, heard "a terrible loud explosion, one that was deafening to the ears." It made his ship "shake, rattle, and roll." Rushing topside, Gourlay discovered that "All hell was breaking loose. All kinds of metal was falling over [our ship], in fact all over the lagoon." Fearing for his safety, Gourlay squeezed behind an upright air duct and waited for the shrapnel to stop falling.[7]

Most of the crew of the Coast Guard vessel, LST #169, was on liberty. As general quarters was sounded and the short-handed

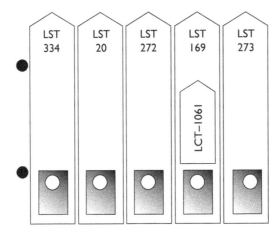

Tare 6. Drawn by Gene Eric Salecker, redrawn by Kristie Buckley. Copyright © 2014 by the University of Oklahoma Press.

crew made preparations to get underway, Lieutenant Kittredge sent two ship's boats out to rescue survivors.[8]

Clyde V. Cook, the chief bos'n mate on LST #272, remembered that seconds after the first explosion he saw men jumping from the burning boats into the water below. "There must have been at least a hundred. Only their heads were showing, and they looked like a large flock of ducks swimming on a pond." Then Cook saw the oil that had spread across the water and around the swimmers catch fire. "The fire swept across the swimming men, and after it passed, not a head was to be seen."[9]

Down below in the tank deck, soldiers from the 27th IDiv Field Artillery Unit were storing their 105mm artillery shells when the concussion from the explosion knocked several of them off their feet. Charlie Danio was thrown down so hard that two teeth were knocked loose. When Danio finally reached the main deck to see what had happened, he saw only smoke and flame. "LST #272 was some distance from the LSTs where the explosion occurred and [you] couldn't see much with the naked eye," he admitted. When the invasion force finally reached Eniwetok Atoll a week later, Danio had the two loosened teeth extracted.[10]

Having been moored at Tare 6 since May 12 in a "disabled condition" because both engines were down, Lieutenant Smith's Coast Guard–manned LST #20 was not prepared for an emergency. At

3:10 P.M., the officer of the deck reported a "loud explosion and severe fire aboard U.S.S. LST 39 and U.S.S. LST 353 berthed in tare docks astern of this vessel." The fire alarm was sounded, the fire hoses were let out, and within minutes the decks were being wetted down. At 3:15 P.M., four volunteers from LST #20 climbed into a rescue boat and went out to pick up survivors. Unbeknownst to all four, they were rushing into a maelstrom of destruction.[11]

The innermost ship at Tare 6 was LST #334. Moored to the tare since May 11, with "forward compartment damage," she also had the port engine down for a major overhaul. Within one minute of the initial explosion, the skipper, Lieutenant Blieden, signaled the crew to break out the fire hoses and set special sea detail. Four minutes later, the officer of the deck wrote, "Commenced wetting [down the] main deck, bridge, conn, and ready [ammunition] boxes." Blieden was not about to lose his ship.[12]

Tare 5

Tare 5, the last major mooring spot within sight of Tare 8, was well over one-third of a mile from the epicenter of the initial explosion. Although in no immediate danger, the crews of the five ships moored at Tare 5 knew the contents of the burning ships at Tare 8. They all realized that at any moment, a devastating explosion might rip those ships apart and send flame and debris over the entire loch. Although seemingly far enough away, all five vessels made immediate preparations to leave West Loch.

Fortunately, the outermost ship at Tare 5, LST #34, was already preparing to pull away from the tare when the gasoline drums exploded on the bow of #353. Within three minutes, Lieutenant Davis had his ship safely on her way down the narrow, winding West Loch channel.[13]

LST #45, with LCT-965 chained to the main deck, was in the number four position at Tare 5 when LST #353 exploded. While General Quarters was being sounded and the crew was rushing to break out the fire hoses and axes, ENS Blanton took eleven crewmen from the fire and rescue party in a ship's boat to see what they could do to help the men jumping into the water. Since the ship's skipper, Lieutenant Gamble, was not aboard, the executive officer

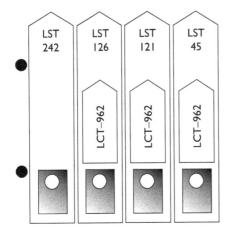

Tare 5. Drawn by Gene Eric Salecker, redrawn by Kristie Buckley. Copyright © 2014 by the University of Oklahoma Press.

ordered special sea detail set and made preparations to get LST #45 out to sea. At the same time, the fire control crew began spraying water across the ammunition boxes and high-octane oil drums stored on the bow.[14]

Unlike so many of the other LSTs in West Loch, LST #121 had the entire crew present and had just brought aboard fifteen tons of provisions. After hearing the first explosion and seeing smoke rising from Tare 8, Lieutenant Devaney took the conn and ordered his crew to make all preparations for getting underway. Stuck in the middle of the nest, however, the skipper knew that he had to wait for the two outboard ships to clear the tare before he could move his own ship. Until then, all he could do was sit and wait.[15]

Lieutenant Krueger's LST #126 was carrying LCT-962 on her main deck. Within a minute of the first explosion, the crew was "wet[ting] down inflammables topside," while the ship's "Small boat [was] dispatched to aid in rescue at the scene of explosion."[16]

BM2/c Hillman was in the mess hall when he heard the explosion. As Hillman recalled, "Everybody cleared out from below decks and headed to the main deck to see what had happened. I could clearly see a large cloud of smoke coming from a group of LSTs moored about 300 yards away in a nest of 8 LSTs berthed at #8."[17]

Donald Lux was by himself in the main engine room when "all hell literally broke loose." As Lux recalled, "Half the crew was on well-earned liberty . . . when the engineering telegraph jangled and down the voice tube came the cryptic command, 'Make emergency preparations for getting underway.'" Although all alone, Lux immediately began working on the engines. Within seconds, "GQ [general quarters] brought [the] crew tumbling down the ladders to lend a hand. From the noises we could hear through the hull, we knew this wasn't a drill."[18]

LST #242 was moored with its port side to the dolphins at Tare 5 when the first explosion occurred. XO J. P. Kennedy was in his room in the deckhouse when he heard the explosion and rushed to the main deck. After spotting "a ship astern of us ablaze," Kennedy, who was the senior officer aboard since the skipper, Lieutenant Winney, was off ship, jumped into action.[19]

"All fire hoses on the main deck and boat deck were broken out and immediately manned," wrote Kennedy. "Ammunition, gasoline, and other inflammables were wet down." Although nobody was present who could navigate #242 through the narrow West Loch channel, special sea detail was sounded, and the crew rushed to get their ship ready to move. In the meantime, a call went out for a qualified pilot to come aboard and get them out of the danger zone.[20]

While the junior officers waited for a pilot they decided to discharge their passengers. "We had a bunch of Marines aboard, and we let them all off," said Fl/c Dale Moore. "They were able to go down the ladders and right on the beach there, just turned them loose there." Additionally, Moore recalled that the crew was actively wetting down anything flammable on the top deck. "And, of course, we had these big 55-gallon drums of aviation gasoline on the main deck, so the bos'n mate came up there and said, 'Well, let's start spraying this stuff down, we gotta water it down.'" As Moore stated succinctly, "'Cause if any shrapnel had hit one of them barrels it woulda blown us sky high."[21]

Tare 3

Far, far away from Tare 8, around the protective curve of Baltimore Point, was Tare 3, the fresh water dock. Moored in place on that Sunday afternoon were two LSTs, #226, tied up to the dolphins,

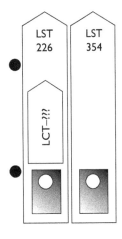

Tare 3. Drawn by Gene Eric Salecker, redrawn by Kristie Buckley. Copyright © 2014 by the University of Oklahoma Press.

and #354, on her starboard side. Although within hearing distance of the explosion, neither ship was in immediate danger and made no preparations for getting underway.

Only a few other major vessels were present in West Loch at the time of the initial explosion. LST #129 was moored in Walker Bay, and the pontoon-carrying LST #128 was in motion, returning to Tare 10 after finding no room at Tare 3 to receive fresh water. Additionally, the minesweeper USS *Terror* was berthed at pier WL-4 below Powder Point, across from Tare 10, the cargo ship *Joseph B. Francis* was docked in front of the ammunition depot unloading 3,000 tons of ammunition, and several LCIs were docked in Walker Bay. When the gasoline barrels on board LST #353 began exploding shortly after 3:00 P.M., each ship and crew was affected differently.

Only about 300 feet ahead of the exploding ships was LCI (G)-371, docked on the western shore of Walker Bay undergoing work on its diesel engines. Only about half the size of the LSTs (158 feet, 5.5 inches long by 23 feet, 3 inches wide), the LCI was in immediate danger from the explosions and flying debris from Tare 8.

"Early in the afternoon, shortly after 3 P.M.," wrote the engineering officer, LT H. D. Goodman, "as we were finishing the tune-up, I heard a muffled bang which sounded like a firecracker." Rushing topside, Goodman was not prepared for what he saw. "Just as I arrived on deck, I saw the LST moored at 'Tare 8,' LST #353 . . . blow up. The forward gun tub was blown high into the air followed by a body. Several others [bodies] appeared to be blown to the deck of the LST. The ship was instantaneously engulfed in flames with many subsequent explosions, most of which were generated by the drums of aviation gasoline lashed to the upper deck." Realizing that LCI (G)-371 was in grave danger if it remained where it was, Goodman rushed below to get his engines back together again.[22]

On the southeastern side of Walker Bay, with its ramp on the shore and its bow doors open, LST #129 was closer to LST #353 than she wanted to be. The officer of the deck reported, "L. H. Benrubi, Ensign, USNR, received [a] slight laceration of left leg caused by shrapnel from nearby explosion." Immediately, the crew broke out the fire hoses and began wetting down all flammable items on the main deck while four volunteers set out in one of the ship's small boats to rescue any people that they could.[23]

Out in the middle of the loch, Lieutenant Walden's LST #128 was just completing a full circle and heading back to Tare 10 when the first explosion occurred. With a clear view of the unfolding disaster, the officer of the deck penned, "Fire spreading on ship [LST #353] followed by another more violent explosion. LSTs nested together trying to get underway. Men jumping over the side of burning ships."[24]

Seabee Frank Craven was onboard LST #128 to help unload and assemble the two pontoons that the ship was carrying once it reached Saipan. He recalled, "We traveled up West Loch towards the [water dock], turned around to come back—boom!" Caught in the middle of the loch, LST #128 had to do some fancy maneuvering. "We had to travel back into the inferno and past it," Craven continued. "You don't stop a ship like you would an auto. Fires from the exploding ships were raining down upon us. We pulled out the fire hoses and kept the topside wet. We had about 80 drums of 100 octane gas topside. We got lucky—no casualties."[25]

Just across the channel from Tare 10, below Powder Point, someone aboard Commander Blakeslee's minesweeper *Terror* immediately notified the Navy Yard of "serious explosions and fire in Tare 8." The same message alerted the Navy Yard that West Loch needed firefighters. Although *Terror* was more than half a mile away from LST #353, Blakeslee had the engine room crew start the fires under his boilers.[26]

MoMM1/c Wood Beeghly recalled, "I just happened to be up on deck looking around, and all of a sudden I see this explosion. . . . Gasoline drums and sailors and Marines and soldiers. You could see them spinning around like a pinwheel and slapping the water." In response to general quarters, Beeghly rushed below and ordered the engines started, a process that would take at least twenty minutes with the old boiler-driven engines.[27]

The only other major ship at West Loch was the *Joseph B. Francis*, moored at the naval ammunition depot dock, at least 3,000 feet southwest of Tare 8. The cargo ship was in no real danger from the falling debris or shrapnel as long as none of the burning vessels drifted southward or the explosions got any worse. Hoping for the best, the depot authorities kept the cargo ship tied to the dock and instructed the civilian stevedores to continue unloading the highly volatile cargo of ammunition.[28]

Two minutes after the first explosion was reported to the Pearl Harbor Signal Tower, the Navy Yard notified the West Loch dispensary to send medical aid to the scene. Already the fire was reported to be spreading. Fire boats and two Harbor Patrol boats were dispatched to Tare 8, and the Navy hospitals around Pearl Harbor's East Loch were ordered to dispatch ambulances.[29]

Up on the banks beside Tares 8, 9, and 10 and about 120 yards from LST #353, Marine PFC Bob Arieta, a member of the military police, was on guard duty with his poi dog, Rebel. Hearing a rumor that Admiral Nimitz was supposed to come through on an inspection tour, Arieta was keeping Rebel, who was a personal pet and was not supposed to be with him while on patrol, out of sight and watching the LSTs when #353 suddenly exploded. "So I'm looking down at 'em, and the first one blows up. Right in front of my eyes." Pieces of flaming debris and shrapnel rained down around him, setting fire to some dry grass along the bank. Reacting quickly, Arieta grabbed a water bucket and raced to put out the fires. Running beside him the entire time was his faithful dog.[30]

Close by was the DUKW carrying Platoon Sergeant Wells, his driver, CPL Harold Reynolds, and the two other crewmen that were going for a few cases of Coca-Cola. "I felt the DUKW shudder and heard an explosion aft," wrote Wells. "I looked and saw a huge mushrooming cloud of smoke boiling above one of the LSTs in Tare 8." Seconds later, Wells ordered Reynolds to pull over.

Before the DUKW even stopped, however, the "Fires had leap-frogged to other LSTs and explosions hurled slabs of metal and other debris high into the air."[31]

Closer to the naval ammunition depot, H. E. Boulware, a chief cook and firefighter, was walking in a hallway on the second floor of the Marine barracks when the first explosion went off. "All of the glass was blown out," he recalled, and something hard hit him in the side. "Believe it or not, it was a silver dollar. It had to have been blown off one of the LSTs." He rushed off toward the ammunition depot to see what he could do.[32]

Another man who rushed toward the depot was EM3/c Harry Spence with the 76th Naval Construction Battalion stationed near Iroquois Point. "Those of us not on liberty were lazing around when there were several very big explosions. We ran outside and saw smoke rising from Westlock [sic]. Two of our trucks came by looking for volunteers to move 5 inch shells and drums of aviation gas off the docks. There were close to 2 dozen of us, and we jumped on the trucks and went to Westlock, which was only a scant mile away."[33]

CDR Bill Meehan, the skipper of USS *Goldsborough* (APD-32), another ex-destroyer converted to a high-speed transport, was on his way in the ship's gig to USS *Waters* when LST #353 exploded. "Around 1500 [3:00 P.M.] I was . . . passing an LST when an explosion occurred," he reported. "My boat was filled with shrapnel, fortunately none of us were hit. We picked up a couple of men who were blown overboard, returned them to the LST, we waited around to offer assistance, and then returned to the *Goldsborough*."[34]

S1/c Alex Bernal was alone in a small motor launch when the first explosion went off. "I was maybe thirty, forty yards away from the ship that exploded and [it] rocked the whole bay. You could see all kinds of debris going up sky high." As Bernal sat watching, a man jumped into the water from one of the LSTs. "So I picked up the first man and then, at last, I had help," Bernal continued. "We looked back, and fire started on the water and then the oil was burning. You couldn't even see the sides of the ships."[35]

Men stationed on ships in East or Middle Loch, or on shore duty around those lochs, also heard and saw the explosion. Some rushed to their battle stations, fearing that the Japanese had returned. Some rushed to hospitals or aid stations to find out what was going on and offer assistance. Some received orders to man their vessels and speed off to West Loch to help in the spreading disaster. Some did nothing.

Ship's Cook 2/c Roy Sannella of harbor tug YTB 129 was playing craps with some fellow crewmen on a pier in Middle Loch when the first explosion went off. "During the game, I heard a very loud explosion and looked at my watch," Sannella wrote. "It was exactly 3 P.M." On a hot winning streak, Sannella continued with the game. "I didn't think about it and kept shooting the dice."[36]

Someone who was more responsive was ENS Bill Clark from LCI (L)-77, whose ship was moored in Walker Bay. At the time of the first explosion, Clark was with a working party gathering provisions at the East Loch supply depot. "We had nearly finished loading our truck with supplies when it happened," Clark said. Although miles away, Clark could hear the explosions and see the smoke and flames. Wanting to get back to their ship as quickly as possible, the work party rushed down to the water. "We went to the depot's docks to get a boat to the ship," Clark wrote. "They refused, as all boats were restricted from West Loch. We would have to find another way back on our own." Leaving their loaded truck with a Marine guard, Clark and his men raced off to catch a bus to take them to another dock where they were hoping to catch a small boat back to LCI (L)-77.[37]

Relaxing aboard a transport ship in East Loch, reveling in the quiet time afforded him before the upcoming invasion, was SGT Harrold A. Weinberger, a member of the Photographic Unit of the 4th MarDiv. Weinberger had fought in World War I, been a professional cameraman for Hearst International Newsreels, and had worked in Hollywood for MGM Studios. Doubling as both assistant director and production manager, Weinberger had worked on such movies as *Too Hot to Handle* (1938) with Clark Gable and Myrna Loy and *Northwest Passage* (1940) with Spencer Tracy and Robert Young.

Shortly after 3:00 P.M., Weinberger, who had enlisted in the Marines at age forty-three as a combat photographer, had just come out on deck when he heard a distant rumble and saw smoke shoot "five hundred feet into the air." Experienced enough to know that something big was happening that needed to be captured on film, Weinberger sprang into action. "First, I ran to a compartment ladder and yelled down for all my crew to double time up to the deck with cameras and film," he said. "Beside myself (a cinematographer), there were three stillmen and two other movie cameramen aboard. In combat, usually a stillman and a cinematographer worked together as a team. Next I rushed to the officer of the deck, showed him my ITEM (intelligence team) identification, and requested a small boat. In five minutes time, I had an LCP with crew and my five men, and we were off to the disaster area."[38]

Four fireboats were quickly dispatched, but they were docked at Honolulu Harbor, 14 nautical miles from West Loch. COX Lindel C. Jones, the skipper of a 55-feet Coast Guard patrol craft, remembered that he was "just lounging around" when he got a call from Pearl Harbor. So far away from the scene, he had not even heard the explosion or seen the smoke. Ordered to take command of Fireboat X1426, Jones and others jumped aboard the four small, tough fireboats and headed west along the shoreline of Oahu toward the entrance to Pearl Harbor. Sadly, it would take some time to get there.[39]

CHAPTER 12 | The Second Big Explosion

As the official court of inquiry report stated, "A second large explosion occurred aboard one of these three LSTs [#353, #39, #179] which threw burning fragments in all directions and set fire to the high octane gasoline, bedding, canvas, and other flammable materials on the decks of the other LSTs."[1]

Whether there was a distinguishable second explosion or not is debatable. Some people recorded it, while others did not. What is known is that the LSTs continued to burn and the gasoline drums and stored ammunition continued to explode. The explosions came fast and furious as boxes of mortar shells, shells for the destroyers, ammunition cans filled with .30 and .50 caliber machine-gun ammunition, Bangalore torpedoes, blasting caps, and even nitroglycerin went up. Each explosion sent shards of metal flying in all directions and flaming debris arching upward and outward. Black smoke blotted out the afternoon sun. To some, the flames, the explosions, and the blackness created a real-life Dante's Inferno.

Tare 8

At the epicenter of the explosions that continued to rock West Loch was LST #353. After the initial explosion, the forward half of LST #353 was engulfed in flames, which quickly began detonating the

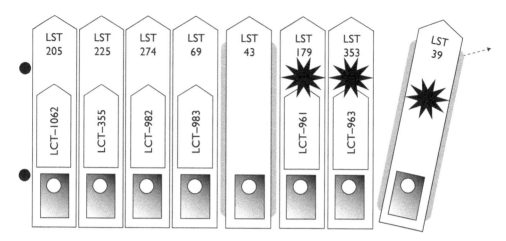

Tare 8: LST #353 is engulfed in flames, LST #39 is on fire and drifting to the right, and LST #179 is on fire. Drawn by Gene Eric Salecker, redrawn by Kristie Buckley. Copyright © 2014 by the University of Oklahoma Press.

gasoline drums stored on the bow and the ammunition stored around and under LCT-963. Heroic but unsuccessful efforts were made to extinguish the flames.

Assistant Engineering Officer Lockwood tried to assemble a fire party but discovered that "very little water was coming from the hose." While he was heading down a ladder to the auxiliary engine room to check on the water pressure, the second explosion erupted and blew him back up onto the main deck. Regaining his composure and glancing to his right, at LST #39, the outboard ship in the tare, he spotted his skipper, Lieutenant Martin, on the neighboring ship trying to get the officers to aim their fire hoses at his ship. At the time, however, #39 itself was burning and exploding.

Rushing back to the deckhouse, Lockwood found several men crowded inside, seeking protection from the falling rain of debris. Although the men wanted to flee to #39, Lockwood knew that it was already doomed. Instead, he sent them toward LST #179 to the left. As the men hurried off, Lockwood joined XO Lieutenant Thomas and another sailor on the fantail and began cutting loose life rafts to drop into the water below.[2]

As Lieutenant Thomas was working on the life rafts, he heard the cries of Lieutenant Martin. Looking over at LST #39, the executive officer noticed that it had broken away on the stern and was slowly drifting away from LST #353. Standing on the fantail, shouting to both Lockwood and Thomas, Martin implored them to do something to get him back on his own ship. Unable to help, and with the fire on LST #353 bearing down on them, the two made sure that "no one was left in sight aboard the ship" and then dropped into the water below. As Lieutenant Thomas recalled, from beginning to end "there was only seven or eight minutes before the ship was an inferno."[3]

As Lieutenant Figaro, the skipper of LST #39, recorded, "Fire immediately spread to 88 drums of gasoline on port and starboard side of forecastle and set off ammunition in ready boxes and rolling equipment [trucks, jeeps, trailers] on top deck." About five minutes after the initial explosion, Figaro reported, "A second tremendous explosion occurred on LST #353 which knocked [away the] causeway on port side and set off 20 mm ammunition. . . . This explosion also damaged the fire main as pressure started to go down immediately." To protect his Marine passengers, Figaro ordered them over the stern and starboard side aft. An instant later, he told his men to flood the aft magazine, where the ship's ammunition was stored. Ten minutes later, and fifteen minutes after the first explosion, Figaro ordered his crew to abandon ship. "[Since] the ship was full of smoke below decks and topside untenable; [and the] cargo ammunition was now exploding; abandon ship was sounded," he wrote. "This was done over the stern and starboard side aft as before."[4]

Marine Richard B. Alsaker had jumped off the fantail with the first group of men after the first big explosion because "All 'hell' was breaking loose on the LSTs." Swimming as fast as he could, he was "petrified with fear." As he headed toward an unidentified LST in Tare 9, it began backing out of its mooring. Fortunately, two sailors suddenly appeared on the open bow ramp, tossed him a line, and reeled him in, undoubtedly saving his life since he admitted that he "couldn't have swam much further."[5]

The communications officer on LST #39 was LT(jg) James Robert Maloney. "Jimmie was on deck and helped to put out the spreading fire, but it was total chaos," reported his cousin, Ernest Lefner. "He & others tried to loosen the ship from its moorings. Abandon ship order came down—and as communications officer, it was his duty to destroy all the ship's communications." According to Lefner, Maloney told a fellow shipmate that as soon as he was done, he was going to "get the hell out of here."[6] While he was gathering up the ship's logs and papers, LST #39 blew up around him.

Still on board at the time was S2/c Chet Carbaugh. "Some other sailors and I were making our way to try and put [out the fire] when the fuel blew up," Carbaugh stated. "It blew the bridge completely off, killing our communications officer, James Maloney. So we all started to abandon ship off the fantail."[7] Perhaps blown into the water by the same explosion was Lieutenant Martin, the skipper of LST #353. Last seen standing on the fantail of LST #39 as the two ships separated, Martin was later found unconscious in the water. He eventually woke up in a hospital and "didn't remember how he got there."[8]

After jumping from LST #39, Carbaugh swam hard to get away from the danger area. He recalled, "I was really just trying to swim away from the falling shrapnel. I don't even know if I was scared or not. Hell, I didn't even know if I was really awake. I remember getting real tired because I was wearing my boots. Luckily a patrol boat picked me up. If not . . . I don't know if I would have made it."[9]

Marine Elster Clements was one of the last men to leave the ship because he could not swim and did not have a life jacket. Standing on the fantail in his underwear, Clements waved his arms frantically until a rescue craft spotted him. He jumped into the water and was quickly pulled aboard. "They went about seventy-five yards when the #39 exploded." Jeeps, trucks, trailers, and all other kind of lethal debris cascaded down all around them, but nobody in the small boat was hurt. Already overloaded, the boat headed for shore to drop off the rescued men and go back to pick up more.[10]

Being downwind of LST #353, Lieutenant Mullis's #179 didn't have a chance. Fiery debris and shrapnel from the first explosion covered the ship from the forecastle to amidships and set fires among the stored gasoline drums on her bow, on the crated ammunition, and inside LCT-961 on her main deck. Although the crew and dozens of Marines fought valiantly to save their equipment and their ship, it was all for naught.

After shielding himself from the shrapnel thrown up by the first explosion, Navajo code talker PFC Thompson tried to help a few wounded men but found "the exploding ammunition was too much to handle." Since "the explosions were getting worse," Thompson decided to head for shore by climbing over and across the ships moored inboard of LST #179. "By now, everyone was trying to get away. Some of the men were jumping into the water while others were trying to escape by going from ship to ship inboard. Some men were screaming for help even though they were wearing lifebelts or jackets." After making his way over to LST #205, the first ship in Tare 8, he "looked down and saw the bodies of men in the oily waters." Thompson recalled, "Some had drowned, some were drowning, and others were trying to swim to shore or just floating while waiting to be picked up." Since Thompson could barely swim, he decided to wait and see what transpired.[11]

Even though crewman Carlyle Harmer had been knocked unconscious by the first blast, the second explosion woke him up. "I tried to get to my feet and discovered that I had a real bad nose bleed and a terrible headache from the concussions. I struggled to my feet and made my way to the main deck and looked at the bow. It was totally engulfed in flames." As further explosions tore the ships apart, Harmer heard someone shout, "Abandon ship. It cannot be saved." Jumping from the fantail along with "dozens of others," he began swimming the 400 feet to shore. "Red hot pieces of steel were landing in the water all around us," Harmer wrote. "There were large pools of burning oil and wounded screaming men dying everywhere. To tell the truth, it was a living hell, and I don't know how I lived through it. I was almost killed."[12]

When Marine Calvin Frawley finally made it topside after the first blast had knocked out all of the lights in the compartments below, he could not believe his eyes. "The devastation was something terrible, fellas with their legs and arms off, body parts, blood, terrible." At first Frawley tried to help fight the fires, but with almost three-quarters of the LST wrapped in flames, he and the others decided to abandon ship. "Everybody just jumped. And then the front end of our LST went up. That was the second major explosion, and it was gasoline, drums and drums of gasoline."

Once in the water, Frawley noticed that the gasoline and oil from the damaged ships had poured down onto the water and had caught fire. "There was gobs of burning gasoline right on top of the water. I looked back to the right and I could see all those boys dying. So I swam out into the harbor rather than going in that direction. I swam out into the harbor. I'd rather drown than get burned to death." Fortunately, the crew of a rescue boat saw the struggling Marine and threw him a life preserver attached to a life line. "Those boys that pulled me in with the life preserver, I never knew them, but they saved my life. Navy boys."[13]

Although flamethrower operator Harry Seehode was used to seeing things burn, he had never seen anything like this. After rushing aboard LST #353 to help an injured man, he was back on #179 going for a stretcher when the second blast blew him through the entrance to the deck house. After regaining his footing, he noticed a group of sailors from his ship rushing forward with a fire hose. A second later, "a great explosion" engulfed everything in a ball of fire. "There were no sailors after that," he remembered.

After helping to pass the word to abandon ship, Seehode moved to the fantail and looked down at the water. "There were a number of men who couldn't swim hanging around the guards protecting the screws [propellers]. The current was drawing everyone in the water back into the ships." Stripping down to his skivvies, Seehode, a strong swimmer, jumped overboard and swam over to help a struggling nonswimmer. Although the man was wearing a life jacket, he was going nowhere fast. Seehode grabbed hold of the jacket and took the man in tow, but the extra effort soon tired him out. Spotting an abandoned lifejacket, the plucky Marine grabbed it and rested for a few seconds. By now, however, the water all around him was aflame.

While Seehode was wondering what to do next, an LCVP Higgins boat zoomed into view trailing a rope. The skipper "hollered to several of the men in the water to hang onto the line" so he could pull them to safety. Needing no further invitation, Seehode and several others, including the nonswimming man in the lifejacket, grabbed onto the line while the LCVP pulled them "away from the fire [and] out to the middle of the stream." Eventually pulled aboard and dropped off on the opposite shore, Seehode, still clad only in his underwear, slowly began walking away from the exploding, burning mess, glancing back every now and then to view an unforgettable sight.[14]

Shortly after the first big explosion, the crew on LST #43 had the fires under control and began fighting the blaze on LST #179 on their starboard side. Within ten minutes, Lieutenant Zuehlke had his engines running and was ready to get out of the nest and away from the three burning ships moored to his right. However, as the log of LST #43 reported, "Attempts to get underway were unsuccessful as fires on forecastle made it impossible to cast off bow cable to either ships, inboard or out. Fires began to spread rapidly due to explosions on outboard ships." Thus when the second large explosion occurred, spreading more flaming debris around the ships at Tare 8, LST #43 was still attached to the exploding ships, trapped in a growing inferno.

While Lieutenant Zuehlke was proud of the crew and Marines of LST #43 who stood and fought the fires, he was disturbed by the sight of the "panicky evacuation" of dozens of Marines and crewmen from the three outer ships who streamed across his deck and impeded the actions of his firefighters. Rushing up to his navigation bridge, Zuehlke grabbed a megaphone and ordered all retreating personnel to stop and help put out the fires. Unbelievably, the panic subsided, and the men turned to help.

Moving up to the conning tower, Zuehlke witnessed "a rather terrible explosion," which seemed once again to come from the bow of LST #353. "Apparently all the gasoline went up," Zuehlke testified, "and this time the flames shot up maybe 75 or 100 feet into the air." This second major explosion once again scattered flaming debris across the main deck of LST #43. In spite of low water pressure, the crew managed to extinguish most of the fires.

Figuring that "things were pretty well under control," Zuehlke climbed down to the wheelhouse and made an "attempt to get the ship underway." Since the fantail of #43 was free of smoke and flames, he could see that his aft lines were clear from the ships on either side of him, but the flames and smoke around his forecastle kept him from knowing whether his forward lines had been cast off or severed. Taking a chance, Zuehlke ordered #43 forward. "By the way the ship reacted," he stated, "I felt confident that the wires which held the bow [of LST #43 to #179] remained on." Realizing that his ship could not move forward, Zuehlke told the engine room to reverse engines, hoping that he would have better luck backing out of the situation.[15]

Perhaps because LST #69 had her bow doors open at the time of the first explosion, the concussion bowled some people over and threw others about. To the men inside, the sound of that first explosion was loud and unforgettable. Up on the main deck, the concussion knocked people off their feet. Still, in spite of being knocked around and shaken up, the Coast Guard crew responded admirably and soon had most of the fires on the main deck extinguished or under control.

Shortly after the first explosion, Lieutenant Gott's crew had at least two fire hoses out, directing streams of water upon "several small fires." Reported Gott, "The deck was covered with camp cots, Marine bedding, and inside the LCT . . . it was the same. Also, there were wooden bulwarks built up for stowage of the ammunition. . . . All of this material seemed to ignite very quickly." The crew tried to keep the fires under control, but continuous explosions on LSTs #179, #353, and #39 constantly sent flaming debris their way. "A fire would no sooner be put out than another one started; a series of them."[16]

After the first explosion, S1/c Ancil G. Dinwiddie joined a gang of sailors with axes trying to chop #69's bow lines free from the ships on either side of them. "The crew cut all of them except for one [wire] cable that was run from the #69 to the #274 [on the port side]," Dinwiddie reported. Going aft to sever the stern lines, Dinwiddie was almost amidships when the second explosion happened. Although uninjured, Dinwiddie recalled that "two other men from the ship's crew were blown over the side from the second explosion." Littered once again with flaming debris and burning gasoline, the fires on LST #69 started to get out of control.[17]

One of the Marine passengers, George Hedges, had been sunbathing with a friend in "shorts and unlaced combat boots" inside LCT-983 when the first explosion went off. As the flaming debris set fire to almost everything inside the LCT, the two quickly abandoned the vessel and dropped down to the main deck. Minutes later, the two were "promptly knocked to the deck" by the second explosion. Hedges remembered seeing men "running everywhere, and wounded . . . lying on the deck." As a second storm of debris came down upon them, Hedges and his friend raced for the safety of the deck house.[18]

Marine Harry Pearce and his pal Sam had rushed to help their injured company sergeant, Paul Bass, who was bleeding from his eyes, ears, nose, and mouth from the concussion of the first explosion. "We picked Paul up," Pearce remembered. "I told Sam, 'Let's get him over to the next LST.'" Pearce grabbed Bass by the legs while Sam grabbed him under the arms. Sam led the way and climbed onto LST #274 to port, but just as Pearce was about to cross over the gap between the two ships, the second explosion hit. "When that explosion went off, it picked me up and took me clear over the LST that Sam was on," Pearce stated. "I came down on one of the guide wires that was holding an LCI on board. It just folded me in double and I went round and round three or four times and fell on the steel deck on my back only to have Sam reach out and grab me and pull me underneath the LCI."

Blown clear across LST #274 and over the piggybacked LCT-982, Pearce was amazed to find his friend there, too. "I said, 'How in the hell did you get here?' He said, 'They blew you over the LST and I [got blown] under the LCI.'" Although physically fine, the concussion injured Pearce's eardrums and left him bleeding from his eyes and ears. Unfortunately, when the concussive blast hit both Marines, they had lost their grip on Sergeant Bass, dropping him between the two ships. "I can remember as I went up in the air," Pearce said, "I saw him hit the water between the two vessels and just disappear, so he was lost."[19]

Down inside the auxiliary engine room, EM2/c Angelich and MoMM2/c Hanna were still manning the fire pumps when they felt the ship shudder. "We were there only five or ten minutes," Angelich remembered, "when the second explosion occurred which shook the whole engine. A few minutes after that one, Chief MoMM Ralph D. Hill, Jr., came to the hatch and called down for [us] to abandon ship." Needing no further prodding, both men rushed topside.[20]

The order to abandon ship had come from the officer of the deck, Lieutenant J. M. Silva. Before making the fateful decision, Silva had tried everything to save LST #69. The ship's magazines were flooded and "hoses were held on the ammunition, but they weren't doing any good," recalled Silva. "The flame was too hot and out of hand. The wooden cases containing the 5' shells were burning. All the life rafts on the bridge were on fire. . . . The #69 was afire and the ammunition stored below the LCT was burning." As he told the court of inquiry, with 750 5' 38 caliber projectiles aboard, he worried about the safety of his crew. When a third explosion ripped through the vessels at Tare 8, Silva gave the order to abandon ship.[21]

One of the complaints that Lieutenant Sard, the skipper of LST #274, had after the disaster was that the firefighting efforts of his crew were hampered by the exodus of the troops and crews from the outboard ships streaming across his deck. In spite of the problem, however, Sard's crew managed not only to extinguish most of the fires on their deck and inside LCT-982 but also to cut the lines mooring her to the outboard ships. Within fifteen minutes of the first explosion, the burning vessels "drifted away and aft" from LST #274.[22]

While the ship's crew continued to fight the fires, the Marines began to abandon ship. Lieutenant Sard claimed that he never gave the order to abandon ship, but in the wild panic of men from the other vessels passing over his deck, some shouting, "Abandon ship," the Marines and some of the crew members of LST #274 undoubtedly became confused. Then when the second large explosion showered an even greater amount of flaming debris atop their vessel, many of the crew thought that their ship was doomed and followed the mad rush across the innermost ships.

E3/c Tidwell from LCT-982 remembered that after the first explosion he abandoned #274 by crossing over the two inboard ships before dropping into the water. "I was in the water when the second explosion went, and I looked around and saw all the debris up in the air and I thought, 'Oh, it's gonna fall on me and kill me,'" Tidwell said. "So I thought, well, if I go underwater and stay underwater as long as I can, when it hits the water, the water will break the force of it and I probably won't get hurt." Diving down deep, Tidwell eventually made it to shore. "When I got to the beach, of course, the coral cut up my feet some, but you didn't feel it because of the adrenaline flow." Finding the beach crowded with fellow refugees, Tidwell and two frightened Marines took off running down the narrow dirt road between the beach and the cane fields.[23]

Tidwell's fellow crewman from LCT-982, S1/c Slater, was on the main deck of LST #274 when the second big explosion erupted. "It created a huge cloud and balls of fire," he recalled. "The concussion would cause the cloud to mushroom outwards, and then shrapnel and other debris would come down on us." As Slater and some of his fellow crewmen from LCT-982 sought cover, a piece of shrapnel sliced into one of the men. "It caused a large hole in the upper chest area, and he was unconscious," Slater stated. "That gash . . . spread from his right shoulder down across his belly button towards his right knee. And he was bleeding." Slater and the gunner's mate of LCT-982 picked up the wounded man and carried him into the galley of LST #274. "We laid him on the steam tables where they served the sailors their dinner," said Slater. "I left him there and went into the sick bay to get a pharmacist to stop the bleeding." Unable to find anybody, Slater and the gunner's mate "took what we could find and wrapped him and were able to stop the bleeding the best we could."[24]

Lieutenant Commander Hoyt, in command on LST #225, also complained about the interference of the refugees from the outboard vessels creating panic and confusion aboard his ship. He, too, was critical of people shouting, "Abandon ship" when, in his opinion, the order was not necessary. He told the court of inquiry that "the troops were as close to panic as I ever wanted to see."[25]

After leaving his shower, Yeoman Rusty Kaiser had been swept up in the panic and had jumped overboard completely naked, with his wallet in one hand and his watch in the other. "I really should not have abandoned ship," he admitted. "Yeah, we heard, you know, the guys shouting, 'Abandon ship,' but it wasn't from any of our officers. They could have court-martialed us for leaving the ship without permission.

"I swam over to the bank and was running through a field when I was suddenly knocked down," he said. Hit in the back by a piece of shrapnel from the second explosion, Kaiser "eventually made it to a hospital area where they cleaned and bandaged my back and gave me shorts and pants and a shirt." Years later, a doctor asked Kaiser about the lump in his back. "He eventually operated and took out a little chunk of metal. He said that if it had been about an inch more to the side it would have hit my spinal cord."[26]

Shortly after the first explosion, the executive officer of #225 had called down to the engine room to start the engines. Although moored as the number two ship at Tare 8, he intended to get out of the nest as soon as possible. Unfortunately, most of his crew was gone. "Panic of troops and naval personnel swarming over LST 225 from outboard ships plus fact that word to abandon ship . . . was passed from ship to ship caused most of crew to desert this ship," the deck officer wrote. With only a handful of crewmen present, it was becoming almost impossible to save LST #225.[27]

Fortunately, Hoyt had no intention of losing his flagship or any other ship for that matter. While he was crossing over the other ships to see what was happening, the second explosion blew him down and out. Eventually regaining consciousness, Hoyt started back to #225. While onboard LST #274, the number three ship, he noticed that Lieutenant Sard and his crew were "doing everything possible in a nasty situation" to save their ship. Speaking about #274, Hoyt testified, "She was heavily afire and her hoses were being continuously cut by flying debris . . . [but the crew] fought the fire with great courage and determination." Spotting the ship's first officer, Hoyt instructed him to move #274 forward, into the wind and away from the blowing debris, and he then crossed back to #225.

Upon reaching his ship, Hoyt was amazed to find that "most of the crew had left." "Her officers were getting the ship underway," he recalled, "two of them in the engine room and two with the few remaining deck hands were clearing lines." When Hoyt asked one of the officers where the rest of the crew was, he was told that "officers aboard [LST #205 to port had] waved their men off and then told [the crew of LST #225] to get the hell off."[28]

Lieutenant Goddard, the skipper of LST #225, had been away from his ship and was on his way back when the first explosion occurred. He later told Commander Hoyt that he was bobbing about in a small boat when the disaster started. "Within thirty seconds of the first explosion, at least two hundred men were in the water, swimming towards shore," he reported to Hoyt. Unable to reach his ship, he could only watch while a handful of his officers and crew and one plucky, angry lieutenant commander tried to save #225 for him.[28]

Although farthest away from the exploding LSTs, the officers and crew of LST #205 reacted the worst to the disaster. Refugees fleeing from the other ships hampered firefighting efforts on LST #205, and just twenty-two minutes after the first explosion, word was passed to the crew to "assist personnel in abandoning ship." Unfortunately, this assistance got out of hand, and everyone began fleeing the ship. Pretty soon there was less than a skeleton crew aboard #205.[29]

CPL Jesse Kirkes, a Marine who had come over from LST #43, four ships away, remembered leaving LST #205. "Someone lowered a rope ladder down the side of the ship so we wouldn't have to jump, but I was in a hurry, so I jumped." Right beside Kirkes was CPL Jim Reed, also a refugee from LST #43. "The water was on fire, oil fire," he remembered. "If you jumped you had to protect yourself in that. There was just no place to go. There was no place to protect yourself. It was just one explosion after another." In a hurry to get ashore, Reed also avoided the rope ladder and jumped overboard.[30]

The second explosion was more powerful than the first, being undoubtedly a mixture of exploding shells, ammunition, and gasoline rather than just gasoline itself. As the officer of the deck on board LST #225 reported, the second explosion started "numerous fires . . . on all ships."[31]

Although the ships in Tare 9 had been splattered by burning debris from the first explosion, the crews quickly contained the fires. The second explosion put the firefighting crews back to work and made it essential that the ships get away from the mooring as fast as possible.

CHAPTER 13 | Escape

Tare 9

The second explosion seemed to do more damage to the ships in Tare 9 than the first. Since hundreds of men were on the main decks of the seven vessels, fighting the fires, more bodies were exposed to flying shrapnel and debris. As the ships in Tare 8 continued to burn and explode, the LSTs in Tare 9 began to peel off from the outboard end and rush to safety.

The two outside ships in Tare 9 did not follow the panicky line of vessels leaving West Loch through the narrow channel but instead turned and headed into the shallow waters of the small boat area west of the naval ammunition depot. Since LST #222 had moored only a few hours before the first explosion, it took Lieutenant Thompson's crew exactly three minutes to get the ship away from Tare 9. As she was backing away from the nest of ships, the second explosion went off. Having broken both ramp chains during the Maui maneuvers and being unable to raise the ramp, Lieutenant Thompson knew his ship was unseaworthy and headed into the shallow small boat area.[1]

Six minutes after the initial blast, the crew of LST #461 cast off the lines to LST #222 on the starboard side and #23 on the port and began "maneuvering to save [the] ship and stand out of danger."[2] Shipfitter Cavalier remarked, "We cut the lines and got

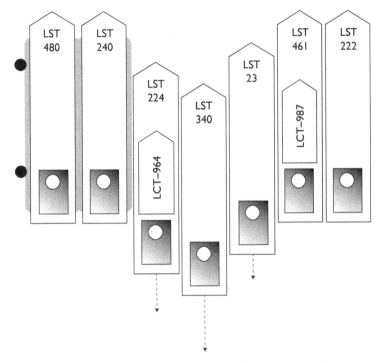

Tare 9: LSTs #23, #224, and #240 break away. Drawn by Gene Eric Salecker, redrawn by Kristie Buckley. Copyright © 2014 by the University of Oklahoma Press.

the hell outta there. Cut the lines with fire axes and we were lucky we were the outside ship because the ones inside were starting to go [burn]." As the ship also maneuvered toward the shallow water area, the third and most violent explosion suddenly went off.[3] LSTs #222 and #461 had picked the right time to move.

After LST #461 peeled away from the right side of LST #23, Bill Montague worked hard to get #23 released from #340 on their left. "Get the axes," he instructed his crew, "do what you gotta do, just cut the damn lines." While the crew was responding to his orders, the second explosion occurred. "Then all hell broke loose," Montague recalled. "Parts and shrapnel flew onto our deck and started fires on the canvas that the Marines had strung up to keep out the sun. . . . The powers of the explosions were like mini atomic bombs."[4]

As Ensign Sortevik remembered, "LT[(jg) M. C.] Darnell and the skipper [Lieutenant Martin] were on the conn giving orders. ... Chief Quartermaster [Willie] Williams took the ship out to sea after the lines were cut with fire axes. One of our lines, a 10-inch hawser on the port side, fell into the water and entangled the port screw." In spite of this handicap, Lieutenant Martin's ship headed down the West Loch channel and out to sea. "The ship continued on one engine."[5]

Like so many of the other crews in West Loch that afternoon, the crew of LST #340 did not wait for the ships on either side to cast off their lines. Instead, they severed them. Executive Officer Tesori recalled that the men "were able to sever hawsers holding [LST #340] to the other ships at the moorage and back away from the most dangerous area." However, as he admitted, "We did not escape entirely unscathed." As the officer of the deck noted, "Another and more intense explosion occurred in Berth 8 strewing our deck with wreckage and burning material. The firefighters of this vessel immediately flooded the entire main deck and the tank deck." Since the bow doors were open and in need of repair, LST #340 could not escape out to sea. Instead, she also headed for the shallow small boat area.[6]

Marine artilleryman Cooper had been bowled over by the first explosion and, after regaining his footing, had been ordered to "keep all of the men below decks to protect them from falling debris." As he was attempting to carry out his orders, the second explosion came. "All these men I was trying to keep below decks came running through the door at the same time. I got knocked down again as they went over the side and into the water."

"By this time," Cooper continued, "the smoke was so thick you couldn't see much in any direction. The water around the LSTs became covered in diesel fuel, and it was beginning to burn. Small boats came in to pick men out of the water, but visibility was so poor that some men were run over by the boats trying to rescue them." After Cooper moved to the fantail of the ship, he was told that there were a number of men hanging onto the guard rail protecting the ship's propellers. "From where I was standing I could see six men in the water hanging onto one of these guard rails," Cooper wrote. Knowing that LST #340 was about to get underway, and that the men would be sucked into the propellers, Cooper tossed a good strong line overboard. "Five of the men caught the line and pulled themselves to safety just as the ship's engine started up to move the ship out of the way. The sixth man was pulled into the screws and killed."[7]

The second explosion went off while Y1/c Frederick Hoffman was on the bow of LST #224 with a pair of earphones reporting on the condition of the ship. "The first explosion after being positioned there knocked me onto the deck," he stated. "I have always blamed my being hard of hearing on that experience." Once back on his feet, Hoffman reported to the bridge that there were "many fires in the cargo on the main deck." He continued, "Of special concern was the 55-gallon barrels of gasoline stored on the jettisoning racks, both port and starboard sides of the forecastle. Phosphorous from the exploding shells in the air ignited almost everything that was flammable, and this gasoline certainly was." Fortunately, crews were soon at work wetting down the dangerous cargo on the bow.[8]

In charge of the firefighting crews was ENS Gene Harter, who received a letter of commendation for his efforts. The letter stated, "His leadership in time of peril enabled the fire to be controlled, the magazines kept cool, and the 88 drums of 100 octane gasoline on the fo'c'sle from igniting." In addition to supervising the firefighters, Harter also "formed a rescue party on the [bow ramp], nearest the explosions . . . enabling the rescue of 34 survivors and casualties from the stricken vessels who were struggling in the water."[9] At a time when some men shrank from danger, Harter stepped forward and shouldered more than his share of responsibilities.

Harter, in turn, had good words for his crew. "Over 50% of our crew were on Liberty, and when the emergency happened, we were very shorthanded," he recalled. "The reason our ship was not burned with the other . . . LSTs was because many of our crew responded to the emergency with complete disregard for their own personal safety."[10] Likewise, Bill Kalencik, a PhM striker attached to the 4th MarDiv, gave "high praise to [the] crew for their coolness and bravery in fighting the fire and moving the ship to safer waters."[11]

To get away from LST #240 on her left side and #340 on her right, the crew chopped the steel mooring cables with fire axes. Radioman Schofield wrote, "I was on the bridge, and I recall the ship's steward [David] Moreland with a fire axe in his hands cutting the hawsers so we could get underway." As LST #224 began to move, the ships in Tare 8 continued to burn and explode. "Another explosion and then another," Schofield wrote. "The explosions just spread from one ship to another."[12]

Marine Bill Simpson (Hq Co., 25th MarReg, 4th MarDiv) agreed with Schofield. "One ship after another blew up which resulted in metal raining down from all over," he remembered. "Oil was burning over much of the water around the ship. . . . Finally, the ship's engines were started, lines were cast off, and the ship backed out into the channel." Undoubtedly the people aboard LST #224 were glad to finally be escaping.[13]

LST #240 was directly in the path of the windblown smoke and debris coming from Tare 8. As two small boats from LST #240 set out to help rescue survivors from other ships, Lieutenant Wells, the skipper, "Got underway to avoid burning debris and burning ships fwd of this vessel."[14]

Unfortunately, LST #480, sporting a pair of pontoons and sitting in the number one position, could not move from Tare 9 until all of the other ships outboard of her got underway first. Covered with fiery debris and shrapnel from the first explosion, the ship was doused once again when the strong southwest wind blew the debris from the second explosion across her decks. While the crew fought gallantly to put out the flames, they waited for the other ships to move and let them out.

"I don't think anybody jumped over from another ship onto ours," reported Radioman Freer. "All the time, as every explosion would go up . . . all this stuff would drizzle down and have little fires, you know, so we just kinda sprayed 'em."[15] MoMM2/c Knebel was at his station in the main engine room when he was called by the bridge. "I was told that 1/3 of the crew was on liberty and they needed me up on the bridge to help fight fires." Coming topside, Knebel was finally able to see what was going on. "Explosions happened every 30 seconds to every 3 minutes," he wrote. "Every time there was an explosion we were showered with all kinds of shrapnel. The noise was so loud that it burst my ear drums." Along with two of his shipmates, Knebel manned a fire hose. "It was our assignment to spray water on the 100 55-gal barrels of 100 octane aviation gasoline that was lashed to the main deck to keep them from exploding. Also to spray water on any material that was on fire that was coming from the other LSTs that were exploding. Several times the concussion of the explosions would knock me down."[16]

Tare 10

Since all of the ships in Tare 10 had been making preparations to let LST #42, the innermost ship, out of the berth, they were the first to break from their moorings and head out to safer waters. Being the last mooring station in line, the five ships at Tare 10 could simply back straight out of their moorage for several hundred yards, then turn slightly west into the shallow open bay area of West Loch.

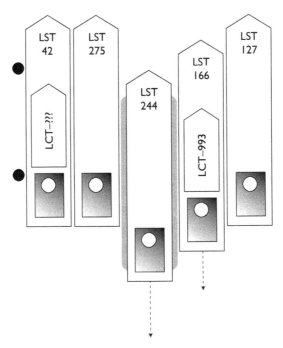

Tare 10: LSTs #244 and #166 break away. Drawn by Gene Eric Salecker, redrawn by Kristie Buckley. Copyright © 2014 by the University of Oklahoma Press.

Lieutenant Bradley's LST #166 may have been the first to move from the tare. She also may have begun to pull the two ships on either side of her out.

"We pulled two of them out with us," said Richard MacNealy, a member of the ship's crew. "One of them, on the one side, had its engine down [LST #244] and the other side [LST #127], I don't think the skipper or whoever's in charge knew what to do so we pulled two of 'em, one on each side out."[17] Actually, the officers on LST #127 were waiting for their skipper, LT Jack Reed, to get back to the ship from a visit aboard LST #166. When #166 began backing away from Tare 10, taking #127 with it, the officers on Reed's ship were still awaiting his return and had not yet cut the hawsers and cables connecting the two ships.

Crewman Alfred E. Erickson wrote in his diary, "The 166 . . . ordered flank speed astern pulling four LSTs away from the fire and explosions. The ships were tied together with steel cables, and some guys were using fire axes to try and cut the steel cables . . . without success."[18] Although Erickson mentions four ships instead of two, there is enough similarity between Erickson's and Mac-Nealy's statements to raise a question. Did LST #166 back out of Tare 10 first, and did she drag some of the other ships out with her?

Once out of her berth, however, and away from all of the ships around her, LST #166 headed for the shallow small boat area. While underway, the crew extinguished "several small fires started by ignited fragments from explosions on the stricken LSTs." The crew's quick actions and the fact that the engines were warmed up and ready to go enabled the officer of the deck to pen, "No damage of any kind suffered by this vessel."[19]

Whether LST #127 was pulled out or began backing out on its own, Lieutenant Reed jumped aboard his ship just before it began moving away from Tare 10. Rushing to the conn, he swung #127 east toward the narrow channel that led out to sea but found the passageway blocked by ships leaving from Tares 5 and 6. Reacting quickly, Reed turned his ship completely around and joined the growing number of vessels heading toward the large, shallow small boat area.[20]

"We backed away from the ship we were tied to," wrote Shipfitter Hillibush, "and they didn't even give us time to throw the lines off. We had to chop them off with axes." After the ship turned around and entered the shallow bay, Hillibush recalled, "we went as far as we could until we beached, hit the ground, which didn't matter, that's what we were built for, and we sat there and sat it out." From where they were, the crew had a panoramic view of the continuing disaster.[21]

Although the officers and crew of LST #166 felt sure that they were the first to leave Tare 10 and pull the adjacent two ships out with them, the men on LT L. W. Aderhold's LST #244, to the left, believed that they were the first to move and had saved the two ships tied to their sides. In the official logbook of #244, the officer of the deck wrote that "we pulled them out with us about 100 yards before they were completely cast off."[22]

Baker 2/c Bernard A. Rupprath certainly believed that his ship had pulled out the two vessels on either side of them. "Our engines were warmed up and our lines to the two LSTs on our port and starboard were being removed," he wrote. After the first explosion, "our LST was moving back to pull out from between the two LSTs and quick thinking we threw the lines back to the two LSTs and pulled them with us."[23] If Rupprath is correct, than the crew of LST #224 actually made a conscious effort to help save the two vessels on either side of them.

Once clear of the other ships, Lieutenant Aderhold maneuvered LST #244 almost straight back along Hanaloa Point, staying "as close to the shore as possible to clear other ships."[24] While the ship was in motion, crewman Henry D. Johnson looked back toward Tare 9. "Men immediately forward of the #244 started jumping into the water, and some were sucked underwater by the screws."[25] Having seen enough, Johnson turned away.

Ten minutes after the initial explosion, after all of the outboard ships had moved away, LT J. P. Dunlavey backed LST #275 out of Tare 10 and into the shallow back section of West Loch. While in motion, the crew finally managed to raise the bow ramp, which had parted with its chains during the Maui maneuvers.[26]

Trapped as they were between the outboard ships and the upright wooden dolphin pilings, the officers and crew of LT Roy Guy's LST #42 experienced some anxious moments before backing away from their berth. With their skipper gone, Captain's Talker Bill Warren remained in the open-topped conning tower helping Ensign Duke back #42 away from the danger area as hot debris fell down around them. "I picked a jagged piece of steel from my Mae West [life jacket]," Warren stated. "I lost track of the number of times I found myself on the deck, never recalling how I got there, but the cause was obviously concussion, as the various ships exploded." Busy with the maneuverings of his own ship, Warren saw very little of what was happening around him. "The only view I recall of one ship was its steel mast, red hot, propelled straight upwards towards heaven."[27]

In a little less than ten minutes, all five ships previously moored at Tare 10 had backed their way out of the nest and into the shallow "small boat area" of West Loch, west of the naval ammunition depot.[28] Seemingly out of the danger area and far away from the exploding ships at Tare 8, all of the crews from the Tare 10 ships waited and watched as the fire and explosions continued.

| Inaction and Indecision

Any ship moored north or east of Tare 8 was upwind of the burning and exploding ships and spared from the thick, choking black smoke that blew to the southwest. Still, several vessels were not far away when the second major explosion threw shrapnel in all directions.

Tare 7

With their firefighters spraying down the entire topside of their vessels, the officers and crews of the high-speed transports *Overton*, *Waters*, and *Stringham* waited impatiently for their boiler pressure to build as the ships in Tare 8 continued to burn. The officer of the deck aboard USS *Overton* recorded the second large explosion coming six minutes after the first and later noted that LST #39, the outermost ship in Tare 8, was "backing into the channel."[1] In reality, the hawsers and cables holding LST #39 to LST #353 had either been released, cut, or burned through and #39 was drifting into the main channel. The uncontrolled hulk was now a threat to any vessel downwind of her.

Tare 6

The five ships at Tare 6 had been pelted with a small amount of fiery debris and shrapnel from the first explosion but had missed the large rain of debris that had struck the downwind ships. The number one ship at Tare 6, LST #334, next to the dolphins, and the number two ship, LST #20, were disabled, causing much anxiety to their officers and crew. On the remaining three ships, confusion seemed to prevail as the crews strove to get their ships underway and into the clear water of the West Loch channel.

It took LST #273, the outermost ship at Tare 6, a full thirty minutes to break away from the nest and head into the main channel, probably because the starboard engine was down and there was trouble with the open bow doors.[2] Still, Lieutenant James was none too happy with the sluggishness of his crew.

S1/c Gourlay was helping to release the lines and cables holding his ship to LST #169 on their port side when James appeared in front of the wheelhouse. "'Get them damn lines off,'" Gourlay quoted James as shouting. "'Chop them if you have to. Use a goddamn axe if you have to!'" Fearful of the wrath of their skipper, the crewmen began chopping at the lines.

As Gourlay was working on the mooring lines, the second blast occurred. "Huge billows of smoke, flames, [and] debris, rose in the air," he wrote, "[throwing] shrapnel onto our main decks." Finally, after thirty-five minutes the mooring lines were cut, the bow doors were closed, and LST #273 got underway. The delay, however, had repercussions. Wrote Gourlay, "Two of [our] high octane gasoline drums were hit by falling debris . . . and in fighting the fire that was on the bow, several of the crew were injured. In fact, one of the men . . . trying to loose the lines was hit, and his leg was injured."

As the ship finally made its way out of West Loch, Gourlay saw sailors and Marines, some with lifejackets, some without, jumping from the exploding ships into "the oil and gasoline covered water." When he saw a few people drawn into churning ships' screws, he quickly turned away. As he stood on the stern of #273 gagging and trying hard not to throw up, he hoped that none of his fellow crewmen noticed.[3]

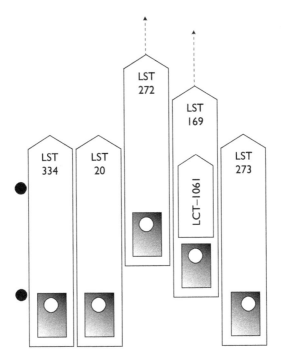

Tare 6: LSTs #169 and #272 break away. Drawn by Gene Eric Salecker, redrawn by Kristie Buckley. Copyright © 2014 by the University of Oklahoma Press.

It took only two minutes from the sound of the initial explosion for the officers of the Coast Guard–manned LST #169 to sound general quarters and begin preparations for getting underway. According to the logbook, the outboard ship, #273, cleared their starboard side in fourteen minutes. Five minutes later, Lieutenant Kittredge started #169 out of her berth.[4]

When the two outer ships moved away from LST #272, moored in the center number three spot, Lieutenant Commander Dore was finally able to move his own ship away from the explosions. A note in the logbook stated that it took thirty-one minutes for #272 to get underway because, according to Chief Boson Mate Cook, there was trouble casting off from one of the other ships. "LST #272, and another ship were moored together," he said, "and one of the men on the other ship refused to cast off the mooring lines which held the two vessels together." Finally Cook grabbed a fire axe and raised it over his head. "Throw off the line or I'll cut it," he shouted. Seeing the look of determination on Cook's face and the axe held high, the man tossed the line over "immediately."[5] Once all of the lines were clear, LST #272 started off on its journey down the West Loch channel.

With both engines down for repair, Lieutenant Smith, on the Coast Guard–manned LST #20, had his crew wet down the deck while he waited for a towboat to rush to his aid. Likewise, with its port engine getting a "major overhaul," Lieutenant Blieden's LST #334, in the number one spot, was in much the same situation.

As the men on LST #20 waited, flaming debris from the second large explosion set fire to the signal flags and flag bag. Five minutes after the outer vessels had pulled away, the tugboat *Hoga* (YTB-146) arrived. Although elated to see the tug, Smith worried that one was not enough. In a communiqué to the Navy Yard he asked, "Please send some more tugs. We are disabled."[6] In the meantime, the two crews worked quickly to attach the necessary lines so that the tough little tugboat could tow the much larger landing ship away from the continuing fury.

On LST #334, LT(jg) S. I. Stern, the officer of the deck, recorded the second large explosion in the ship's log. "Explosion occurred on LST 39 drifting toward vessels in Tare 9." As the outboard ships eventually pulled away and the tugboat helped #20 away from the tare, the officers and crew of #334 had an unobstructed view of the fires burning fiercely "on four unidentifiable LSTs in Berth's Tare 8 and 9."[7]

Tare 5

Within three minutes of the first blast, Lieutenant Davis's LST #34 was safely on her way to a berth in Pearl Harbor's East Loch. The remaining four vessels at Tare 5 were not far behind.

Ten minutes after the first explosion, the executive officer, in the absence of Lieutenant Gamble, had LST #45 "underway [and] proceeding out of Westlock [*sic*] in company with several other LSTs."[8] In order to escape so quickly, the "crew chopped the lines

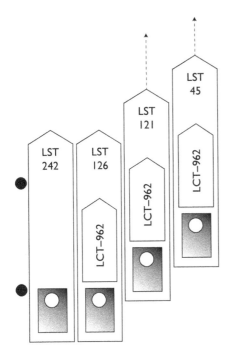

Tare 5: LSTs #121 and #45 break away. Drawn by Gene Eric Salecker, redrawn by Kristie Buckley. Copyright © 2014 by the University of Oklahoma Press.

that held [the ship] to another [LST #121] to get underway and out of the Loch," recalled crewman Philip Moses.[9]

LST #121, with Lieutenant Devaney at the conn, was underway only two minutes behind LST #45. Because of problems with her bow ramp and doors, #121 was ordered to a berth in East Loch, far away from the growing disaster in West Loch.[10]

As if following a schedule, Lieutenant Krueger had LST #126 away from Tare 5 two minutes after #121.[11]

BM2/c Hillman was aboard LST #126 and wrote, "I had no sooner reached the deck when explosions began to rip the invasion fleet apart. All hell was breaking loose. Explosions were sending fiery debris high into the air, and onto the decks of nearby moored ships causing a chain reaction of fire and fury. . . . Unless we got underway, it was only a matter of time before we became part of the conflagration."

Before #126 left the nest, however, Hillman and Seaman Steven "Sack" Sacoolidge were called upon to man one of the ship's

LCVPs. "We didn't need to be told twice. Scampering down the Jacob's Ladder, I rushed to the engine controls and started the engine while Sack hurriedly untied the lines." Without looking back, Hillman and Sacoolidge turned the Higgins boat toward the dozens of bobbing heads in the oily, fiery water around the burning ships in Tare 8.[12]

At the same time, Lieutenant Krueger took LST #126 in the opposite direction. "We slowly got clear and when we began to move forward freely, I went to the escape hatch and stuck my head out . . . and was given another view I'll never forget," recalled MoMM Lux, who had been working in the main engine room. "Hatch covers, magazine parts and all kinds of debris were hurtling into the air and explosions and black smoke went sky high." He noticed an LST in Tare 8 "fiercely burning and . . . red hot along the water line." As #126 was pulling away from Tare 5, Lux recalled that "large pieces of debris thundered down on us."[13] The third large explosion had just gone off among the burning ships.

In the absence of their skipper, Lieutenant Winney, or anyone else capable of navigating the ship down the narrow West Loch channel, the officers and crew aboard LST #242 could only sit and wait while the outer ships broke away and rushed to safety. Finally, forty minutes after the first explosion, LCDR R. L. Green, USNR, a qualified pilot, arrived.[14]

Having been down below when the first explosion went off, F1/c Dale Moore rushed topside where he had a perfect view of what was happening. "I saw all these explosions and, my God, bodies flying through the air and everything." Looking around, he noticed that the men on his own ship had "started spraying [the gasoline barrels] down with the fire hoses and meanwhile there's explosions one after another, just kept going, and then we were trying to get the other four ships alongside of us outta there." As he admitted, "Of course, we had to wait for each one to get off by himself, start their engines and everything."

"We couldn't move 'til we got ahold of fleet landing," stated Moore. "We had to signal for a pilot 'cause our skipper was ashore, and nobody could run the ship. So by the time they got a pilot out there and got the thing running . . . they kept telling us on the radio to get that thing outta here." Finally, with pilot LCDR

Green at the helm, LST #242 headed down the channel. As Moore admitted, "It was pretty doggone touchy there for a while, you know."[15]

Seventeen-year-old S1/c Karl Koehler was on the port side near the aft mooring line that held the ship to the dolphin pilings when Commander Green finally arrived. As Koehler remembered, "I climbed out onto the dolphin and awaited orders to free up the line." In the meantime, the bow lines had all been released so when the last ship next to them, LST #126, finally moved away from their starboard side, the suction drew the bow of LST #242 outward. Koehler recalled, "This caused a strain on the aft hawser, which I was to throw off when ordered. The order came and I could not remove the hawser from the dolphin, because the strain was so great and I thought the line was about to part. I knew if it broke I could possibly be decapitated or cut in two, because this was a three-inch hawser strained to the point of water misting out." At that exact moment, the third and most violent explosion erupted over the waters of West Loch.

"I hugged that dolphin real hard, and if I could have squeezed in between the poles I would have," Koehler admitted. "I could almost feel the hot shrapnel hitting my back, which thankfully none did." While the young sailor was atop the wooden pilings dodging the falling shrapnel, the executive officer was yelling at him to cast off the line. "I was yelling back that it was too tight and I couldn't," Koehler said. "The exec then issued the order to cut the line and with the ship at that moment out of reach for me to board, I would have been marooned on the dolphin if the line were cut. Fortunately, also at that moment the strain on the line caused the bow of the 242 to swing back toward the shore, which eased that strain and now with obvious great motivation I managed to cast off the line. The ship practically bolted away from the dolphin, and I took the leap of my life and managed to grasp the ship's lifeline (railing) and some crewmen hauled me aboard."

Koehler's knees were bruised when he banged against the side of the ship. "That was a small price to pay when the alternative was being left on the dolphin and having to wait for a pick up or jump into the water (think very brackish water and deep mud) and wade to solid ground."[16]

Tare 3

The crews of LSTs #226 and #354 sat at Tare 3 around the protective curve of Baltimore Point and watched the explosions going off at Tare 8. Too far away to be hit by shrapnel or debris, both crews were eyewitnesses to the pageant of fleeing ships and the panorama of a broadening disaster.

On Lieutenant Henry's LST #354, the officer of the deck recorded the second explosion. "Smoke and flame billowed into the air and it was not possible to distinguish which or how many LSTs were damaged," he wrote. "However, from the number and general direction of subsequent blasts it was assumed that no less than five ships had blown up."[17]

While almost all of the ships moored closest to the epicenter of the explosions were trying to get away, LST #129 in Walker Bay had no intention of moving. Moored with its bow ramp up on the beach northeast of Tare 8, Lieutenant Prince's ship was far upwind and safe from most of the burning debris and shrapnel. Still, they were not completely out of danger.

"The water's surface was burning with oil spilled from the explosions," a crewman wrote. "I was training the fire away from our ship with a hose when a . . . minute later the water stopped flowing through my hose. I looked back to figure out what had gone wrong, and discovered that a shot from a 20mm gun had landed right behind me, severing the line. It will give you an idea of the chaos going on around me too when I say I didn't even know it had hit until I saw the cut hose."[18]

On the other end of the loch, below Powder Point and the naval ammunition depot, the minesweeper USS *Terror*, which was loading up with ammunition, could not move into the shallow back bay area west of the depot because she had a draft of almost 20 feet. Instead, as the conflagration at Tare 8 continued to grow, Commander Blakeslee called for a tugboat to help tow him out to sea.[19]

Only about 300 feet from the exploding ships, along the northern shore of Walker Bay, was LCI (G)-371, which was having its engines overhauled. After witnessing the devastation taking place to the south of him, the engineering officer, Lieutenant Goodman, had rushed down to the engine room. "I ordered our motor mechanics to 'button up' the last two diesel engines on which they were working and start them as soon as possible," he wrote. "Within 20 to 30 minutes, a ranking Naval Officer arrived on the scene in a small boat to direct rescue operations. . . . Lt. Gooding of our ship returned within an hour after the first explosion and took command. Shortly thereafter, the Fleet Command at Pearl Harbor ordered our ship to get underway and leave Pearl Harbor for the open sea."[20] Leaving at such a late time, LCI (G)-371 would meet a parade of rescue vessels rushing into the loch through the narrow West Loch channel.

| The Rescuers

Within two minutes of the second explosion, the Pearl Harbor signal tower received a report that two ships were now on fire at Tare 8 and that "the whole nest will be soon." One minute later, the tower got a call of another "large explosion in [the] vicinity of [the] fire. Flames shot 1,000 feet in the air."[1]

At 3:20 P.M., LCMs (Landing Craft, Mechanized) (larger versions of the LCVP or Higgins boat) with fire pumps were en route to West Loch. At 1523 hours, CAPT Craven, USN, the duty officer at the time with the title of Yard Craft, Commandant, Yard Master, responsible for the movement of all major vessels within the environs of Pearl Harbor, ordered all available tugboats to "save as many ships as possible." When an unknown LST asked the signal tower to "Rush fire tugs," the tower responded, "Affirmative. Fire tugs already en route."[2] One Coast Guard and four Navy fireboats were on their way, but they were coming from Honolulu Harbor and would take more than an hour to arrive.

Closer to the scene was the large harbor tug *Osceola* (YTB 129), whose crew was still shooting craps on a pier in Middle Loch. "It was 3:15," wrote Roy Sannella. "Then we heard sirens and ships' whistles blowing. We hurried to our boats. By the time we headed out to the bay, a third explosion occurred. Now it was 3:30."[3] The crew had wasted precious minutes by continuing with their crap game.

Already in West Loch was Seaman Bernal. Alone in a small motor launch at the start, he had already plucked a handful of men from the water when the second explosion went off. "It was just one big mass of fire, and smoke, and debris," Bernal stated. "So you couldn't figure out what was going on . . . it was scary. . . . [W]e were out about 30 or 40 yards, and [the fiery debris] still rained in our boat. I told the personnel to get into the water where they would be protected. Lots of times we would jump into the water to protect us from the debris, until it finally stopped raining on us. Then we'd jump into the boat and continue."[4]

One thing that Bernal would never forget was the burning water. "The fire ignited the water," he remembered, "you know, the oil, it would cover the whole ship. You couldn't even see the ships anymore."[5]

One of the small boats scurrying around the burning vessels contained four volunteers from the Coast Guard–manned LST #20 at Tare 6. GM2/c Joseph Tezanos, S2/c Joseph F. Hammond, S1/c John E. Bloomfield, Jr., and S1/c Harry M. Church would later receive the Navy & Marine Corps Medal, awarded to "any person who . . . distinguished himself or herself by heroism not involving actual conflict with any enemy." Each award read, "Under conditions of great personal danger from fire and explosions, he assisted in rescuing 42 survivors, some of whom were injured and exhausted from the water and from burning ships." Additionally, the award for Seaman Bloomfield noted, "He dived overboard and brought one severely injured man to safety."[6]

What was not said in the citations, however, was the fact that after rescuing forty-two survivors in two trips back and forth to dry land, the men were going out a third time when their LCVP "was swamped and lost." Bloomfield, Church, and Hammond managed to return to LST #20 before nightfall, but Tezanos had to be taken to a first aid station "for treatment of burns." He remained in a hospital for a few days before returning to #20.[7]

Other Coast Guard rescuers included PhM2/c Johnson, S2/c Arbuckle, and two other volunteers in an LCVP from LST #69. "My boat went around the sterns of the eight LSTs in [Tare 8] and we began picking out of the water men who jumped or were blown off the ships," Johnson wrote. "Some were badly wounded. . . . Men were jumping into the water from all the ships and the fires were spreading to all the ships like wildfire. Things were really hot there. No one had time to get helmets or life belts, so many of the fellows drowned as soon as they hit the water. . . . Ours was one of three or four boats picking up survivors.

"My boat was rescuing men when a second large explosion occurred. It threw equipment, men, and shrapnel all over the harbor. . . . I jumped out of the [LCVP] and held my hands over my head in the water. Shrapnel landed around me, but none hit." Climbing back into the boat, Johnson and the others continued pulling men from the oily, burning waters.[8]

Boatswain's Mate Hillman and Seaman Sacoolidge were in an LCVP from LST #126 at Tare 5. "Once in mid-channel, we could clearly see the disaster that was taking place about 300 yards away," Hillman explained. "Red-hot fragments showered the clustered LSTs . . . igniting gasoline drums lined up on their exposed forecastles. Ships everywhere were burning. The sky was quickly filling with thick black smoke."

Moving alongside LST #39, the outermost vessel at Tare 8, Hillman watched in horror as panicked sailors and Marines began jumping directly into his LCVP. "I'm sure many suffered broken arms or legs, but at the time, no one seemed to care," he wrote. "They were safe and that's all that mattered." When the boat could handle no more, the two rescuers took the LCVP over to the ammunition depot and deposited the rescued men ashore.

While his boat was being unloaded, Hillman looked back and saw hundreds of men still in the water. "Realizing that certain death awaited them in the flaming, oil-soaked waters, I asked several of the men we had pulled from the water if they would stay and help us rescue them," remembered Hillman. "No one refused." With a crew of willing hands, Hillman raced back into the maelstrom.[9]

Another rescuer was PLT SGT Wells, with 2nd Platoon, 2nd Amphibious Truck Company, who had been in a DUKW with three other men going for some Cokes when the first explosion occurred. After watching for several minutes, Wells and his driver, CPL Harold Reynolds, ran back toward the DUKW park along Hanaloa Point. "About halfway there we were stopped by two MPs, a very young 2nd lieutenant and an enlisted Marine," Wells wrote. "The lieutenant informed us that no one was allowed to go into the area." Although Wells explained that they were with the

DUKW company and intended to "drive them to haul casualties to hospitals," the officer would not let them through. Becoming irritated, Wells said, "Lieutenant, my unit is right in the middle of that and we're going in!" Just as stubbornly, the officer responded, "I said you are not going into that area!"

When Wells insisted a second time, the officer drew his pistol. What happened next surprised Wells. The Marine MP, the older of the two guards, suddenly yanked his own pistol and pointed it at the officer. According to Wells, the older MP said, "Lieutenant! If they're willing to go, let them! It's their necks they're risking. Now put the damned pistol away!" Slowly, the young lieutenant lowered his pistol. "All right, you can go." Without another word, the two would-be rescuers hurried toward the DUKW park.[10]

A short distance away was eighteen-year-old Marine PFC Arieta, who had been on MP duty with his poi dog Rebel and was busy fighting some grass fires started by the first explosion. "I was now about 50 yards away from the burning ships with my dog and—boom—another one went off," Arieta wrote. "It sent me and my dog 20 or 30 feet. We laid there for a while. He yipped a couple times. I felt this burn in my leg. We stayed there about five minutes." With a ruptured eardrum and an injured leg, Arieta took Rebel in tow and retreated from the area. Eventually his commanding officer arrived and ordered him to take the MP jeep and go down to help out. "The scene was so horrible," he remembered. "There were heads, legs, arms, body parts. So many men in the water."[11]

A major threat to the swimming men was the burning oil atop the water, which continued to spread and caused authorities at the ammunition depot to order the removal of the tons of ammunition stored on the dock. Seabee EM3/c Harry Spence, who had just arrived with a dozen other Seabees from near Iroquois Point, immediately began pitching in to move the ammunition. "We moved the shells and drums of gasoline which were in danger . . . out of the way," he recalled. "Many sailors volunteered to help. . . . They were from many units and commands around Pearl."[12]

While the Seabees and volunteer sailors were moving the ammunition, Marine cook Boulware and the volunteer firefighters from the nearby Marine barracks were put to work "on a portable water pump spraying water on the hull of an ammunition ship which was being unloaded." Undoubtedly, this was the *Joseph B. Francis,* which was still loaded with about 350 tons of ammunition. While all of this was going on, small boats and LCVPs began arriving at the depot dock with dozens of survivors, including many wounded. Boulware immediately took "a truckload of men who were wet and covered with fuel oil" back to the Marine barracks for some clean, dry clothes.[13]

Far away, aboard an LCP in East Loch, SGT Harrold A. Weinberger and his crew of five photographers and cinematographers still did not know the exact location of the billowing clouds of black smoke that could be seen to the west. "Explosions occurred continuously, as we churned the waters," he wrote. "Whatever it was, it was immense and devastating." Eventually Weinberger managed "to pin the conflagration to West Loch." Throwing caution to the wind, the LCP carrying the photographic unit headed toward the loch.

"As we entered the narrow waters south of Ford Island [but still in East Loch], a Navy picket boat intercepted us and ordered us to turn back. We ignored them, and I ordered the cox'n to stay on course and continue," Weinberger wrote. "The picket boat made a tight U-turn and quickly overtook us. They drew alongside us. We did slow down, and the skipper [of the picket boat], a Navy Lieut., demanded to know in very choice language what the hell we were doing." Weinberger showed the lieutenant his intelligence team (ITEM) credentials and lied that he had a pass from Admiral Nimitz. "Actually," Weinberger said, "Admiral Nimitz's signature was on my ITEM card." Believing the bluff, the Navy lieutenant cleared them through to West Loch, and the LCP sped off.[14]

At 3:30 P.M., word of the disaster reached the Intelligence Unit, Naval Air Station at Barber's Point, southeast of the entrance into the Pearl Harbor channel. Immediately LTs Edward Turner, Clarence G. Shea, and Robert B. Flannigan were dispatched to West Loch. It was their job, as intelligence personnel, to "determine whether or not the disaster was the result of an act of sabotage."[15]

By this time, two other important figures were on their way toward West Loch, one by tugboat and one by automobile. Jumping into a tugboat to see the disaster firsthand was Vice Admiral Turner, the commanding officer of the Joint Expeditionary Force and in control of the Saipan invasion. Informed that there were fires and explosions among the combat loaded LSTs at West Loch, Turner boarded the nearest tug and sped off.[16]

Admiral Nimitz, commander in chief of the entire Pacific Fleet, was on an inspection tour with his bodyguards and driver when they noticed the smoke and heard the muffled sound of explosions. Nimitz ordered his driver to take him toward the smoke.[17] Both admirals were on their way when the third and most destructive explosion tore through West Loch.

CHAPTER 16 | The Third Explosion

The third explosion was much more powerful and damaging than the previous two. Historian Howard E. Shuman placed the time of the second explosion at 1522 hours, fourteen minutes after the first. Shuman wrote, "It was heard 15 miles away, showering burning metal and debris over more than 1,000 yards, created a massive mushroom cloud, and endangered not only the ships but the naval ammunition depot itself."[1]

The third explosion sent large pieces of metal tumbling through the air, landing miles away. Marine cook Boulware recalled, "A huge chunk of one of the LSTs was blown over the [Marine] barracks [near the ammunition depot] and landed on the grass in front of the barracks. It was still too hot to touch the next day, and they had to cut it up in order to haul it away in trucks." As many as twenty buildings were damaged by the blast, some having only broken windows but others sustaining 3-foot holes in their roofs from thrown debris. Jeeps, trucks, trailers, and pieces of vehicles were hurtled high into the air, coming down, in some cases, with deadly effect. Unexploded shells rained down.[2] In an instant, no spot close to West Loch seemed safe.

Tare 8

By the time of the third explosion, the outermost ships at Tare 8 were doomed. The fire and explosions that had started on the fore-castle of LST #353 had quickly spread to the two adjacent ships. Although the crew of LST #39, on the right, put up a determined fight, there was just too much damage to save the vessel. In the end, the crew had to abandon ship.

On the left side of #353, Lieutenant Mullis's LST #179 per-haps burned the most furiously. The prevailing wind, coming out of the northeast and blowing hard to the southwest, pushed burn-ing debris and flaming gasoline over three-quarters of the upper deck. LCT-961, chained atop the main deck, never stood a chance. Doused with the fiery rain, the smaller vessel was engulfed in flames within seconds.

The crews of the two middle ships at Tare 8, LSTs #69 and #43, had fought back gallantly against the first two explosions, but fleeing personnel from the outboard ships hampered firefighting efforts. As the refugees raced across their decks, more and more crewmen from the two vessels joined in the exodus. When the third explosion came, throwing even more burning debris and shrapnel over the two ships, there were fewer firefighters available. Faced with the inevitable, the crews of both #69 and #43 abandoned ship.

LST #353 was wrapped in flames from stem to stern. Explo-sions continued to rock the vessel as ammunition stored further down along the main deck caught fire and exploded. By the time of the third big explosion, LST #353 had been abandoned.

With her mooring lines either cast off or burned through, the crew of LST #39 had tried to get away from Tare 8 and put out the fires. Unfortunately, the blaze could not be controlled, and the crew had to abandon ship. Floating free and assisted by the stiff 23 mph wind coming out of the northeast, LST #39, with her bow doors wide open, her ramp down, and her top and insides ablaze, began drifting backwards and to the southwest, toward the few remaining ships at Tare 9.[3]

The sailors and Marines aboard Lieutenant Mulliss's LST #179 may have been among the first to abandon ship. Wrapped in flames from the very start, the crew tried to put out the fires on the main deck and inside LCT-961 but could make no headway.

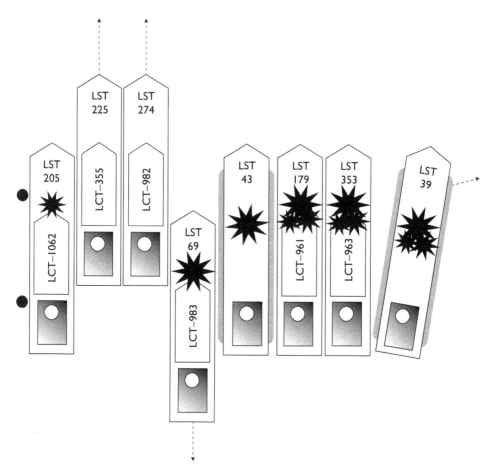

Tare 8: LSTs #179, #353, and #39 burn; LST #43 has been abandoned; explosions occur on LST #69 before it is abandoned and begins to drift towards Tare 9; LSTs #274 and #225 are shored; and LST #50 is on fire. Drawn by Gene Eric Salecker, redrawn by Kristie Buckley. Copyright © 2014 by the University of Oklahoma Press.

Understandably, men began to break away and flee across the inboard ships or leap into the water from the fantail. By the time the official order was given to abandon ship, there were very few people still on board.

In spite of an injured back, legs, and buttock from being blown atop an LVT through a collapsed elevator hatch, Marine PhM3/c Sheppard had jumped from the ship and was in the bottom of an

LCVP when the third explosion erupted. As Sheppard recalled, "Hot stuff was flying around, and a corpsman held a life jacket over both of us for protection."[4] Eventually Sheppard was taken to shore and rushed to a hospital.

The men on LST #43 were fighting valiantly to save their ship. Although they had tried to get underway, blazing fires raging across their bow had prevented them from severing the bow cables holding her to the other two ships. Lieutenant Luehlke had tried to move #43 both forward and back but to no avail. As the fires "began to spread rapidly," the third explosion occurred. Written in the logbook was the line "Tremendous explosion on an outboard ship knocked down all fire-fighting personnel, ruptured fire main in several places . . . commanding officer, officer of the deck, and all bridge personnel knocked unconscious."[5]

Lieutenant Zuehlke, the skipper, was one of the men knocked out. "[It] was for a short time," he told the court of inquiry, "a couple minutes or maybe five." When he regained consciousness, he discovered that all of his clothes had been blown off. Uninjured, except for some minor shrapnel wounds, he assessed the damage from the third explosion.

"The main deck was burning and smoking," Zuehlke testified, "which heretofore had not been a problem. . . . From that time on the situation looked hopeless." Several of his firefighters had been badly hurt. With his ship encased in flames and his crew down and out, Zuehlke made the hard decision to abandon ship.

One by one, the men rushed to the fantail and dropped into the water below. Lieutenant Zuehlke personally helped a quartermaster whose arm was "shot off pretty badly." Fortunately, a small boat soon picked up Zuehlke and the survivors of #43. As he sat in the rescue boat, the skipper looked up and saw Lieutenant Sard's LST #274, the third ship in line, moving forward "with both her engines in operation." A few seconds later, Zuehlke collapsed. Taken to the naval ammunition depot dock, he was eventually sent to the dispensary.[6] He had done all that he could to save his ship.

The engines were down on Lieutenant Leary's LST #69, and she could not move under her own power. The first explosion had done little physical damage, and the crew had responded quickly, extinguishing most of the fires on the main deck. When the second explosion came, it did a lot of damage. People fighting the fires were bowled over, hoses were ruptured, and fires were started anew. The men tried to cut loose from the burning ships to their right, but the raging fires on #43 prevented this. When the flames started eating into the wooden ammunition crates on #69, people began to leave the ship. After the third explosion roared out of LST #353, engulfing the ships near her in flames, LST #69 was doomed. As the ammunition inside LCT-983, chained to the deck, began to explode, the order was given to abandon ship.

After the third explosion, Engineering Officer Anderson felt that "things on board were out of control." With the ammunition boxes burning and nobody fighting the fires anymore, Anderson figured that the order to abandon ship was about to be given, and he sent Chief Hill down to warn the men in the engine room. When the court of inquiry asked Anderson who had given the official order to abandon ship, he stated that he did not know but felt "that all the officers did at once."[7] Actually, the first officer to give the order was LT(jg) J. M. Silva (USCGR). As officer of the deck, and with the skipper gone from the ship, Silva had deemed the situation bad enough to order abandon ship.[8]

Lieutenant Gott was still trying to fight the fires on the bow when the third explosion came. The concussion hit him squarely in the back, throwing him across the bow. The same explosion lifted the lowered elevator of LST #69 from the floor of the tank deck up to the main deck and then dropped it back down again.

With the fire raging all around him and the boxes of ammunition starting to explode, Gott headed for the fantail. "The LCT was afire inside," Gott recalled. "All those cots were a blazing inferno and underneath the LCT, where we had bunked the Marines, all of those cots and bedding were afire and . . . [fire was] around the boxes that the ammunition was in."

By the time Gott reached the fantail, he was all alone. Having never heard the order to abandon ship, he was puzzled by the absence of anyone else. As he stood alone, he noticed that LST #274 to port was moving forward. With his LST #69 blazing around him, Gott climbed over the port railing and jumped onto LST #274. Behind him he left a floating, drifting, burning, exploding hulk.[9]

Although Lieutenant Sard seemed willing to pull LST #69 clear with his own ship, he first had to fix the problems on his LST

#274. As the men were preparing to get underway, it was discovered that the ship's steering mechanism had been jammed by the first explosion. After most of the fires were extinguished on their own deck and inside their own LCT, the firefighters turned their hoses toward the ships on either side of them. After fifteen minutes, with LST #69 wrapped in flames, the ship was cut free, and it began to drift away with the other burning ships to outboard. Five minutes later, after rigging emergency steering, LST #274 started dead ahead. After going 200 yards, the ship beached itself, "with bow doors open and ramp half way up." In control of the ship at this time were two officers and thirteen to fifteen enlisted men. The rest had all abandoned ship.[10]

"[We] had about twelve or thirteen fires at one point which the Old Man had told me to take care of," recalled Lieutenant Broadwell, the stores officer. While the men were fighting the fires, the mass exodus of men fleeing from the burning ships to outboard panicked the men. "At some point I'm sure somebody gave the word to abandon ship," Broadwell explained. "I know that Sard never gave the word, but a number of people on our ship did abandon. Some went over the sides, some ran onto other ships."[11]

Marine PFC Ellis had been blown off of LST #274 by the first explosion but had swum back to the open bow doors. "I got back aboard the LST, but by this time the fire had also reached the rest of the LSTs lined up there," Ellis remembered. "The word was to abandon ship, so I jumped back in the bay and swam to shore."[12]

Out on the fantail, S1/c Slater and a gunner's mate, both from LCT-982, were trying to help a sailor who had been gashed across the chest and stomach. "We didn't know what to do, and another explosion went off," Slater said. "That was about the third explosion that went off, and we backed inside [the deck house] and waited until the shrapnel cleared. It was raining everywhere." After the shrapnel and debris stopped falling, Slater and his friend started moving the wounded man onto LST #225.[13]

When it was discovered that the ship's steering mechanism was jammed, Lieutenant Broadwell went down to work the emergency steering. "We'd lost control. I don't remember how. Somebody said the concussion. I don't know how the concussion could have done it."[14] Before long, Broadwell had LST #274 ready to move away from Tare 8.

"The captain told us to get out of there, so we cut the lines off and pulled out and put it on the beach," said Chief Birch, who had been down in the engine room. "Guys on topside cut the lines, and the captain called down for full speed, and I gave it to him." Pulling away slow but steady, LST #274 went about 200 yards straight ahead before striking the northwest shoreline of Walker Bay. "Went right into the beach as hard as we could go," recalled Chief Birch. "There were shells flying everywhere, while they was exploding. It looked like the whole world was on fire."[15]

Already hampered by a rush of Marines, Seabees, Army personnel, and sailors from the outboard vessels shouting, "Abandon ship" as they fled across the deck, a number of crewmen from LST #225 lost heart and joined the crowd. Seconds later, to make matters worse, the "ammunition in the ready boxes on LCT-355 and in gun tub #46 began to go off." Fortunately, enough bravehearted personnel were still aboard who wanted to save their ship. "Remaining officers and men," noted the officer of the deck, "attempted to put out [the] fires." Only then did the remaining crewmen discover that the third explosion had damaged the fire main, causing a decrease in water pressure in the fire hoses. Just then, when everything looked bleak, the ship got underway. All lines were cast off from LST #205 to the left, and in a matter of minutes the plucky LST nosed into the beach "next to LST 274."[16]

It was a skeleton crew that saved LST #225. Marine radioman John B. Hovis (Co. B, 25th MarReg, 4th MarDiv) had originally abandoned ship, but he returned when he realized that #225 was not going to sink. According to Hovis, "Only four Navy crewmen stayed on board and were able to move the ship a short distance until it got stuck on the bottom." In reality, there were more than four loyal crewman. There were actually a few people in the engine room, a few officers on the bridge, and a few men fighting the fires when the ship went straight forward into Walker Bay.[17]

Since it was the number one ship, moored securely to the dolphins, Lieutenant Buchar's LST #205 was the natural springboard for every person fleeing from ship to ship to shore. While Buchar ordered his men to "assist [the fleeing] personnel in abandoning ship," some officers began ordering everybody ashore—those fleeing, those fighting the fires, and those on the ship next to theirs, LST #225.[18]

As the sky over West Loch filled with smoke, LST #205 filled with refugees. Marine Harry Pearce and his buddy Sam had come over from LST #69. "We finally got to the last boat, and it was anchored to [the] shoreline, probably 75 or 100 feet off of the shore," he noted. "The shore was a mud bank, maybe 2 foot wide at the bottom and then went up a steep incline, probably 15 feet. There had been enough men go up that mud bank that it was as slippery as a greased eel." By the time Pearce and his buddy arrived on the edge of LST #205, the oily water was afire. "Down below I could see Navy personnel, some with Kapok lifejackets on, just bobbing in the water, some without any lifejackets," Pearce said. "Their heads were going under and coming back up, and they were fanning the water. . . . I suppose there were probably two hundred men in the water below us." After watching for a few minutes, Pearce and Sam dropped down into the water and headed for shore.[19]

After S1/c Slater and the gunner's mate that was helping him got their wounded sailor across LST #225 and onto LST #205 from #274, they had to get the man safely to shore. "The gunner's mate slid into the water," Slater remembered, "and I slid this sailor in with him. We swam him ashore and after we got him to shore we were having trouble carrying him. A Marine who was on an LVT there, there were several LVTs there, parked there . . . took his fatigue jacket off and gave it to us so we could make a stretcher. So we were able to start carrying him up through the sugar cane field to safety."[20]

As Slater and the gunner's mate started out across the sugar cane field with the seriously wounded sailor, LST's #274, the number three ship, and #225, the number two ship, cut loose and pulled forward, away from Tare 8. LST #205 was now all alone at Tare 8. Although fires still raged across her main deck and inside LCT-1062, and ammunition continued to cook off, LST #205 was still salvageable. Unfortunately, by now there were only a few people left aboard to save her.[21]

CHAPTER 17 | Another Victim

After LSTs #274 and #225 loosed their mooring lines and pulled ahead into Walker Bay, the burning vessels to outboard were set adrift. On the far outside end, LST #39, burning fiercely, had tried to move off on her own before the fire forced the crew to abandon ship. All alone, she floated slightly away from the other ships, occasionally being bumped by LST #353. Eventually, #39 drifted toward the south while #353 began to drift toward Tare 9.

From the middle of Tare 8, LSTs #69, #43, and #179 all began to drift southward toward Tare 9. LSTs #43 and #179 remained together, perhaps stuck by unsevered cables, but #69 broke away and, pushed southwest by the current and the wind, headed straight for LST #480, the number one ship in Tare 9.

By the time of the third explosion, most of the ships at Tare 9 were gone. The ships could not back straight out or go straight ahead but had to jockey back and forth to get away from the tare. Although all of the crews fought hard to save their ships, in the end one would be lost.

When LST #461, which was straddled with LCT-987, left Tare 9, Lieutenant Geis headed toward the shallow small boat area. Executive Officer Futterman was in the bridge with Geis. "We didn't have any maps or anything, and so we started upstream [toward the shallows], to get away from it, to limit our exposure," Futterman said. "We went upstream and . . . then we came to a

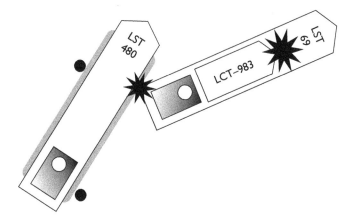

Tare 9: LST #69 has drifted from Tare 8 and collides with LST #480. Drawn by Gene Eric Salecker, redrawn by Kristie Buckley. Copyright © 2014 by the University of Oklahoma Press.

point where it became apparent that upstream was not the way to go; we were running out of water. So we turned around and we went downstream."[1]

While LST #461 was going down the West Loch Channel, LST #45, pulling out of Tare 5, collided with her starboard side. Since the collision was only minor and no damage was done to the hull, #461 continued down channel and eventually out to sea.[2]

Although LST #23 had a 10-inch hawser line fouled around her port propeller, Lieutenant Martin's ship headed directly down the channel and therefore was the first from Tare 9 to escape West Loch. As LST #23 turned into the main channel at Waipio Point, a call went out to the Navy Yard: "We require a doctor immediately." Five rescued men, including four African American soldiers from the 29th Chemical Decontamination Company, had been brought aboard #23 prior to her leaving Tare 9.[3]

Backing at full speed out of the number four spot, Lieutenant Haskell's LST #340 moved directly into the small boat area and dropped anchor only twenty-five minutes after the first explosion. When the explosions became more intense, Lieutenant Haskell moved his ship into the upper reaches of the shallow bay. Before backing away from Tare 9, however, #340 had taken aboard 127 survivors, many in need of minor medical attention.[4]

As LST #224 cleared Tare 9, her personnel were throwing life-jackets down to the struggling swimmers. Executive Officer John McDowell Beall, who was in the conn in place of the skipper, Lieutenant Pugh, at first attempted to get out to sea, but he found the narrow West Loch channel too crowded. Turning the ship completely around, Beall took #244 into the small boat area. When a headcount was taken of the personnel, it was discovered that thirty-four had been rescued but that four crewmen were missing and nineteen Marines had abandoned ship. A short while later, thirteen casualties, including MoMM3c Garbitt, who had been horribly burned by an exploding phosphorus shell, were "transferred to the emergency hospital set up on the shore."[5]

As Lieutenant Wells's LST #240 was trying to get away from Tare 9, the officer of the deck recorded "a third tremendous explosion on LST's fwd of this vessel, burning chunks of shrapnel and debris falling on this ship causing many small fires." By the time the ship entered the narrow West Loch channel, the crew had the fires under control. Shortly thereafter, four injured men were deposited at the Hickam Field Hospital. LST #240 then proceeded out to sea.[6]

To the officers and crew of LST #480, the escape of the outboard ships must have seemed excruciatingly slow. By the time all of the outer ships had moved away, LST #69 from Tare 8, wrapped in flames, was bearing down on #480.

Twenty-year-old R2/c Arthur T. "Art" Freer was with a young radioman striker fighting the fires on the starboard side of the bow when the third explosion erupted. "It went big up into the air and it made a beautiful, big smoke ring and the smoke in this smoke ring was going in circles. It was just a memorable thing," he recalled.

Freer and the younger sailor had been working a fire hose since the first explosion, trying to keep their ship alive as they waited for the outboard ships to move away. "There was probably six ships to the right of us and just behind us, so we couldn't move," said Freer. "And you see, by the time those ships moved beside us . . . [LST #69] drifted into our bow . . . and set us off." After #69 drifted in beside #480, Freer turned to the young radioman. "I said to him, 'Let's take this hose back of the wheelhouse,' figuring it would be safer." Eventually, the two men made it to the fantail and jumped overboard. "We weren't excited," said Freer. "You know we didn't realize we were in such bad shape as we really were. It was stupid really."[7]

MoMM2/c Harold J. Knebel was still manning a fire hose when #69 bumped #480 and exploded. A split second later, he was struck in the lower part of his back with a 5-pound piece of angle iron. "The explosion sent the angle iron like an arrow," Knebel recalled. "It struck me with such force that it tore me loose from the fire hose, threw me 6 feet into a steel bulkhead, and rendered me unconscious. I don't know how long I was unconscious. It must have been quite some time." Fortunately, while Knebel was out, a couple of shipmates had located a pharmacist's mate who bandaged the wound and put tape over it to protect it from the polluted water. By the time Knebel regained consciousness, the abandon ship order had been given. Feeling no pain, the motor machinist mate sat on the deck wondering if his friends down in the engine rooms had received word to leave.[8]

The skipper of LST #480, Lieutenant H. William Johnson, had tried to move his ship while the outboard ships were fleeing but had somehow ended up on the other side of the dolphins, between the pilings and shore. Snagged and unable to move, #480 had been a sitting duck for the drifting, exploding #69.[9] "A derelict burning ship drifted into us on our starboard," remembered Shipfitter Art Sacco. "Soon our ship was ablaze. . . . Flames covered the whole deck, we couldn't see the bridge. I made everyone jump over the port side and swim under the burning oil to get to shore."[10]

After MoMM2/c Knebel regained his feet, he climbed down to the two engine rooms. "The men were still there," Knebel remembers. "I told the men that the order to abandon ship had been given some time ago as the ship was exploding and sinking." Understandably, everyone immediately rushed topside.

"By this time there was a lot of aviation gasoline and diesel oil on fire on the water," said Knebel. "I proceeded to jump over the port side of the ship into the burning aviation gasoline and diesel oil fire on the water. I prayed and then jumped feet first into 'HELL.' When I jumped into 'HELL' I lost everything. On the other hand, I did not lose my life."[11]

With LST #480 now wrapped in flames, the few remaining crewmen fled to the fantail. "We were the inboard ship in our nest and were trapped when a derelict ship settled alongside our outboard side just as the ship next to us cleared our stern," remembered ENS Phil Kierl. "We had to abandon ship losing only one man."[12] Had there been ten or fifteen minutes more, #480 might have gotten clear of the dolphin pilings and the drifting, burning #69. Unfortunately, they were never given that additional fifteen minutes.

From atop a small bluff on Hanaloa Point, northwest of Tare 8, Admiral Nimitz watched the whole sad affair, accompanied by three Marine bodyguards, a physician, and a driver. When he ordered his driver to take him closer to the action, one of his bodyguards, eighteen-year-old CPL Loren F. "Sonny" Paulus, overruled him. "Shrapnel was already landing near us on top of the bluff," Paulus remembered. "If we'd gone down that trail we would've been hit for sure. I ignored the admiral and ordered the driver the hell out of there."[13]

Much later, Admiral Nimitz went through the disaster area in his personal boat. "About two hours later Admiral Nimitz in his gig came through the fire and smoke, at least that [was] who we thought it was," wrote Alfred E. Erickson, a sailor aboard LST #166.[15] Undoubtedly concerned that the disaster might delay, cripple, or even cancel the upcoming invasion of Saipan, Nimitz was worried and wanted firsthand knowledge of what had happened and what was being done about it.

CHAPTER 18 | Safely Ashore

The eastern shoreline of Hanaloa Point was about 75 feet from the dolphin pilings of Tares 8, 9, and 10. Behind a 5- or 6-foot-wide beach, there was a slight rise, from 8 to 15 feet high. Running along the top of the rise was a single-lane dirt roadway, flanked on both sides by wide, sandy flats. Beyond the flats were the sugar cane fields of the Oahu Sugar Company. It was on the sandy flats on either side of the roadway that the DUKW and LVT crews parked their vehicles side-by-side.[1]

As hundreds and hundreds of people fled from the various ships, either jumping from the fantail for a long swim to shore or moving from ship to ship until reaching the innermost vessel for a short swim, they had to scramble up the slight rise to the open flats when they reached shore. Once there, some sought shelter behind the armored amphibians, some ran up the road, but most fled westward through the newly harvested cane fields. "The cane had been cut, leaving stubbles about six to eight inches high that were cut at an angle and sharp," recalled Marine Harry Pearce. Most of the men had taken off their shoes prior to jumping into the water. "It cut our legs and our feet all to pieces," said Pearce. Radioman Freer concurred: "Going through the cane field without any shoes was tough on the feet."[2]

Although many of the refugees felt that they would be safe once they reached the cane fields, they soon found otherwise. "You see,"

Seaman Walter Slater stated, "a lot of guys went up through the sugar cane fields, and that's where a lot of them got killed. Because the shrapnel, when the explosions would go off, it would go up high in the air, and there'd be big chunks of sheet metal flying, spiraling, and coming down, showering, and it would mushroom out."[3]

When Marine CPL Jim Reed reached shore, he had trouble getting up the steep, muddy bank because of an injured ankle. "Somebody reached down and pulled me out of the water," Reed related, "and then piggybacked me through the cane fields, and while he was doing that, there was shrapnel falling all around us, jeep motors and all kinds of shrapnel. Fortunately, we never got hit by any of them." The stranger didn't put Reed down until they were out of the danger area. "I had never met this man. I have never seen him since," Reed said. "He was just like a guardian angel to me."[4]

Marine refugee George Swallow, from LST #69, ran through the cane field and spotted a fellow Marine missing both legs below the knees, the victim of a jeep or truck engine catapulted from one of the exploding LSTs. Another Marine, CPL Jack Lamb, found the cane field "dotted with men who had been cut down by flying metal from the explosions." Like Swallow, he came across a man missing both legs. While he was putting a tourniquet on the man, two fellow Marines came up and dragged the man away. Years later, Lamb was still amazed by the freakish accident. "The chances of losing both limbs by such a blast would probably be a million to one," he said.[5]

As improbable as the accident may have been, it seems to have happened more than once. Joseph Wachter, from LST #43, found a terribly wounded Navy crewman one and a half miles from the exploding ships. "His legs were torn off by a piece of machinery, and two medics were tending to his wound."[6] Marine PFC Stan Ellis recalled, "One of my friends, named Van Ness, . . . was already ashore and trying to run away from the explosions. Part of an amtrac motor went sailing through the air like shrapnel, cutting off both his legs. The poor guy bled to death before anything could be done for him."[7]

Harry Pearce and his buddy Sam climbed up the muddy bank and then turned to help another man reach the high top. "Sam and I got the man up and shoved him over the top and just as we did a jeep engine came down from out of nowhere and cut both of his legs off just above the knees," recalled Pearce. "We grabbed the man and a couple of sailors went by and we got their belts from them and tied their belts around his two stumps." After applying the tourniquets, Pearce and Sam carried the man through the cane field, all the time trying to avoid the rain of debris.

Eventually they got the injured man to a small house. "When we came into the yard, the woman saw the man with his legs off, and she ran into her bedroom and took her sheets off . . . and she began to bind up his stumps the best she could." As she was doing this, more and more refugees arrived. Her husband brought out his old Model-T Ford and drove the wounded men to the hospital. "We put ten guys in there and he started the thing and took them into Hickam Field. There was a base hospital there someplace," Pearce remembered. "In the meantime, more guys were coming into the little house where we were, most of them with very severe burns. One Navy guy with a Kapok lifejacket on asked me to help him get his jacket off. I went to take the Kapok lifesaver off, and the meat on his shoulders and back was coming off. It was stuck to the Kapok lifejacket, and he was as black as the ace of spades, just burned all over." To try and alleviate the suffering, the wife gave Pearce and Sam a pail of lard to smear on the burns. "When we had no more lard," Pearce went on, "I used . . . axle grease to smear on their wounds." Eventually Navy trucks arrived and began taking the rest of the wounded to nearby hospitals.[8]

Electrician Tidwell, off of LCT-982 on LST #274, was running through the cane field beside two Marines. Then "the third explosion went off and all that stuff's in the air and I didn't know what to do, but the Marines jumped down the ditch and started plowin' their heads up under the dirt," said Tidwell. "So I stuffed my head under one of them's armpit and went with them!" When the debris stopped falling, Tidwell and the Marines started running again. When they finally reached safety, they turned and watched the LSTs continue to explode. "There were several more explosions," Tidwell remembered. "When that 100 octane went up, most of it went up in the air as a vapor, and it sort of exploded."[9]

Harold Knebel, the MoMM2/c who had been badly injured by a piece of flying angle iron, suffered burns while swimming ashore. "After swimming 100 yards thru and under the burning aviation gasoline and diesel oil fire on the water, I finally swam out of the fire," he wrote. "I thought I was safe until more shrapnel fell around me. I started to swim under the water for longer periods. I was exhausted." When Knebel reached shore, he "ran thru the cane field with shrapnel still falling around me." Knebel had moderate burns on his face, neck, arms, chest, and back. Said Knebel, "Thank God the Navy had previously instructed me how to swim thru burning oil on the water and survive."[10]

Seaman Slater and the gunner's mate who was helping him with the badly wounded crewman from LCT-982 made it safely to shore but then ran into more trouble. "The explosions continued, and we'd stop and try to shield ourselves in a bank or anyplace that was available because the shrapnel was so heavy," Slater stated. "Anyway, the gunner's mate that was with me got hit, but he was still able to carry on." Instead of moving through the cane field, the three men moved up the one-lane roadway beside the loch. "The ambulances and fire trucks were coming down this lane alongside the sugar cane field," said Slater, ". . . and an ambulance picked us up and took us to a Navy hospital." Thanks to the quick actions of both Slater and the gunner's mate, the badly wounded sailor survived, despite having had his chest and groin cut wide open. "As a matter of fact," noted Slater, "he was medically discharged."[11]

While Marine Jack Claven and a few other men were helping to load one of the ambulances, LST #69, which had drifted toward LST #480 and was now close to shore, suddenly exploded. "The ambulance was totaled," Claven wrote, "and those who were left took off running in high gear." Having done all that he could, Claven took off with the others.[12]

While other men saw jeeps and trucks and parts of vehicles thrown sky high, Marine rifleman James T. Cobb heard a "horrendous blast" behind him and turned in time to see an entire LCVP Higgins boat hurtle through the air and land only a few feet away. As Cobb stated, this is no "sea story."

Scared out of their wits, Cobb and about two dozen other men ran through the cane field until they finally reached the small town of Waipahu, almost two miles northwest of the exploding ships. Spotting the local saloon, the men rushed inside "and proceeded to do some serious beer drinking." Later that afternoon, a Navy shore patrol rounded the men up and took them back to a transit center.[13]

While hundreds of men fled through the cane field, a few others decided to stay close to the LSTs and protect themselves by hiding among the parked LVTs. Navaho code talker Thompson had reached shore and was running close to the parked LVTs when "the main engine room of one of the ships went up, causing parts of engines to rain down." Seeking shelter, Thompson and a few others dove under the nearby amtracs. When things slowed down, they all "took off again and headed for the sugar cane fields."[14]

Although the amtracs and DUKWs were convenient items to hide behind, they were also an important cog in the invasion of Saipan, whose beaches were ringed by a coral reef and only accessible through the amphibious vehicles. While dozens of men tried to hide under and behind the armored amphibians, some of the crews were trying to save them. Sergeant Wells and Corporal Reynolds were two men from 2nd DUKW who tried to save the DUKWs and at the same time transport wounded men to nearby hospitals.

"Massive explosions were hurling huge chunks of steel, vehicle parts, and other debris our way," Wells wrote. "We ducked behind the road bank until the mammoth pieces had passed overhead and then leaped to our feet and ran until the next explosion." Once the two reached the parked DUKWs, just above Tare 8, they found most of them gone and only one man, CAPT James L. George, standing by. "He was very calm and seemingly oblivious to the danger," noted Wells. George ordered Wells and Reynolds to try to get some of the thinner-skinned amtracs out of the danger zone, but when the two DUKW men could not figure out how to start their engines, they switched tasks and began helping the constantly arriving casualties.[15]

Just above the area where 2nd DUKW was parked, eighteen-year-old Marine MP Bob Arieta was trying to help the wounded. "Things happened so fast," Arieta recalled. "They started bringing guys that were wounded. I took guys in my jeep to sick bay. When I got up there, it was like that scene in *Gone with the Wind*, with all the bodies laid out." Arieta did not know how many trips he made, but he remembered the brutality of the situation. "Some guys were missing arms and legs. I'd put two or three guys in the jeep, as much as I could. The doctor would take 'em out, and I'd turn around and go back for more."[16]

Pearce also recalled the *Gone with the Wind* look of the hospital. "The hospital and the Navy sent trucks out to pick people up along these roads and in the sugar cane field to take them into the base hospitals and to care for them," he said. "They were taking the wounded in and dumping them out right in front of the women's nurses quarters. The women, of course, came to the windows to look out, and here were Marines and Navy boys—some naked, some in shorts, some wounded. They couldn't figure out what was going on."[17]

Among those taken to a hospital was MoMM2/c Knebel, suffering from the puncture wound near his spine. "The hospital was full of patients. I was given one of the last Army cots that was placed in the hallway. Every available space was taken." Feeling no pain, Knebel sat quietly and watched the frenzied activity around him. "The hospital staff was quite busy. Men were dying, amputations were being made, bones were being set, burns of the faces, hands, and arms were being treated, and other wounds were being treated."[18]

Opposite Tare 9, where LST #480 was snagged and set afire by the drifting LST #69, was the amtrac park. Arthur J. Auxer and Merle B. Carpenter, both with 2nd Armored Amphibious Battalion, were awarded Navy & Marine Corps Medals for braving the continuous rain of shrapnel and debris to save the men and LVTs. The citation for Auxer stated, "As he was moving away from the enveloping blaze and explosions, his vehicle caught fire, which was immediately put out by his prompt actions, saving the casualties and the armored amphibian. Later, he returned again, heedless of his own personal safety, and assisted in driving four other armored amphibians away from the burning ship." Carpenter's citation was identical.[19]

After BM2/c Hillman and S2/c Sacoolidge took a boatload of rescued men to the naval ammunition depot dock, the two men and a few eager volunteers returned to the burning ships. "We headed for the middle of a burning group of LSTs," said Hillman. "About 100 yards from it we began pulling men from the water. However, the oil slick that now covered the bay made it hard getting the men into the boat." Out of the corner of his eye, Hillman noticed that another rescuing LCVP had lowered its bow ramp, allowing the crew to stand on it and, in the words of Hillman, "literally 'scoop' men out of the water." Wrote Hillman, "It looked like a good idea, so I followed suit."

There was, however, an inherent danger in maneuvering an LCVP with the bow ramp down. "Putting the ramp down in the middle of the harbor, even in the best of situations, was not without its risks," explained Hillman. "All that was needed to sink us was a small wave." Sure enough, with the bow ramp down, the LCVP was hit by a big wave created by an escaping LST. "As the boat filled with water, the sight of my LCVP sinking to the bottom of the bay flashed before my eyes," wrote Hillman. "Sack [Sacoolidge] and I jumped to the cable winch that raised the ramp and cranked for all our worth. By the time we got the ramp closed, we had about a foot of water over the floor boards."

Although their boat was now full of water, and the propeller had become fouled with debris, Hillman, Sacoolidge, and the others continued in their rescue efforts. Twenty-five minutes later, when the oil on the water around them began to burn, Hillman headed back to the ammunition dock. For their heroic actions on May 21, 1944, Hillman and Sacoolidge were awarded the Navy & Marine Corps Medal.[20]

Another man awarded the Navy & Marine Corps Medal was S1/c Alex Bernal, who had taken his small boat into the center of the disaster to pull men from the burning waters. "We just stayed there until we couldn't stay anymore," Bernal recalled. "The fire in the water drove us away." As he left the area, Bernal collapsed. "That's when I blacked out. I just passed out until I got to the hospital, and they found out there was something wrong with my ears. I had a broken eardrum." It was probably ruptured from the very first explosion. Bernal had performed all of his lifesaving work with an injury that should have caused him constant pain. "I got the Navy Commendation Ribbon [later the Navy & Marine Corps Medal], and to me it was a big honor to be singled out," he said. "It was just a thing that any other man in my same position would have done 'cause there was nowhere to run."[21]

CHAPTER 19 | # The Drifting Menace

Some thirty-five minutes after the first explosion was recorded at 1508 hours (signal tower time), the Coast Guard finally asked the Pearl Harbor Yard fire dispatcher to send all "available waterborne firefighting equipment to West Loch."[1]

A little more than an hour after the first explosion, LSTs #45 and #126 (both from Tare 5), #169 and #272 (both from Tare 6), and #23, #240, and #461 (all from Tare 9) were at sea. All seven ships were ordered to remain within 15 miles of the Pearl Harbor entrance. The command ship for the little group became LST #272 with LT CDR John Dore at the conn. "As we lay off Pearl," wrote Donald Lux, aboard LST #461, "we watched the endless explosions and hurtling debris through the night." Eventually, a number of small combat craft came out to protect the slow moving LSTs and escort them in a prescribed grid around Oahu.[2]

In spite of a 10-inch hawser twisted around her left screw, LST #23 went out to sea with the others. After falling into column, Lieutenant Martin shut down the engines and Ensign Sortevik went "over the side with a knife" to cut away the troublesome line. Unfortunately, the attempt failed. With only one engine and a handful of wounded men aboard, the ship returned to the Pearl Harbor entrance where she was met by a U.S. Navy salvage tug, which was there to assist in maneuvering the ship up the winding main channel to the repair docks in East Loch, and by a Navy picket boat, which dropped off a medical officer and four pharmacist's mates.[3]

Forty-one minutes after the first explosion (signal tower time), Navy Yard personnel were still trying to get firefighting equipment to respond. At 3:49 P.M., the fire dispatcher logged a request to send a Landing Craft, Mechanized (LCM) to the firefighters school to "load foam supplies," since they were fighting oil and gas fires. Two minutes later, the same dispatcher asked the Pearl Harbor Receiving Station to send a work party to the school to help in loading the foam supplies.[4]

It was almost 4:15 before LST #242, under command of Lieutenant Commander Green, the qualified pilot, left Tare 5 and started down the narrow West Loch channel. Although ordered out to sea, the radioman informed the Navy Yard, "Ship not in condition to go to sea" because of trouble raising the bow ramp. When the Navy Yard responded, "Proceed to sea," Commander Green shot back, "Ship unseaworthy request instructions. Signed Pilot Green." This time, the Navy Yard sent the ship to a berth in East Loch.[5]

Even after many of the LSTs had managed to leave the danger area, the fire and explosions continued.[6] At 1630 hours, when it was reported that some of the exploding ships were drifting south toward the ammunition depot and the cargo ship *Joseph B. Francis*, three PT boats from Motor Torpedo Boat Squadron 26 were dispatched from East Loch toward West Loch with orders to torpedo and sink, if need be, any drifting LST that might reach the depot.[7]

SF Ed George was in an LCI trying to get out of West Loch when the PT boats raced by. "When we were coming out, there were two [sic] PT boats that came down each side of the channel," George stated. "While we were coming back, they were coming in and they almost sunk us because of the wake."[8]

Out of the five ships from Tare 8 that began drifting south, LST #69, with a burning LCT-983 still strapped to her topside, drifted back and to the left, eventually colliding with LST #480, which had become entangled in the Tare 9 dolphins. After #480 was set on fire, both ships drifted down about 200 yards, past the Tare 10 pilings, before a courageous tugboat crew shoved LST #480 aside and stopped her from drifting any further.[9]

Around 4:50 P.M., LST #353, which was still carrying LCT-963 on her burning, exploding main deck, sank in about 30 feet of water about 70 feet from shore and almost straight east of the Tare 10 dolphin pilings. Only a large part of the remains of her deckhouse and a small section of her forecastle remained visible above the water.[10]

When LST #353 sank, LST #39, which had been drifting alongside her, came to a stop, perhaps fouled in the wreckage of #353. With her bow doors open and her ramp down, and a pair of long pontoons on either side of her hull, LST #39 continued to burn and explode.[11]

After colliding with LST #480 and turning her into a flaming wreck, LST #69 continued to drift southward. Close by were the burning and exploding LSTs #43 and #179, carrying LCT-961.[12] These three ships became the major threat to the naval ammunition depot, the *Joseph B. Francis*, and all ships and personnel nearby.

People at the ammunition depot had been working to remove ammunition from the exposed docks. In the words of truck driver Otto A. Bohlmann, there was "great confusion and excitement that prevailed there." The biggest excitement came from the civilian cargo ship *Joseph B. Francis*. Still loaded with 350 tons of her original load of 3,000 tons of ammunition, she had been moored alongside the depot dock with her hatch covers off when the first explosion occurred. For more than an hour she remained moored in place but eventually got underway on her own power. At 4:20 P.M., however, as she was leaving the depot, a huge explosion pelted her top deck with white phosphorous shells, sending at least one shell into one of the open hatches. Seconds later, a fire started. The crewmen sprang into action, spraying water into the burning cargo hold and getting the fire under control. *Joseph B. Francis*, at first ordered out to sea, was eventually sent to a berth in Middle Loch because of her open hatches.[13]

At 5:05 P.M., while *Joseph B. Francis* was making her way up the main channel, one of the phosphorous shells reignited, sending flames and black smoke billowing out of the forward bay. Fearing that the ship might explode among the dozens of warships moored in East Loch, the Navy Yard started moving ships out of the way. At 5:20 P.M., the escort carriers USS *Long Island* (CVE-1) and USS

Copahee (CVE-12) were ordered to get out of East Loch immediately. Two minutes later, however, the skipper of *Joseph B. Francis* reported, "Present fire out." To be on the safe side, two Marine Corps fire inspectors boarded the cargo ship and inspected the entire vessel. At 7:14 P.M., the inspectors reported "Fires positively out and all fires secured."[14] Miraculously, another disaster had been averted.

Although the minesweeper *Terror* was moored around the bend from the ammunition depot, she was unable to proceed on her own and was awaiting a towboat as the burning ships began to drift toward the depot. Around 4:30 P.M., shortly after *Joseph B. Francis* left, the Navy-chartered tug *Mikimiki* pulled up on the port bow and quickly tossed lines to the big minesweeper. Within nine minutes, *Mikimiki* pulled *Terror* away from the loading dock at WL-4 and cast off the tow lines. Then, with Commander Blakeslee at the conn, the minesweeper traveled down the West Loch channel and out to sea.[15]

Back inside West Loch, the three burning ships—LSTs #43, #179, and #69—continued drifting toward the ammunition depot. Docked nearby, at the mouth of the shallow small boat area, were a number of refugee LSTs.

"Late in the afternoon," recalled LT(jg) Seymour Tabin of LST #127, "three exploding and burning LSTs came drifting into view out of the bay." Acting quickly, the crew of LST #127 freed the ship from the mudflats and moved to a safer berth about a mile deeper into the bay.[16]

Another ship that moved further into the small boat area was LST #244. After backing out of Tare 10 and entering the shallow bay, Lieutenant Aderhold had brushed up against one of the ammunition barges near the ammunition depot, sustaining a cut "about 10 inches long in the hull of the ship and 5 feet above the waterline." For the next forty-five minutes, Lieutenant Aderhold repeatedly dropped first his stern anchor and then his bow anchor and "crabbed" his way deeper into the back water area. Near 5:00 P.M., the ship dropped both anchors for good. In spite of their new location, "All hands [were] kept at special sea detail, and the decks were continually sprayed with water."[17]

Henry D. Johnson, a crewman on LST #244, watched from the main deck as his ship moved deeper into the small boat area and a drifting ship moved ever so slowly toward the ammunition depot. "This ship was afire," Johnson wrote, and the crew feared that the ship might drift all of the way to the depot and "cause more ammunition to explode." Recalled EM Milo F. Crankshaw, "That's when the PT boat came in to torpedo them."[18] Fortunately for all present, cooler heads prevailed.

By the time the PT boats arrived in West Loch, the situation had changed. The swift little plywood boats had been sent out from East Loch with orders to torpedo any drifting, burning LST that might threaten the ammunition depot. However, torpedoing one of the combat loaded ships might have caused an even bigger explosion, showering the entire area with live ammunition and burning phosphorous shells. It had to be avoided at any cost. Fortunately, by the time the three PT boats arrived, numerous tugboats and fireboats were already at work. Instead of torpedoing and sinking the LSTs, the PT boats stood by and let the tugs and fireboats try to push the three drifting LSTs into shallower waters and extinguish the blazes.

"Capt. Craven ordered torpedo boats not to take action until advised," noted the signal tower officer at 1640 hours, at the exact same moment that the five fireboats from Honolulu Harbor finally entered West Loch. A few minutes later, the three PT boats were told, "Do not take action unless further ordered." Luckily, the message was received before any damage could be done.[19]

Although the PT boats would never fire their torpedoes, they did assist in the rescue of survivors. ENS Bill Clark and his crew, which had gone to get fresh provisions for their LCI anchored in West Loch, were still in East Loch trying to get back to their ship when the motor torpedo boats returned. "A PT boat approached at full speed," Clark recalled, "stopping just in time to keep from ramming the dock. It had injured on board who were immediately transferred to waiting ambulances." Prevented from getting a boat to West Loch, Clark and his men had to wait until early evening before returning to LCI(L)-77.[20]

Fortunately for all, just before the PT boats entered West Loch, about a dozen specialized boats arrived to help extinguish the fires and stop the drifting ships. As the small seaplane tender USS *Swan* (AVP 7), capable of fighting fires, and the five responding fireboats began spraying the burning LSTs with water, the tugboats spread out to do what they could. While some tugs began helping the ships grounded on the mudflats or pushing out vessels still sitting at their moorings, a few rushed in to stop the burning ships from reaching the ammunition depot.[21]

SM3/c Charles E. Schiering, serving on *Swan*, recalled, "On the day of the explosion [our] ship was coming in from sea and approaching the channel to Pearl Harbor." Schiering contacted the Navy Yard signal tower and requested a berth in East Loch. "The tower sent back a message, advising the *Swan* to proceed to West Loch to help fight the fires and explosions on LSTs there." In spite of the fact that the *Swan* was carrying 5,000 gallons of aviation fuel and hundreds of aviation bombs and rockets, the skipper headed toward the scene.[22]

One of the first tugboats to reach the area of the disaster was the 124-foot-long harbor tug *Osceola* (YTB-129). On board was ship's Ck2/c Roy Sannella. "I saw three landing ships, or LSTs, burning and many dead Marines and sailors floating in the water," Sannella wrote. "I attempted to haul some of the survivors onto the tug, but the skipper yelled that we could not stop." Rushing in among the burning ships, the tugboat crew assisted LSTs #225 and #274 to go forward out of Tare 8. "After we cut the lines of two LSTs, we tried to untie the rest of the LSTs and separate them," Sannella continued. "Because of explosives flying all over us, we had to break off the effort. While the crew was busy manning hoses, I managed to lift several Marines and sailors, some wounded, into the boat." Many years later, he stated, "To this day I don't know how I did that, since I was an 18-year-old sailor weighing only 118 pounds."[23]

In command of fireboat X1426 was Coast Guard COX Lindel C. Jones. After the boat entered the West Loch channel, they were stopped by a small boat carrying Vice Admiral Turner. "The admiral directed each boat to a certain area," Jones wrote. "He sent a couple of boats to the ammunition dock and sent us to the center of the loch. About this time, a half dozen [*sic*] LSTs were adrift." Racing in, Jones's crew began pumping water onto one of the fiercely burning ships, probably LST #39, and pushing the LST out of the channel and closer to shore. When the LST ran aground, Jones backed his fireboat out and headed toward another burning ship.

"On the way back, the boat picked up considerable clothing in her screws," Jones remembered. Coming to a stop because of the fouled propellers, and because the strainers and suction lines that drew water from the loch to feed the fire hoses had become clogged with debris, S1/c Roland H. Noack, Jr., and S1/c John C. Livingston "jumped over the side into burning oil and gasoline covered water and freed the strainers and lines [and propellers], thus keeping [their] ship in action when it was so vitally needed." The actions of the men earned each of them a Navy & Marine Corps Medal.[24]

Coxswain Jones was not the only individual to encounter Vice Admiral Turner that day. Marine Corps COL Robert Hogaboom recalled, "Admiral Turner boarded a tug and personally led the fight to save what could be saved. At great personal danger, he personally supervised the operation until the fires were suppressed." During the height of the disaster, Turner ordered a small tugboat to assist in fighting the fires aboard the drifting vessels near Tare 9. Recalled the boatswain mate in command of the tug, "I received an order from Admiral Turner to proceed to T9 . . . and put out the fire there. Due to the fact that ammunition was exploding, I backed away." In his written report the boatswain added, "The Admiral came to me and said: 'Go back in there and stay or I will shoot you.' Four or five LSTs were at T9, all of which were burning and terrible explosions were occurring but I carried out my last order, as I had been told."[25]

While Seamen Noack and Livingston were underwater removing the debris from the propellers and strainers of Coxswain Jones's fireboat, an officer in a small boat pulled up alongside. The officer thought the crew on Jones's boat were "goofing off" and began to chastise them until Jones managed to explain the problem. "The officer seemed satisfied with the explanation and directed the [fire]boat to an LST which was burning fiercely," Jones said. "The officer directed the fireboat to be run upon the LST's ramp, which was down. As the officer and his cox'n pulled away, he shouted, 'Hurry up! What do you want to do, live forever?'" Jones instantly shot back, "You're not kidding!" Then, as Jones watched, the LST with the open ramp exploded, knocking the officer in the little boat into the drink. Jones quickly rescued the officer, who then climbed back into the little boat and sped off in another direction.[26]

When the fireboats first arrived in West Loch, a few were sent to the three LSTs still in the vicinity of Tare 8. LSTs #225 and #274 were already beached on the shore of Walker Bay, but LST #205 was next to the Tare 8 dolphin pilings. All three LSTs were burning.

"One of [the fireboats] secured itself to the port side of the #274 and very quickly and skillfully brought her fires under control," noted Lieutenant Commander Hoyt, watching from LST #225. "Another fireboat came up behind the #205, which was the inboard vessel at Tare 8. She sent a party [aboard] to help fight the fire on the LCT. The officer in charge of this party was extremely competent and knew his business. . . . With the arrival of the fire boats, the fires on the #274, #225, and the #205 were quickly extinguished and no further incidents appeared on those three ships."[27]

After extinguishing the fires on LST #205, the fireboats helped the ship move away from the Tare 8 dolphin pilings and into Walker Bay, to the left of LSTs #225 and #274. Although the three ships were out of danger from the burning, drifting ships, they were still threatened by the oil-soaked water. "It looked as though the LST was going to be surrounded by the burning oil and gas on the water which was heading towards [us]," wrote John B. Hovis, a Marine aboard LST #225.[28]

With the fire on the water drawing nearer, all three ships decided to move further north into Walker Bay. However, LST #205 was blocked in by LST #225 and #274. In a repeat of the earlier situation, where LST #205 had been hemmed in against the dolphin pilings at Tare 8 by the outboard vessels, Lieutenant Buchar's ship would once again have to sit tight and wait until LSTs #225 and #274 moved out of its way.[29]

Rushing in quickly, tugboats began pushing and pulling LST #225 and #274 deeper into Walker Bay. During the move, the ships bumped against one another, but no serious damage occurred. Once both ships were out of harm's way, the little tugboats returned for LST #205 and helped push her away from the burning oil. Much later, when a headcount was taken on LST #205, a Coast Guard ship, it was discovered that one crewman was dead— a steward's mate who had "apparently abandoned ship and was burned to death in the flaming water." He was the only Coast Guard fatality during the entire West Loch disaster.[30]

While the tugboats were working to save the three LSTs, the crews aboard the three high-speed transports moored at Tare 7, *Overton*, *Waters*, and *Stringham*, were awaiting some tugboats of their own. Aboard *Overton*, the outermost vessel, five men had already been seriously wounded and several more had "received minor cuts and bruises" by flying debris from the second explosion. When the oil on the water caught fire, the crew flooded the ship's after magazines and looked around once again for the tugboats.

Eventually, four small fire tugs arrived and immediately began spraying the burning oil. On board *Overton*, it was soon discovered that fuel oil had somehow leaked into the water system and was coming out of the fire hoses. In spite of the inherent dangers, the crew continued to use the oily water to wet down the decks. About this time, the third big explosion occurred, once again showering *Overton* with debris. Among the pieces that hit her was a 10-foot chunk of steel that impacted on the fantail, denting one of the on-deck depth charges. After the detonator was removed, the damaged depth charge was jettisoned over the side.[31]

The second ship in line at Tare 7, *Waters*, was shielded from most of the thrown debris by *Overton*. Still, the second "terrific explosion . . . filled the air with debris and flying shrapnel" and wounded one sailor in the head. Trapped in the middle of Tare 7 when the third major explosion went off, *Waters* was showered with debris and hit hard by the concussion, in spite of her somewhat protected position. Damage consisted of "a few sprung doors, cut cables, some sprung bulkheads, a bent yardarm brace, and a slightly damaged hull frame."[32]

Morris Folstad was on board *Stringham*, the third high-speed transport and the ship tied to the Tare 7 pilings, when the third big explosion went off. "Pieces of steel went flying through the area," he recalled. "A signalman standing between myself and another signalman was hit by a piece of steel in his forehead and killed instantly." Three other crewmen were injured by flying debris, and several were blown overboard by the concussion.[33]

While the crews of the three high-speed transports waited and watched, LSTs #69, #43, and #179 drifted closer to the ammunition depot, the two moored ammunition barges, and some of the grounded LSTs still at the mouth of the small boat area. One of the threatened ships was LST #224, which had moved out of

Tare 9 and into the back water bay. "Three LSTs on fire from T-8 began drifting out into the channel," the officer of the deck wrote. Minutes later he logged, "Fire and Rescue ship two points off on starboard bow began spraying drifting ships with water."[34]

Dutch Williams, a motor machinist's mate on LST #224, had come up from the engine room once the ship stopped. "We could see the ships that were on fire. We saw two [sic] ships still tied together drifting toward the ammunition warehouse. All of a sudden they stopped, and we thought that it was because the fire had caused the stern anchor to release." Ensign Harter from LST #224 was also watching. "One of the LSTs that was burning was being driven by the current and wind directly into the ammunition dock. Just before it reached the dock, somebody was either still alive on the fantail and dropped the stern anchor, or possibly the brake burned and released the anchor. This prevented the vessel from being blown into the ammunition dock."[35]

Whatever the cause, the three wayward vessels suddenly came to a halt about 500 feet from the ammunition depot. First one stopped, then the second ship got fouled on the first. Finally, the third got fouled on the other two. They all continued to burn and explode.[36]

CHAPTER 20 | # The Last Big Hurrah

Although the three drifting ships had been stopped, they were still a menace as they continued to explode and throw flaming debris, shrapnel, and white phosphorus shells around the area. Additionally, the burning oil on the water was a threat to ships moored anywhere inside West Loch as the northeast wind continued to move the flames toward the ammunition depot, the moored ammo barges, and the ships at the mouth of the small boat area.

Bill Simpson, a Marine telephone man on LST #224, which had moved to the shallow back bay area, watched the fireboats fight the flames on the water. "One fire boat disappeared into the fire several times. Each time they backed out with their rope bumpers smoking or on fire. Finally, it went into the holocaust one more time, and this time it was never seen again."[1] Doing tremendous work, the fireboat and tug boat crews placed their lives in peril numerous times in order to save the lives of others.

By the time Sergeant Weinberger and his fellow photographers and cinematographers reached West Loch, the three LSTs had stopped drifting northeast of the ammunition depot. LST #43, with her steel pontoons still attached, had exploded, keeled over, and capsized. The other two ships continued to burn and explode, creating a magnificent panorama for the photographers. "Three of them moored together were totally involved in towering flames.

Munitions were exploding constantly," Weinberger remembers. "Our cameras were in operation from the instant we entered the loch. Many men were in the water and were being helped by Navy personnel onto a nearby quay only fifty yards from the burning ships. All of my crew landed on the quay, while our LCP continued in the rescue work, picking men, sailors, and Marines out of the water." His crew alternated between shooting movies and still photos, both black-and-white and color, and helping with the rescue work.

Around 5:05 P.M., LST #69, which had stopped near the ammunition depot, suddenly exploded in a terrific ball of smoke and flame that shot over 200 feet into the air, throwing deadly pieces of metal all around the loch. All of it was captured on film. "We had to keep alert and on the move to avoid debris constantly spewed into the air by the explosions," Weinberger wrote. "At one point, as I looked through the camera finder I saw a huge piece of metal arcing toward me. Like an outfielder tracking a fly ball and maneuvering to get under it, I did just the opposite to avoid being under it. It was a section of the hull, roughly 8 feet long by 4 feet and of 1-inch thick steel. It still had an orange glow from the heat and landed 10 feet away from me. We kept shooting until we exhausted our stock of film and stayed on the quay until dark."[2]

While Weinberger and his crew were filming the devastation, the small seaplane tender *Swan* arrived and headed over to LST #480, the last ship to catch fire. SM Charles E. Schiering recalled, "[Our skipper] brought the bow against the LST and tried to push it over in the water. There were two Navy men on that LST, and before [we] could get the men off, it exploded, killing the two men and injuring several crew members of the *Swan*." According to Schiering, the LST disintegrated. Later, the crew of *Swan* found part of a watch from one of the Navy men and parts of an electric potato peeler from LST #480 on their deck. Heavily damaged and with several injured men aboard, *Swan* left West Loch, "hobbled into the Navy Yard for repairs," and spent the next six weeks in dry dock.[3]

The burning ships had separated into two groups. LSTs #39, #353, and #480 were near Tares 9 and 10 while LSTs #43, #69, and #179 were in mid-channel, about 500 feet northwest of the depot. In the first group, LST #353 had sunk around 4:50 P.M. near Tare 9. LSTs #39 and #480 had drifted further south until a few courageous tugs pushed #480 close to the shore. Still carrying her pontoons, LST #480 continued to burn and explode and make a nuisance of herself. LST #39, also with a pair of pontoons, stopped a little to the right and a little behind #480, where she continued to explode and throw shrapnel and fiery debris in a wide arc.[4]

LSTs #43, #69, and #179 also continued to burn and explode. Eventually, LST #43 capsized. When she did, one of her two pontoons, which was aflame, came loose and began drifting toward the moored ammunition barges. Fortunately, some yard tugs rushed in and towed the ammunition barges deeper into the shallow small boat area while a few fire tugs doused the wayward pontoon.[5]

Near 7:00 P.M., the Coast Guard fireboat X58276, the diver class rescue and salvage ship USS *Valve* (ARS-28), and the yard net tender tugboat *Tamaha* (YNT-12) arrived. For four hours, *Valve* fought the fires but was eventually ordered to leave the loch after an explosion erupted from LST #39. The terrific blast completely wrecked *Tamaha*. Fearful that the same fate might befall *Valve*, the valuable little diving ship, which would see plenty of work in the months ahead, was ordered to safer waters.[6]

A witness to the explosion that wrecked *Tamaha* was Boatswain's Mate Hillman, now aboard LST #274 in Walker Bay. "A tug boat [actually *Tamaha*] was alongside [LST #39] pumping hundreds of gallons of water a minute onto her in a desperate attempt to put out the fire raging on her deck. It was like spitting into a fire. As flames lapped at the deckhouse [of LST #39], the control center of the ship, her 3" magazine exploded. Remarkably, the tug survived."[7]

The officer of the deck aboard the high-speed transport *Waters* also witnessed the deadly explosion that damaged Tamaha. "1930 [7:30 P.M.] A violent explosion occurred on the LST #39 which was 250 yards astern. The bridge was blown wide open and part of it falling on a medium tug [*Tamaha*] pinned it to the LST. Several of the smaller tugs being slightly damaged. A large tug took the tug pinned in tow to get [it] loose but only succeeded in pulling the whole LST #39 down the channel about 1,500 yards, thus making three separate fires."

The large unknown tugboat that tried to pull *Tamaha* out from under LST #39 had been pushing LSTs around in the shallow small boat area when it was ordered to rush over to help. Its crew struggled to free the small net tender from the deathlike grip caused by the fallen bridge of LST #39. After fifteen horrendous minutes, the Tamaha was pulled free, and the burning, exploding hulk of LST #39 was pushed over to the west bank of the channel, below Tare 10.[8]

At this point, Coast Guard Coxswain Jones, after clearing his propeller and strainers of debris, moved over to the open bow doors of LST #39 and ran the bow of fireboat X1426 up onto the lowered ramp. "We proceeded to put foam and water into the interior of the tank deck," Jones wrote. "Bullets were going off and bouncing off the tank deck. This was unbelievable, but not one of [our] crew was hit." Once most of the fire was extinguished and the bullets stopped flying, Jones and his crew entered the charred tank deck looking for survivors. "We found a number of people, but none was alive," he recalled. "We found men in the chain and rope lockers who had gone in there to escape the fire but suffocated in there."[9]

On the shore above Tare 8, at 2nd DUKW park, Sergeant Wells saw a boat move up to the open bow doors of LST #480.

As evening approached, a Navy tug, equipped for firefighting, approached an LST in Tare 8. [Actually Tare 9.] The captain nestled the tug's bow against that of the LST right where the bow doors met in the center. Shortly after the tug began pouring torrents of water on the raging fires aboard [#480], a tremendous explosion erupted. I dived behind a DUKW and crouched there until the concussion and shrapnel passed. Then I cautiously peered under the DUKW's bow. I stared in astonishment because the tug's superstructure was in shambles! The LST's bow doors had blown open right where the tug had nestled against them. Every man topside on the tug had disappeared. I carefully scanned the water near the tug and some distance forward of the LST, but not a single man or body was visible. The tug was floating slowly and silently away. The tug's superstructure destruction had been caused by the last of the most violent explosions.[10]

By late evening the authorities had the disaster under control and the other ships out of the danger area. Three of the eight ships in Tare 8 had managed to pull ahead into Walker Bay. Only one ship out of the seven originally moored in Tare 9, LST #480, had been unable to get away, and it fell victim to the five burning and exploding vessels from Tare 8. In Tare 10, all five ships had made a miraculous exit, sustaining only superficial damage. In retrospect, the disaster could have been worse, much worse.

At 7:47 P.M., it was determined that "apparently seven [*sic*] LSTs [are the] only vessels involved in situation." The other ships were all safe. Still, the four burning LSTs that remained afloat, #39, #480, #69, and #179, continued to burn well into the night. The log of the Pearl Harbor signal tower looked like a scratched record that kept repeating itself: "1955: Another explosion original scene," "2003: Series of explosions at original scene," "2006: Large explosions on LST adrift in West Loch stream."[11]

Throughout the night, dozens of firefighting boats, tugs, and harbor patrol craft dotted the surface of West Loch. At one point, it was reported that eleven harbor patrol boats were in West Loch. The burning oil on the water continued to be a menace to the rescue craft as well as to the ships and boats moored to the south and west. Unignited oil was almost as much a problem as the burning oil. A heavy coating of unignited fuel oil and gasoline lodged under one of the piers near the ammunition depot. Firefighting teams went to work with hoses to break the sludge apart and keep it from igniting until the ebb tide carried it out of the area.[12]

Just after 9:00 P.M., the high-speed transport *Waters*, sitting idle at Tare 7 between *Overton* and *Stringham* and northeast of the fires, contacted the Navy Yard in regard to the burning oil. "Request additional chemical firefighting equipment be sent. A change in wind would endanger nest of the APDs." Already overwhelmed, the Navy Yard thought to minimize the danger by moving the three transports to safer berths. "Is it possible for you and other APDs to get underway and clear?" the Yard asked. "Negative," *Waters* came back. "Channel is blocked with wreckage."

The Navy Yard was doing all that it could to control the continuing "minor explosions" and contain the fires and was hard-pressed to send additional firefighting equipment to help the trapped transports at Tare 7. "What is progress controlling fire

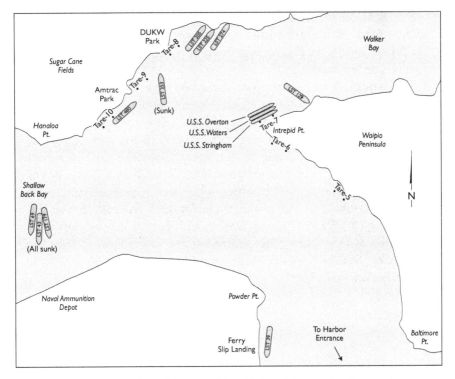

West Loch, Pearl Harbor, 6:00 A.M., May 22, 1944. Drawn by Gene Eric Salecker, redrawn by Bill Nelson. Copyright © 2014 by the University of Oklahoma Press.

nearest you?" the Yard finally asked *Waters*. "Fire in Tare 9 is about the same," *Waters* responded, indicating the fires aboard LSTs #39 and #480. "There appears to be no one fighting it. Believe it could be reached from shore. Have seen nothing but water used on fires today. Urge foam or chemical." The Navy Yard responded to part of this information, and land-based firefighters were soon spraying streams of water onto the two grounded and burning LSTs.[13]

Of the four remaining upright and burning LSTs, the one that gave the firefighters the most trouble was LST #39, lodged just below Tare 10. At 9:52 P.M., LST #39 burst into roaring flames again, spraying burning debris onto the nearby shore and causing a couple of uncontrolled grass fires. At 10:30, the signal tower was able to report that the "two shore fires [are] under control and burning themselves out" but that LST #39 was "burning again." The efforts of the exhausted firefighters finally paid off, and at 11:34 P.M., the signal tower reported, "Fire on LST #39 still burning but under control."[14]

Firefighters continued to soak the burning vessels, aided by six portable lighting sets that managed to turn night into day. Around 1:30 A.M., LST #480 began smoking again, and the fire crews quickly switched their hoses from LST #39 to the new threat. At 5:10 A.M., as the sun began to brighten the eastern sky, the signal tower reported, "Fire and smoke still visible at Tare 8 [sic]." It was the last report containing any mention of fire or smoke. More than fourteen hours after the initial explosion had erupted aboard the forecastle of LST #353, the West Loch disaster came to an end. At 7:15 A.M., the duty officer in the signal tower entered into his logbook, "Sandwiches and coffee for 50 men sent to Tare 8."[15] It was time for Pearl Harbor to get back to preparing for the invasion of Saipan.

Exploding LST at West Loch, May 21, 1944. The boat in silhouette at center was trying to aid in the rescue effort. Courtesy of the NPS USAR Collection, VALR-3404.

LST #39 on fire. Courtesy of the U.S. National Archives. Photo# SC 185701.

LVT Park and burning LST #480. Courtesy of the Fourteenth Naval District Photo Collection, National Park Service.

Firefighters attempting to extinguish the fires on an LST carrying pontoons. Courtesy of Real War Photos Galleries.

Firefighting ships at West Loch. Courtesy of the NPS USAR Collection, VALR-3406.

Fireboats fighting fire on burning pontoon in West Loch. Courtesy of the NPS USAR Collection, VALR-3403.

Fire tugs fighting fire on floating pontoon. Courtesy of Real War Photos
Galleries.

Nighttime explosion aboard one of the burning LSTs. Courtesy of Real War
Photos Galleries.

The West Loch explosions left an array of floating pontoons and smoldering ships. Courtesy of the NPS USAR Collection, VALR-3409.

LST #480 burned out and grounded on Hanaloa Point, West Loch, on May 22, 1944, with USCGC *Woodbine*. Courtesy of the U.S. National Archives.

The sunken hulk of LST #39 seen after the disaster. Note the pontoon hanging on the side. Courtesy of the U.S. National Archives.

Rescue personnel inspecting the insides of LST #39. Courtesy of Real War Photos Galleries.

Overhead view of the burned-out hulk of LST #39 in West Loch. Courtesy of the U.S. National Archives.

The remains of LST #480, still visible in West Loch today. Courtesy of the U.S. National Archives.

Wreath-laying ceremony at the site of LST #480 in commemoration of the West Loch disaster. Courtesy of the U.S. Navy photos.

CHAPTER 21

The Next
Twenty-Four Hours

Shortly after the disaster began, the gears were in motion to discover what had gone wrong and who, or what, was to blame. At
3:45 P.M., just a little more than thirty minutes after the initial
explosion on LST #353, the three investigators from the Naval Intelligence Unit, Lieutenants Turner, Shea, and Flannigan, arrived
at the naval ammunition depot, determined to discover if the first
explosion was an act of sabotage. Upon their arrival they could see
the fires and explosions from the LSTs at Tare 8. Through obser-
vation and questioning, as the ships continued to burn and explode
and survivors were brought ashore, it was noticed that the entire
area around West Loch was "readily accessible to any person without supervision."[1] Definitely, security was at a minimum.

Of a more serious matter were the "countless maps, papers,
and secret and confidential publications [that] were scattered by
the explosions and blown by the prevailing winds across the naval
ammunition depot, West Loch, cane fields of the Ewa Plantation
Company, the Marine Corps Air Station, Ewa, and the Naval Air
Station, Barber's Point." Almost immediately, instructions went
out for all commanding officers to turn in "all maps, papers, and
debris from any of these ships, collected in the area under their ju-
risdiction."[2] With an invasion in the offing and the destination still
unknown to most officers and personnel, the intelligence unit was
hoping to gather up any and all material that might indicate where

such an invasion would occur. If papers fell into the wrong hands, the whole operation could be jeopardized.

Over the next few weeks, the Intelligence Unit poured through hundreds and hundreds of documents, maps, and scraps of paper. Eventually, the Unit would find enough "secret, confidential, and restricted publications" to fill "two large packing boxes."[3] No one knew, however, how much was not found and whether any vital information on the upcoming invasion had leaked out. Only time would tell.

The three intelligence officers spoke to eyewitnesses. On 27 May, the collected material was submitted to the official court of inquiry that had been convened on 22 May, indicating that "there was no evidence or indication that the fires and explosions of the LSTs in West Loch, Oahu, T.H. [Territory of Hawaii] were the result of an act or acts of sabotage."[4] Although the officers did not know exactly what had caused the initial explosion, they felt certain that it was not sabotage.

As the sun rose on Monday, 22 May, four of the LSTs were still burning. Although a few small explosions occurred, the heavy detonations were over and the smoke had cleared. What was left behind, however, was devastating. Marine PFC Carl Matthews (23rd MarReg, 4th MarDiv), recalled, "Many bodies were found in the sugar cane fields, blown there by the explosions. . . . When the smoke cleared there was no doubt that we had suffered a serious disaster."[5]

Of the seven LSTs that had been hustled out to sea, LST #23 had returned to Pearl Harbor late on the evening of 21 May because of the problem of the line wrapped around her port screw. "At 2005 the '23' returned through the sub nets and moored to the starboard side of LST 29," wrote a crewman. "The exploded ships were still burning." LST #23 had been in Tare 9, directly behind the worst of the exploding ships, and had been pelted with debris, shrapnel, and human remains. The crewman remembered, "The next day the entire crew turned to cleaning blood and body parts off the deck."[6]

The remaining six LSTs that had escaped Pearl Harbor and had gone to sea—#45, #126, #169, #240, #272, and #461— continued to cruise a grid about fifteen miles outside of the Pearl Harbor entrance throughout the night of 21 May and far into the next day. At 4:21 P.M. on 22 May, LST #272, with Lieutenant Dore at the conn, slipped back into West Loch and moored with her port side to the Tare 4 dolphins. Over the next few hours, LSTs #169, #461, and #240 pulled in beside it, extending the number of ships moored at Tare 4 to four.[7] There they were far enough away from the smoking derelicts to be safe, yet close enough to see what was going on.

LSTs #45 and #126 returned to West Loch just before 5:00 P.M. Both were eventually assigned to Tare 2 along the northern shoreline of the West Loch channel. Already tied to the dolphins was LST #226, which had moved from Tare 3, the water depot, in the early afternoon. LST #126 slipped into the number two position, and somehow LST #224, which had spent the night in the shallow boat area, slipped into the number three position before LST #45 arrived. By 7:45 P.M., there were four ships moored at Tare 2.[8]

Donald Lux was aboard LST #126 when it came up the West Loch channel to moor at Tare 2. He would never forget what he saw. "When we were cleared to reenter the harbor, it was a frightening sight," he wrote. "Body parts of the Marine tank crews and infantry could still be seen afloat in the harbor." Philip Moses, aboard LST #45, also witnessed "the torn bodies . . . the headless bodies . . . [that] the rescuers were bringing out of the water and placing on the dock."[9]

The gruesome task of gathering up and identifying the dead of the West Loch disaster had begun with first light on Monday, 22 May. Around 7:00 A.M., Coast Guard COX Lindel Jones took his fireboat X1426 back to one of the burned-out LSTs. Anchoring in front of the open doors and lowered ramp, Jones and his crew went into the tank deck. "The ship was completely gutted," he wrote, "and there were dead bodies all over the ship . . . they never had a chance."[10]

Four LSTs, three high-speed transports, and a handful of smaller LCIs had spent the night in the area of Walker Bay, unable to evacuate because the exploding, burning ships had been too close to the main channel. LSTs #205, #225, and #274 had fled from Tare 8, while LST #129 had been moored in the bay since before the explosions began.[11]

LST #205 had been the last ship to leave Tare 8 and only after firefighters had rushed aboard to help put out the fires in

LCT-1062. It was eventually moved to East Loch and found to be too badly burnt to participate in the attack on Saipan. Late Monday, the crew of LST #205 began unloading cargo from the tank deck.[12]

The first vessel to move forward from Tare 8 to save herself had been LST #274, surging ahead under emergency steering. At 6:00 A.M. Monday, the main steering was finally repaired and Lieutenant Sard moved the badly burnt and scarred ship, carrying an equally burnt and scarred LCT-982, into East Loch.[13] Damaged beyond immediate repair, they too would miss out on the invasion.

Although LST #225 and her piggybacked LCT-355 had sustained considerable damage, Lieutenant Commander Hoyt had managed to move forward into Walker Bay in spite of the fact that almost everyone aboard had abandoned ship. Deemed salvageable, in spite of a 5-foot slice in her side from striking LST #274, the ship was sent to a dry dock in East Loch where work began immediately to get her combat ready. When the other LSTs finally steamed toward Saipan, LST #225 was with them.[14]

James T. Cobb was a Marine rifleman on LST #225 who had abandoned ship with the others. As a passenger on LST #225, Cobb felt that the Marines "had no knowledge of what was expected of [us] in this situation" but knew that the officers of LST #225 had higher expectations for their crew. As Cobb remembered, Lieutenant Goddard was none too happy with the actions of his crew and the Marines. "The Captain of the ship expressed extreme displeasure that they had abandoned ship without his orders to do so," Cobb wrote, "but it seemed like a good idea at the time."[15]

Another Marine from Cobb's company, John B. Hovis, was not worried about the Marines getting in trouble for leaving the ship, but he wondered about the crew. "Most of the crew was subject to a court-martial, because they had abandoned ship without orders to do so," Hovis said. Since Vice Admiral Turner was already going to be short on men, materiel, and ships for the invasion of Saipan, Lieutenant Goddard was restrained from pursuing such action. With every able-bodied man needed, the courts-martial, if they came at all, would have to wait. Fortunately for the crew of LST #225, they never came.[16]

While the number one, two, and three ships at Tare 8 had moved forward into Walker Bay to avoid the five exploding outboard ships, ten LSTs from Tares 9 and 10 had fled into the small boat area west of the naval ammunition depot. All five ships from Tare 10 and five from Tare 9 had managed to back into the shallow bay. Although the crew of each ship had spent a fretful night on guard, watching and listening to the explosions, their ships were well out of range of any further debris or shrapnel. They all remained at anchor or grounded in the shallows until orders arrived for them to begin loading for the upcoming invasion.

Lieutenant Haskell's LST #340 sat in the shallow back bay area with 127 refugees, many from LST #353. Around midmorning on 22 May, all of the survivors from LST #353 were separated from the other survivors and taken off the ship. The rest of the survivors began to trickle back to their ships. On Tuesday, 23 May, LST #340 finally moved out of the small boat area to continue her combat loading.[17]

Near 1:00 P.M., LST #127, with Lieutenant Reed at the conn, moved out of the shallows to moor in East Loch. A half hour later, Lieutenant Buchar's LST #205 arrived. The difference in appearance between LST #127, which had been the outermost vessel at Tare 10 and had escaped, and LST #205 was dramatic. LST #205 had suffered extensive damage to the vehicles and materials on her main deck as well as to LCT-1062, chained to her top. In contrast, LST #127 had suffered only minor burns.

About a half hour later, however, when Lieutenant Sard's LST #274, another badly scarred survivor from Tare 8, pulled in beside #205, Lieutenant Buchar's ship looked like a beauty queen by comparison. Lieutenant Commander Hoyt, who was an eyewitness to the fires on LST #274, remembered how she had looked during the height of the flames and explosions. "[I do] not think there was any ship in the nest that was more heavily afire except the #353 than the #274," Hoyt told the court of inquiry, "and yet she was saved by her officers and crew." In praise of Sard and his crew, Hoyt added that LST #274 "was a good example of a ship that stands and fights."[18]

Once the shallow back area of West Loch was clear and the three high-speed transports had finally moved from Tare 7, life settled down to a somewhat normal routine at Pearl Harbor. While

Admiral Turner and his staff scrambled to find men, weapons, equipment, supplies, gasoline, LSTs, LCTs, amtracs, etc., to replace everything that had been lost, the crews of the LSTs returned to the tasks of preparing their ships. Still, after such a harrowing experience, many of the men were a bit jumpy. GM2/c Harry Horn, on LST #242, became extremely nervous when his heavily combat loaded LST tied up beside a much larger warship. As Horn recalled, he was worried that someone from the taller ship would toss a lit cigarette onto the aviation fuel drums stored on the forecastle of his ship. The thought of another careless catastrophe became, for Horn, the "biggest scare of my life."[19]

On the other hand, while Horn became deathly afraid of cigarettes, Marine LVT driver Harlow Lunney felt that he needed a cigarette to help calm his nerves. As his LST was moving out of West Loch, Lunney and a friend lit a cigarette apiece. Suddenly the two Marines heard a shrill announcement over the ship's public address system. "The next S.O.B. to light a cigarette will be shot." Without a word of protest, Lunney and his friend quickly put out their cigarettes.[20]

In the wee morning hours of Monday, 22 May 1944, SGT Harrold Weinberger and his cameramen finally returned to East Loch, exhausted but excited about the images they had captured. "It turned out that there was no other photo coverage of the holocaust," Weinberger wrote. As the adrenalin rush began to wear off, Weinberger and the others retired below decks to get some rest. Unfortunately for Weinberger, it wasn't meant to be. "About forty minutes later, after I had had some chow," he wrote, "Capt. De Vinna [the commanding officer] paged me. The Navy had been told of our coverage and signaled that they wanted all the film, motion pictures, and stills taken to the laboratory at once. So I gathered all negatives, was given a canvas dispatch bag, and was promptly on my way." He would spend the night at the Honolulu Eastman Kodak Laboratory, developing the precious film.[21]

The official investigation was underway.

CHAPTER 22 | The Court of Inquiry

Marine SGT Harrold Weinberger of the Photographic Unit, 4th MarDiv, and his assigned driver raced through the empty nighttime streets of Honolulu toward the Eastman Kodak Laboratory. Beside him was the canvas dispatch bag filled with undeveloped pictures and movies of the West Loch disaster. "It was a strange feeling being out after curfew, on Oahu," Weinberger remembered. "We had the streets and highways all to ourselves. Brownout conditions prevailed, and we drove without lights. We passed only two vehicles on the entire [10-mile] trip. Both were military police patrols. One challenged us. The other did not, probably assuming we were on official business."

Upon reaching the lab, which during World War II was under the control and operation of both Eastland Kodak and the Armed Forces, the Marine cinematographer began developing the film. "Our three cinematographers had exposed over 2,000 feet of 16mm Kodachrome film," Weinberger explained. It took him all night to develop the film and in the morning he sent it off to Navy Headquarters. Then he returned to his ship for some much needed sleep.[1]

Early on the morning of 22 May, less than twenty-four hours after the first explosion on LST #353, RADM John Franklin Shafroth, Jr., USN, received an order from Admiral Nimitz entitled "Court of inquiry to inquire into the circumstances surrounding the explosions which occurred at West Loch on May 21, 1944." As instructed by Nimitz, Shafroth as president, and assisted by RADM Malcolm F. Schoeffel, USN, and CAPT Samuel R. Shumaker, USN, with CAPT Elmer A. Turbutton, USN, as the judge advocate general, were to convene at 10:00 A.M. at the Navy Yard, to investigate the "circumstances connected with the explosion in the USS LST 353." The court was ordered to make a thorough investigation into the "causes thereof, damage as to property resulting therefrom, injuries to personnel incidental thereto, and the responsibility therefore." And should the court find that "any offenses have been committed or serious blame incurred," they were to "specifically recommend what further proceedings should be had."

When Nimitz named Shafroth to head the court of inquiry, he chose the right man. Shafroth had been born in Colorado in 1887 and had graduated from the U.S. Naval Academy in Annapolis in 1908. He commanded a destroyer in World War I, winning a Navy Cross, and had commanded a cruiser division in the Southwest Pacific early in World War II. In 1943, he had received the Legion of Merit for his part in helping to plan the Southwest Pacific campaign, and in March 1944, just two months before the West Loch Disaster, he had taken over the duties of inspector general of the Pacific Fleet and Pacific Oceans Area.[2]

At 2:40 P.M., Shafroth and his team met behind closed doors to begin their inquiry. Over the next sixteen days, they interviewed and read the testimony from close to sixty eyewitnesses.[3]

Among the witnesses called was Sergeant Weinberger. After both the photos and films had been developed, they had been passed on to the court. Weinberger was needed to give some input into what was going on in each scene, where the shot or shots had been taken, the approximate time, etc. "All of this film was run for my comment and identification," he recalled. "That was the last I ever heard of the matter."[4]

On 25 May, while the court was still in session, Admiral Nimitz issued a press release to explain what had happened at West Loch on 21 May. As Howard Shuman noted, "At least 250,000 people on the ships and ashore at Pearl Harbor and tens of thousands more from Honolulu to Ewa saw the black smoke and fires and heard the blasts at West Loch. The disaster was not unknown." Trying not to expose the buildup of ships in Pearl Harbor for the upcoming invasion of Saipan, but knowing that he needed to offer some sort of explanation, Nimitz issued the following statement: "An explosion and fire which occurred while ammunition was being unloaded from one of a group of landing craft moored together in Pearl Harbor on May 21, 1944, resulted in destruction of several small vessels, some loss of life, and a number of injuries. Further information will be announced later. A court of inquiry has been convened of which Rear Admiral John F. Shafroth, U.S. Navy, is president."[5]

This was just enough for the newspaper reporters and curious citizens to tide them over until the court released the whole story. By admitting that something had happened, though woefully understating the scope of the disaster and the loss of several major transport ships, Nimitz had put a beautiful little spin on a devastating accident.

BKR2/c Bernard A. Rupprath of LST #244 recalled, "The many explosions got people up in arms. Hickam Field had aircraft ready to take off. Ships in Pearl Harbor manned battle stations and at Honolulu, 11 miles away, people were running around looking for information with the assumption that there was another attack on Pearl Harbor."

As Rupprath knew, something had to be forthcoming from the Navy. He did not, however, expect the curt press release. "The fear was so great," he continued, "that the Navy had to come out with a statement that was, in my opinion, the greatest understatement of the war. . . . The official statement was so unsatisfactory and insufficient that those on the island who were not directly involved thought the Navy was trying to cover something up. Of course, we were preparing for the invasions of Guam and Saipan, which could have explained the Navy's unwillingness to explain the entire story."[6]

On 12 June, Shafroth and the court wrapped up the testimonies and presented their findings to Admiral Nimitz. Two days later, Nimitz's office issued another press release.

The Commander in Chief, Pacific Fleet, has issued a preliminary report from Rear Admiral J. F. Shafroth, U.S. Navy, president of a board of inquiry convened to investigate an explosion and fire which occurred on May 21, 1944, among a group of landing craft moored in Pearl Harbor.

The following casualties were caused by the explosion of ammunition being unloaded and the subsequent fire: Dead; Army 8, Navy 9, Marine Corps 10. Missing; Army 53, Navy 21, Coast Guard 26. Injured; Army 56, Navy 143, Coast Guard 3, Marine Corps 159, civilian 19.[7]

Once again, the press release was a beautiful understatement. Mimicking the earlier press release, this announcement repeated the fact that the accident had occurred "while ammunition was being unloaded," so there was no need, in the eyes of the Navy, to provide any further explanation. There was also no need to point out a responsible party. The whole little affair had been a mistake, caused by some mishandling of ammunition while it was being removed from a landing craft. Although 27 people were reportedly dead, 100 missing, and 380 injured, everything was under control, and there was nothing to get excited about.

The final summation released by Admiral Shafroth's court of inquiry was much more detailed. Although any conclusive evidence was lacking, the court decided that the cause of the explosion was the detonation of a mortar shell aboard LST #353 at 1508 hours on Sunday, 21 May. Unfortunately, even the court realized that this was conjecture, since "those closest to the explosion, who might have been able to give more precise information, were among the casualties." In reporting on the scope of the disaster, the court found that the reason why a single detonation was so damaging was because of "the stowage of gasoline in the immediate proximity of high explosive ammunition" and the "nesting of numerous combat loaded vessels at one berth."[8]

As far as major material losses, it was determined that six LSTs had been destroyed: #39, #43, #69, #179, #353, and #480. Three LCTs had been lost: LCT-961 aboard LST #179, LCT-963 on LST #353, and LCT-983 on LST #69. Seventeen LVT amtracs had been destroyed inside one of the lost LSTs, and eight 155mm howitzers had been destroyed inside another. LST #205 and #225 were badly burned while waiting to escape from Tare 8, and they were deemed unsafe to make the 3,200-mile trip to Saipan.[9]

In a monumental effort to replace the much needed material, Admiral Nimitz and his staff began searching for replacements. Several LSTs that had been earmarked for transporting reserve troops or garrison troops to the battle area were now moved to front line duty. LST #19, skippered by LT(jg) Howard K. Heath, USCGR, was bumped up from carrying Army troops for the invasion of Guam to carrying Marines for the invasion of Saipan. On 23 May, a work party came aboard and began changing the chains and lashings that held down LCT-357. While the men were working, the first load of Marines began filing aboard.[10]

Another replacement vessel was LST #127, commanded by Lieutenant Reed, which had undergone dozens of repairs while the other ships were participating in the Maui maneuvers. "We knew nothing about being a replacement or even that we were going to Saipan until we were several days at sea," recalled SF Francis Hillibush. Having undergone numerous upgrades, replacements, and repairs, and with a new skipper at the helm, LST #127 would now be making the trip to Saipan.[11]

LST #461, commanded by LT Charles Paul Geis, USNR, became another replacement vessel. "It turned out we were supposed to be one of the LSTs that was not to be included in the next invasion," said XO Jack S. Futterman. "But we were still running, and some of the others that were supposed to be in this were disabled or gone. And so we went west."[12] In all, eleven LSTs became replacements for the six LSTs lost in the fire and explosions, the two that were badly burned before exiting Tare 8, for LST #71, which had lost LCT-999 during the Maui maneuvers, for LST #244, which had suffered what appeared to be a minor fire in the galley around Maui and a puncture of her hull when she brushed up against one of the ammunition barges, and for one other LST. It was a fanciful bit of scurrying, but Nimitz and his staff pulled it off.

"Since the LSTs were scheduled to sail on 24 May," wrote Vice Admiral Dyer, "it took a bit of doing to put the various LST task units and troops back together with all the necessary amtracs and DUKWs and replacement personnel. Departure of the LSTs took place on 25 May, and the sturdy craft made up the lost day while en route to the assault area."[13] Marine Corps MAJ Carl Hoffman was equally impressed with the work that was done to assemble the replacement LSTs and get them on their way just one day behind schedule: "The LST's were to sail on the morning of 24 May, less than three days after the costly fire. It was apparent that a delay would be demanded. But for how long? The gears of the attack machine were meshed to an established target date; delays could upset the smooth timing. Concern along these lines was soon relieved, however, as efficient staff work paid off. Ships, personnel, equipment, and supplies were replaced in four short days and [the] LSTs sailed only 24 hours late, with the lost day being made up en route."[14]

Along with the eleven replacement LSTs, Admiral Nimitz also sent out four LSTs as backup. LST #274, which had been badly burned and had a large gash in the hull after being hit by LST #225, did not participate in the invasion but was there nonetheless. "We were supposed to leave with a flotilla," stated Electrician Tidwell of LCT-982 on LST #274, "but since we got that big hole in the back and I guess there were three other craft, LSTs that got damaged, we had to delay there in Pearl Harbor and they had to patch us up. So we left there four days later than the regular flotilla going to Saipan. We had destroyer escorts and all, even though we were just four, and we finally caught up with them, see, and we got to Saipan about the same time that the rest of the bunch got there."[15]

S1/c Walt Slater, a crewmate with Tidwell on LCT-982, also recalled the delay and change of status for LST #274. "We had a gigantic hole in the starboard side, which was above the water line, and the workers were able to weld it up and within two days we were ready to go. They took the Marines away from us and sent them to some other craft, and when we were repaired, they put an Army engineer outfit on and these were the guys that built the B-29 bases. We were able to become seaworthy and we met the 58th Task Force in the Marshall Islands."[16]

"The morning of the 25th we left Pearl Harbor and formed a convoy," wrote MoMM1/c Richard MacNealy from LST #166. "We were all happy to get away from there, the fires were still burning, and the area was a smoldering mess." Although the LSTs were leaving West Loch, the memory of the tragedy would stay with them. Added MacNealy, "No one on our ship was injured, but this experience scarred those of us aboard for life."[17]

Aboard LST #224, even leaving Pearl Harbor did not quell the tragedy. During the height of the explosions, pieces of phosphorus shells had landed among the gasoline drums strapped to the forecastle. Although the burning phosphorus had been put out, the chemical had the ability to reignite once it dried out. To prevent this, a fire hose had been rigged above the gasoline drums to keep a constant spray of water washing over the barrels. The water was not turned off until the barrels were carted ashore sometime after the invasion of Saipan.[18]

Besides the damage caused to the invading fleet, numerous ships that called Pearl Harbor their home were also incapacitated. While fighting the raging fires and the continuing explosions on the burning LSTs, the large harbor tugboats *Osceola* (YTB 129) and *Hoga* (YTB 146) were damaged. The medium harbor tug *Geronimo* (YTM 119) and the six little harbor tugs, YTL 233, 306, 307, 308, 309, and 339, all "suffered varying degrees of damage." The valiant little net-tender (tug class) *Tamaha* (YNT 12), which had tried to put out the fire on LST #39, had been heavily damaged when the bridge from the larger transport had been blown overboard onto her. And finally, the Navy-chartered civilian tugboat *Mikioi* also sustained some damage.[19] Eleven vital yard tugs, each called upon every day to muscle big warships into berths and moorings, would all be missing for days and, in some cases, weeks to come.

While Admiral Nimitz had been able to replace the LSTs with suitable substitutes, the same could not be said of the replacement personnel. Although new men were quickly assigned to fill the gaps left by the dead and wounded, their experience and expertise could not be replaced. As Marine Harry Pearce recalled: "Forty-eight hours after the explosions we had new personnel, both officers and enlisted men. . . . [We] now had new personnel where [before] I knew every man by his first name. Now I didn't know any of them. They were just faces. We were not sure which platoon was going to get which man and what each man coming in was qualified to do. But we were getting men that were going to have to be flamethrowers that as far as we knew had never had a flamethrower in their hand. We had men that were going to have to be bazooka men that had never fired a bazooka. We had problems right fast."[20]

MAJ GEN L. R. Jones, who commanded the 23rd MarReg, 4th MarDiv, which had suffered the biggest loss of personnel from the disaster, admitted that although the regiment received enough troops to replace the number lost, the new men "were not trained to carry out the functions of those lost."[21]

Pearce said, "I don't think it affected morale so much as the feeling of intensity that we've got to train these men somehow aboard ship to fire these things before we go into combat. He's got to know what his weapon is and what it'll do before he goes into combat. I think this thing was preying on our minds more than anything else." Before invading Saipan, the flotilla of warships stopped at Kwajalein Atoll, about 1,000 miles from Saipan, to conduct a few practice landings.[22]

Along with the hundreds of new men, many of the assaulting Marines and soldiers had to receive all new equipment and weapons. Everything aboard the lost LSTs was gone, and hundreds of other men had lost web gear, backpacks, canteens, clothes, and their weapons. Donald Owens with Co. E, 6th MarReg, 2nd MarDiv, recalled the replacement equipment. "We thought the explosions would hold up our operation, but they issued new equipment to those of us who had lost some," he wrote. "Some things were in short supply. I remember that entrenching tools in particular were hard to come by. Marines had to share shovels or picks with their buddies."[23]

Some of the items were brand-new, which presented a problem. Harry Pearce recalled that "the rifles came packed in cosmoline. We had no way of cleaning the cosmoline out of them. We had no way of sighting in our weapons at sea to see how accurate they would shoot. . . . We fired mortar rounds out to sea. We fired rifles and pistols out to sea, and we didn't know whether they'd shoot straight or crooked or upside down or what. This was the best we could do."[24] In spite of the new equipment, the untested firearms, and the lack of some items, the 2nd and 4th Marine Divisions and the Army's 27th Infantry Division made a successful assault on Saipan, capturing the island in twenty-four days.

Although Admiral Shafroth's court of inquiry felt that the cause of the explosion was the premature detonation of a mortar round, they concluded that "no specific offenses contributory to the disaster have been committed" and that they were "unable to ascribe to any individual or organization the responsibility for this explosion." As A. Alan Oliver pointed out, "In reviewing the volumes of testimony by Naval and Coast Guard personnel . . . many errors and deficiencies were noted and several skippers were called to account for inadequate reactions to the emergency. However, the nerve-shattering shock of the explosions and the inability of most vessels to be able to quickly slip their lines under such torturous conditions was taken into account with instructions to revise and improve certain training regimens." There would be no courts-martial or career-ruining letters of reprimand in anyone's file, in spite of the fact that many people had abandoned ship or issued the order to abandon ship without direct orders from commanding officers.[25]

In their report, the court of inquiry stated that one of the reasons why so many LSTs were lost or damaged was because of the "nesting of numerous combat loaded vessels at one berth." Said the court, "A disaster comparable to the loss of a great battle may occur at any time in Pearl Harbor as the result of an accident when the harbor is filled with combat loaded vessels as it was on May 21, 1944." However, the court also realized that in war, certain risks had to be taken. "The crowded conditions of Pearl Harbor, the berthing of combat loaded vessels near the ammunition depot, and the loading of the LSTs themselves were dictated by the necessity of accepting certain risks in order to move more rapidly against the enemy and to do the best that could be done with the means that were available."

Among the court's recommendations were more tugboats, more tugs equipped with firefighting equipment, fire protection consultants to inspect and advise the crews, and the establishment of more firefighting schools. The court also recommended that the heavily combat loaded ships be sent to other locations between the last date of rehearsal and the date of departure, thus minimizing the threat to the vital Pearl Harbor facilities. Once vessels were combat loaded, the court suggested that "they be not nested in groups but sent to an anchorage where they can be separately berthed and protected. Numerous atolls are held by us to the westward of Pearl Harbor where such vessels can be accommodated if such anchorages are not available in the Hawaiian Group."

Through their days of collecting testimony, the court found that "there was a deplorable lack of observance of elementary safety precautions in connection with open lights [i.e., smoking] on LSTs generally, but particularly on the 353, 39, and 179, although this did not cause the explosion." The court also noted: "There was a lack of appreciation in all ranks of the hazards involved in stowing gasoline and ammunition in close proximity to each other in vessels whose crews were largely composed of young and relatively inexperienced personnel." The court did, however, recognize the fact that both ammunition and gasoline stored in any location were always a volatile and dangerous cargo to carry.

On 29 June, after reviewing the report, Admiral Nimitz sent a letter to the judge advocate general in which he generally agreed with what the court had found and recommended, but he decided to modify one finding. Although the court felt that the cause of the explosion was a mishandled mortar shell, Nimitz wrote, "There is some evidence which might lead to the opinion that the initial explosion could have been caused by gasoline vapor."

Also, Nimitz flat out rejected the court's recommendation of berthing the LSTs in smaller nests or at distant locations between the last rehearsal and departure. Nimitz stated that the vessels needed to moor at Pearl Harbor because it was the only anchorage outside of the continental United States that offered vital facilities. "During this period, repairs, water-proofing of equipment, and final preparation of personnel and material for assault necessitate proximity to facilities which are not available at atolls and other anchorages." He added, "It is a calculated risk that must be accepted." As commander in chief of the Pacific Fleet, Nimitz was willing to accept the risk.[26]

One step above Nimitz in the chain of command was ADM Ernest J. King, commander in chief of the U.S. Fleet. In his review of the court's findings and recommendations, King was highly critical of the actions and reactions of anyone and everyone involved with the LSTs. From the task force supervising officers to the shipboard officers and crews, no one escaped his wrath. "The organization, training, and discipline in the LSTs involved in this disaster leave much to be desired," he wrote. "The lack of proper understanding and compliance with safety precautions when handling ammunition and gasoline, particularly in LST 353 where the first explosion occurred, is also noted. It is perfectly apparent that this disaster was not an 'Act of God.'"[27] Admiral King expected better from his Navy.

In spite of everything that Nimitz wrote in his letter to the judge advocate general, a survey was made and published on 13 July 1944, entitled "LST Bow Loading and Mooring Berths and Anchorages in the Hawaiian Area." Among other things, the survey was conducted "for use in making plans for a wider dispersal of LSTs during Combat Loading so that they will not have to be nested close together in loading berths while loading highly inflammable petroleum products and ammunition." Although the Navy had hoped to find mooring places outside of West Loch for forty-four ships, they eventually found spots for only sixteen. Unfortunately, some of the spots were deemed to be "in close proximity to important installations," some had "no railroad connections," and a few were on "three outer islands."[28]

Oddly enough, the sixteen ships would still be berthed in clusters. There were two spots in busy East Loch, one for three ships and one for two, one spot near Iroquois Point for five LSTs, and one spot in Kewalo Basin, southeast of Honolulu Harbor, where six ships could berth. "This will permit spacing the LSTs in loading berths sufficiently to prevent fires from quickly spreading to adjacent vessels in case of fire or explosion," noted W. B. Phillips, Commander Administrative Command, Amphibious Forces, U.S. Pacific Fleet, who undertook the survey.

The survey also suggested that "the loading of cargo gasoline on the main decks of the LSTs be done at the Iroquois Point loading berths and at the Kewalo Basin berths so as not to endanger important Pearl Harbor installations in the vicinity of [East Loch]." Although the Shafroth court had determined the cause of the 21 May explosion to be the mishandling of a mortar shell, suddenly everybody was concerned about gasoline and the very combustible gasoline vapors.

The survey also found only twenty-one berths available at Tares 1 through 7 in West Loch, "Nested 3 abreast." Suddenly, nesting more than three ships to one set of dolphin pilings was frowned upon, since one of the things that the court of inquiry questioned was whether the pilings were strong enough to safely hold more than three ships at one time. Likewise, it was suggested that only three ships be moored at Tare 8, which had held eight ships on 21 May, and that no ships be moored at Tares 9 or 10. In explanation for the exclusion of the last two tares, Commander

Phillips wrote in the remarks column, "Partly obstructed." The sunken hulk of LST #353 and the partially submerged wreck of LST #480 off Tares 9 and 10 made it impossible to use either tare.[29]

The Navy Department also acted upon the court's recommendations to equip "numerous tugs and vessels as fire boats for the protection of harbors and anchorages." Fifty-two fire protection consultants were soon trained to "assist ships during periods of availability in reducing shipboard fire hazards, inspect firefighting equipment, and advise Commanding Officers of the latest firefighting practices and techniques." By the end of the year, eleven Class A and fifteen Class B fire schools were established at "Naval Training Centers, Navy Yards, and Advanced Bases for the training of personnel in approved firefighting techniques with standard firefighting equipment."[30]

On 17 July 1944, 320 sailors and civilians were killed and another 390 wounded by an explosion and fire that occurred during the loading of ammunition aboard a ship docked at Port Chicago, near San Francisco. These two catastrophes led to significant changes in the way the Navy began to handle ammunition. In 2009, CAPT Drew Mogart, director for Logistics Current Operations for the U.S. Pacific Fleet, stated, "The Navy has learned many valuable lessons from the events of 65 years ago." For instance, Mogart noted, the Navy no longer moors ships in large nests and all munitions handlers undergo specified training and certification before touching live ammunition. Additionally, modern-day munitions have been redesigned to make them much safer to handle.[31] At least some good has come out of the West Loch and the Port Chicago disasters.

| Salvage

Six ships were lost during the West Loch disaster of 21 May 1944. All six were stricken from the Navy list of active ships on 18 July 1944. The three LSTs that had drifted toward the naval ammunition depot, #43, #69, and #179, had all sunk a few hundred feet north of the depot. They became underwater hazards to ships entering and exiting West Loch, especially deeper draft vessels such as the APDs.

LST #353 had sunk about 70 feet out from the Tare 10 dolphins in only 30 feet of water with a part of her forecastle and deckhouse visible above the surface. LST #480, which was the last to catch fire, had drifted down below Tare 10 and had been beached by some tugs with her bow up on the southeastern shoreline of Hanaloa Point. LST #39, which had continued to burn and explode throughout the night, had finally been dragged over to the ferry boat slip below Tare 5 along the West Loch channel. For the next two or three days, fire boats kept a watch on #39, continually spraying water into the smoldering remains.[1]

Almost immediately, the Navy realized that they had to remove the sunken wrecks. The war was far from over, and the vital West Loch anchorages were still in use. The diver-class rescue and salvage ship USS *Valve* (ARS-28), commanded by LT W. D. Mooney, USNR, began salvage operations on LST #353. From 31 May until 30 August, a span of forty-one days, her divers, wearing hard-hat diving helmets, special suits, and weighted belts and shoes and attached to the ship through oxygen lines and safety ropes, made 225 dives salvaging fifteen tons of live ammunition, ten LVT am-tracs, and a large amount of wreckage. On 30 August, *Valve* was called away to aid another ship but returned on 5 September. By 8 October, the salvage had been completed, and the ship's hulk was destroyed underwater.[2]

The USS *Vent* (ARS-29), under LT Howard H. Bothell, USNR, arrived in Hawaiian waters from California on 27 June and immediately began salvage work above the ammunition depot. Unlike her sister ship, *Vent* spent only a short time before moving on to the South Pacific on 23 July.[3]

Ray McNaught was a diver first class for the Navy and remem-bered the condition of the sunken ships. "When they blew up [on 21 May], they had enough holes in them to sink," he wrote. Going down into the murky waters of the loch, McNaught and the other divers brought up whatever they could from the wrecks. "Some pieces weighed a ton or two." When enough material had been removed from one of the three hulks, the divers raised it back to the surface. "One LST we were able to raise by 'dewatering' the compartments with compressed air," McNaught explained. "We towed it into the beach [with] beaching gear."[4]

Perhaps the ship that McNaught and the others brought up was LST #39, which had been towed close to the ferry slip near Powder Point before it sank. In spite of being the host of some of the most horrific explosions, the ship was in relatively good shape. Although the main deck and center of the ship were burned away, the hull was salvageable. Navy divers eventually managed to refloat LST #39. Converted into a "spare parts issue barge," the ship was redesignated YF-1079. Unfortunately, it did not lead a charmed life. On 9 October 1945, one month after the war was over, YF-1079 and dozens of other ships were badly damaged when they were thrown against each other and then up onto Buckner Bay, Okinawa, by Typhoon Louise. Stricken from the Naval Register in February 1946, YF-1079 was destroyed the following August.[5]

Navy diver Paul Greenwell worked on the three sunken LSTs in the middle of West Loch. "Every morning, we had two barges that we worked off of," he stated, "and we went up to those barges about 8:00 in the morning and we got back down to the [Fleet Ship Salvage Base] about 5:00 in the afternoon. . . . We may have as many as ten, twelve divers down at one time." The divers were working in a relatively calm body of water, and the bottom of the loch was covered with a thick layer of silt, which was easily disturbed by the actions of the men. "Everything we did, or probably 90 percent of the work that we did," said Greenwell, "if you put your hand like that in front of your face plate, you couldn't see it. You could not see your hand. It was all by feel. Everything we did was by feel primarily."

Since the vessels had been badly damaged and mangled by the numerous explosions, dangers awaited the divers at every step. "We did have a few [divers] that . . . would punch a hole in their [oxygen] line," Greenwell remembered. "They'd get on a piece of the bulkhead some place and they'd cut that. And once in a while you'd get your hose caught going through one of them passageways."[6]

During a dive on 17 February 1945, two divers were working at a depth of 40 feet, in 20 feet of mud, using a water jet nozzle to tunnel under the wreckage of one of the LSTs with the intention of eventually passing a steel cable through the tunnel and under and around the LST so that the ship could be winched to the surface. While the men were working, however, some of the steel wreckage from the bottom of the ship caved in and trapped them. Hearing their calls for help via the hard-hat radio communication line, Navy diver BM2/c Owen Francis Patrick Hammerberg rushed to their assistance.

Plunging into the pitch-black water, Hammerberg used an additional jet nozzle and, "despite the certain hazard of additional cave-ins and the risk of fouling his lifeline on jagged pieces of steel imbedded in the shifting mud," he began digging into the original excavation point. Using nothing but instinct and feel, Hammerberg eventually reached the first man and managed to untangle his fouled lines and send him to the surface. He then began work to save the second man.

For the next several hours, Hammerberg remained below the surface of the loch, digging a shaft beneath the sunken LST with the water jet, flushing away the "oozing submarine, subterranean mud in a determined effort to save the second diver." Miraculously, he reached a spot above where the second man was trapped and worked hard to wash away the mud until the steel plate that held the man in place could be moved. At that moment, however, another cave-in occurred. Another heavy piece of steel dropped from the bottom of the LST, directly above Hammerberg and the other diver, crushing down upon them. Somehow, before the plate settled, Hammerberg maneuvered his body enough so that he was crosswise to the other diver and took the full impact of the blow, shielding the other man but "placing the full brunt of terrific pressure on himself." Although both men were eventually rescued and brought to the surface, Hammerberg died in agony eighteen hours later.

For his unselfish actions, BM2/c Owen Francis Patrick Hammerberg was awarded the Medal of Honor, the highest award given by the U.S. military. The citation for his award read, "Hammerberg, by his cool judgment, unfaltering professional skill and consistent disregard of all personal danger in the face of tremendous odds, had contributed effectively to the saving of his two comrades. His heroic spirit of self-sacrifice throughout enhanced and sustained the highest traditions of the U.S. Naval Service. He gallantly gave his life in the service of his country."[7]

Hammerberg's death occurred in February 1945, but the salvage operation went on. On 21 July, LST #267 arrived at Pearl Harbor to be converted into an ammunition ship in preparation for the envisioned invasion of Japan. As the ship came into West Loch, the officer of the deck recorded in the ship's logbook, "Several sunken LSTs being raised from catastrophe of 21 May 1944 where 6 LSTs exploded, burned, and sunk."[8]

On 6 August 1945, the United States dropped an atomic bomb on Japan. Three days later, after Japan refused unconditional surrender, America dropped another one. On 15 August, World War II officially ended when Emperor Hirohito surrendered. With the end of hostilities, hundreds of vessels of all kinds began bringing millions of men back to Pearl Harbor. Among those that returned was O. H. Wright, a submariner. "With the war over, my submarine was 'killing time' at Pearl Harbor, when the Navy Bureau of Ordnance brought forth a new magnetic exploder," Wright related. "It was decided that our sub would make the very first test firing with a live warhead on the torpedo. Our target was to be one of the damaged LSTs." The LST that was raised from the depths in November 1945 to be used as target practice for the new torpedo warhead was LST #179.[9]

As Wright remembered, "The LST was towed out to sea with a couple of big pumps pumping like mad to keep her afloat. Experts from the Bureau of Ordnance prepared the torpedo on our sub. Many high-ranking observers were aboard." Not knowing what might happen from the concussion caused by the new warhead, the skipper of Wright's submarine elected to fire the torpedo from a stern tube and then race like mad to get away from LST #179. "We fired the torpedo, then went ahead as fast as you can get a 1,500-ton ship to move from dead slow," wrote Wright. "The torpedo evidently ran in a vertical circle, not approaching the target and exploding when deep under us." Fortunately, the submarine was not damaged, but the test had been a dismal failure. And what happened to LST #179? "The pumps ran out of fuel, and the LST sank," said Wright.

Surprisingly, LST #179 was not the only victim of the West Loch disaster to be used for torpedo practice. LST #43, which had gone down beside LST #179 just north of the naval ammunition depot, was eventually raised but "deemed beyond economical repair." The hulk was subsequently towed out to sea and "sunk by torpedoes in 1945."[10]

Although LSTs #39, #43, and #179 had been raised and re-used, three LSTs, or parts of them, remained at West Loch. Almost all of the reusable and serviceable equipment and machinery had been removed from LST #353, sunk near Tare 10, before her hull was blasted into smaller pieces. LST #69, which had sunk just north of the ammunition depot, had salvage work done on her, and presumably she too was blasted into smaller pieces when her hull could not be raised. LST #480, which had been shoved up onto the beach on the southeastern shore of Hanaloa Point, was left alone. Resting with her slightly tilted forecastle above water, her rusting carcass still lies just north of the old naval ammunition depot, which today is the Naval Magazine Pearl Harbor. She is the only visible remains of the West Loch disaster still around today.

The West Loch Disaster had been a hard pill for the Navy to swallow, but fortunately, in spite of some initial heel dragging, lessons had been learned. New mooring berths were located and improved, the facilities for loading gasoline and ammunition were separated, and safety precautions were implemented. For the victims of West Loch, the changes came too late, but if their deaths could bring about much needed change and caution, then at least they did not die in vain.

CHAPTER 24 | Censored

Although the Navy admitted in their 14 June 1944 press release that they had suffered 27 dead, 380 wounded, and 100 missing, a total of 507 casualties, they later amended the release. On 17 June, CINCPAC issued press release no. 447, which was a "corrected report . . . regarding casualties" of the 21 May fires and explosions. Instead of 9 dead sailors, there were actually 10, and one Coast Guardsman had also been killed. Among the Marines, the number of killed was changed to 8 instead of 10. According to the release, total dead remained 27. The release continued, "In the missing category, the 26 Coast Guard personnel listed as missing should have been listed under Marine Corps. The total missing category therefore remains the same."

In reality, nobody knew how many men had actually been killed, injured, or were missing. The Intelligence Unit from Barber's Point, which began investigating the disaster only hours after the first explosion, issued a report on July 24, 1944, stating that there were 27 people killed (the exact same figure as the CINCPAC press release), 74 missing, and 377 injured, a total of 478, 29 less than reported by CINCPAC.[1] Evidently, because of the mad scattering of all of the ships in West Loch during the disaster, as well as the exodus of the ships toward the Marianas invasion a few days later with all of the Army, Navy, Coast Guard, and Marine Corps personnel involved in the incident, it was difficult to come up with definitive numbers.

Almost two years later, on 27 February 1946, a document entitled "Report of Explosion at West Loch, Pearl Harbor, T.H., 21 May 1944" was issued by the Navy. It once again proclaimed that the "probable cause" of the explosion was the detonation of a mortar shell and that there "were 127 killed and missing and 380 injured," the same total of 507 as in the press releases. Two years after the event, the Navy was still laying claim to the exact same numbers that it had issued on 12 June 1944.

However, the preeminent Naval historian, author, and retired admiral Samuel Eliot Morison looked into the Navy's final numbers while compiling volume 8 of his monumental work, *History of the United States Naval Operations in World War II*. Allowed access to classified Naval documents, Morison recalculated the casualty figures to show the number of dead and missing as 163, and the number of injured at 396, for a new total of 559 casualties.[2] These figures have been the recognized casualty numbers ever since. Recently, Pearl Harbor historian Ray Emory challenged the official figures, claiming that the number 163 dead or missing is too high. "No one single list is complete," argues Emory. "When you take the various lists and add them up, it comes to 132."[3]

Emory, a Pearl Harbor survivor, worked for years to get a law changed that allowed for the date and ship name to be placed on the headstones of unknown sailors who had died in the explosion and sinking of the USS *Arizona* during the infamous December 7 attack. He was also the key factor in getting the U.S. Department of Veterans Affairs to change headstones in Hawaii's famous National Cemetery of the Pacific at the Punchbowl area of Honolulu from "Unknown" to "Unknown; West Loch Disaster; Pearl Harbor; May 21, 1944." In 2006, thirty-six grave markers of West Loch victims, located in four sections of Punchbowl, were thus changed.[4] While Emory contends that the number of West Loch dead and missing is lower than the official numbers indicate, most survivors contend that the number is way too low. Almost to a man, the survivors of the West Loch disaster claim that the figures have been doctored and should be much higher.

Bill Warren, a crewman aboard LST #42, does not believe the official tally. "I accept the casualty statistics with the same grains of salt as I do the official cause of the explosion," he wrote. "I later learned that ambulances were kept busy most of the night shuttling from West Loch to the area hospitals. Only 163 dead and 396 injured? . . . If you believe that, I have some fine grazing land for sale in the James River, tides are receding, and in just a few years, it is guaranteed to be high and dry, excellent tax shelter."[5]

LT Phil Kierl was aboard LST #480, which was trapped and burned at Tare 9. Kierl wrote, "There were reports circulated that total casualties exceeded two thousand." Marine BAR-man Joe Drotovick and his friends on LST #42 also felt that the "death toll would reach two thousand men." PhM2/c William L.C. Johnson from LST #69, who had gone out in an LCVP to rescue dozens of men, managed to get a letter home to his mother with word of the disaster in spite of the censors. "They have estimated the loss of men at one thousand, although nothing has been told in the newspapers about it," he wrote. "I saw plenty of them dead, fellows with their arms and legs off and plenty of them nervous wrecks. I get plenty scared now when I hear any loud sudden noise."[6]

Four men from LST #274, which had been badly burned while in Tare 8 before moving ahead into Walker Bay, felt that the casualty figures were doctored. S1/c Walt Slater called 163 a very conservative number. "It was so devastating. You have no idea the intensity and the devastation that was involved. I think 1,400 is a closer figure."[7]

Marine PFC Albert G. Sutcliffe was a member of Company F, 25th MarReg, 4th MarDiv on LST #274. He recalled that his company alone lost about twenty men. The company also suffered two killed, including "a machine gunner named Van Nest . . . [who was] hit by a jeep engine some distance from the shore." According to Sutcliffe, the "replacements were flown from boot camp near San Diego," given weapons and equipment, assigned to Company F, and "left for Saipan a couple of days later."[8]

Another member of Company F, PFC Stan Ellis, also remembers the loss of men from LST #274. "One of my friends, named Van Ness . . . [lost] both his legs . . . [and] bled to death before anything could be done for him. There were several other men killed from my LST, but I can't give you the exact number. I do know it was a horrifying experience, no enemy to fight, just plenty of dead Marines and sailors." Added Ellis, "And remember, I'm talking about my LST. There were six others that also went up. It affected not only our outfit [the 4th Marine Division] but also the

2nd Division. They also lost plenty of men. I think it was probably the most dreadful accident of the Pacific during the war."[9]

Another survivor from LST #274 had a hard time believing the official death toll of 163. "From what some of them were saying and talking about [there were] so many soldiers that couldn't swim and even Navy guys that couldn't swim," said Electrician Kenneth Tidwell of LCT-982. "There were so many in the water pulling each other under and drowning, it's a little hard for me to believe 163. I just don't know. I just don't know the answer to that question."[10]

SF1/c Ed George, with Portable Maintenance Unit 19, an eyewitness to the beehive of activity of ships rushing out of and into West Loch during the incident, was never told the official death toll. "We could never find out," he said, "and we were there! We thought there were more than 163, and they really censored our letters after that. Nobody ever found out what really happened."[11]

A Marine from Company B of the 25th MarReg, 4th MarDiv, John Hovis, who had been on LST #225 in Tare 8, remembered that his company "lost twelve men as casualties along with all weapons and personal equipment that was stored on the main deck." He did not know how many of the twelve were killed.[12]

In the official 4th Marine Division Operations Report for the invasion of Saipan, it was noted, "On May 21 . . . three (3) LSTs assigned to RCT [Regimental Combat Team] 23 were destroyed by fire and two (2) LSTs assigned to RCT 25 were damaged to such an extent as to require replacement. LSTs 19, 84, 223, 128, and 487 were substituted without delay and the necessary adjustments were made in embarkation. This adjustment involved the replacement of casualties (112 officers and enlisted men) and of all supplies and equipment previously loaded in the five (5) LSTs destroyed and/or damaged."[13] Accordingly then, if the 4th MarDiv admitted to a loss of 112 men, than the 2nd MarDiv must have lost the other 81 men killed, injured, or missing out of the total of 193 Marine Corps casualties reported in the CINCPAC press releases.

However, the 2nd MarDiv reported a loss of 95 men, not 81. MAJ Carl W. Hoffman, who wrote the Marine Corps historical monograph *Saipan: The Beginning of the End*, had access to both the 2nd MarDiv and 4th MarDiv reports on the campaign and wrote, "The 2nd Marine Division lost a total of 95 men and the 4th

Marine Division 112 in this disaster." Another Marine Corps historian, Richard W. Johnston, who wrote *Follow Me! The Story of the Second Marine Division in World War II*, also confirmed that there were "ninety-five casualties among Second Division Marines."[14] The total number of casualties among Marines then is 207 and not 193 as given in the press release. If the Navy had made a mistake in calculating the loss of personnel among its Marines, which had fewer bodies aboard the different ships at the time of the disaster, could it also have miscalculated the loss among Navy personnel, which had thousands of men on board?

During the battle to capture Saipan, hundreds of Marine casualties were brought back to the hospitals around Pearl Harbor for treatment and recuperation. Many returned to find themselves lying beside men who had been injured in the West Loch disaster. SGT Les Groshong (Hq Co., 8th MarReg, 2nd MarDiv) was wounded on Saipan and shipped back to Pearl Harbor. "What I remember most about [the West Loch disaster]," he wrote, "was that when I arrived back as a wounded Marine at Aiea Heights hospital a few weeks later the hospital was full of wounded from that explosion."[15]

One of the victims of the West Loch disaster still in a hospital when the Saipan wounded began to return was MoMM2/c Harold Knebel, who had suffered hearing damage and had been struck near the spine by a piece of angle iron while fighting the fires onboard LST #480. Knebel remained in the hospital for seven days before being discharged and sent back to the States. On the way stateside, he had to report to sick bay every day for five days for treatment. Sent back to another LST after a thirty-day leave was up, Knebel continued to suffer from his West Loch wounds until the end of the war. "I did not have any duty that required anything physical," he remarked. "I still had pain with movement around my shrapnel wound and spine." In January 1946, Knebel was given an honorable discharge. "Today," he wrote in 2008, "I am receiving a 40 percent service connected disability compensation for hearing loss and disintegrating joint disease in my spine."

In addition to the hearing loss and back injury, Knebel, like so many other West Loch survivors, suffered nightmares long after he left the service. "All thru the years I have had the same nightmare," he wrote. "I was standing on the edge of the ship, then I jumped into 'Hell' and started swimming. My wife woke me up when I started swimming in bed. When I wake up I am sweating."[16]

MoMM1/c Richard MacNealy, of LST #166, also suffered nightmares. "This experience has caused me many sleepless nights and many nightmares," he wrote. "I knew I was going to die, wither from smoke inhalation or by one or more of those bombs and other projectiles that was flying off those burning ships. I shudder and relive those few horrible days whenever the occasion arises that causes me to recall or think about the experience." MacNealy had always loved the 4th of July fireworks but not after witnessing the West Loch explosions. "When you see human beings tossed into the air and either back into the smoking mess or into the water you don't forget it," he said. "Neither do you forget the flying missiles of fifty gallon drums of gasoline or the exploding ammunition. The 4th of July fireworks displays have always been something that I avoid since that happened. It brings back too many memories."[17]

Another longtime sufferer was MoMM3/c Ernest J. Garbitt, Jr., the sailor from LST #224 who had received a horribly burned arm from an exploding phosphorous shell. "One day in 1947," recalled Bernard Schofield, who had been a radioman second class on LST #224, "I was walking through the city of Brockton, Mass. (Ernie's hometown and my birthplace as well) and a man stepped out in front of me at a bus stop. He inquired about my name, and when I told him who I was, he identified himself as Ernie Garbitt. To be sure, he had had skin grafts galore. His life was changed forever. In spite of all his medical treatment and care and being disfigured, Ernie never received a disability of any percent, nor was he awarded any compensation for his permanent injuries."[18] It was as if the government and military were trying to minimize the casualty list by ignoring many of the injured.

Many of the West Loch survivors felt that due to the fire and explosions, many victims were burnt beyond recognition or blown to pieces. "I saw men flying through the air and bodies floating everywhere," a sailor aboard LST #129 wrote, "and I have always felt that the number reported as dead seems too low to me." Roy Sannella, who had worked on the tugboat YTB-129, *Osceola*, assisted in the cleanup. "The next two days I was on another tug, recovering bodies," he wrote. "It took three days to remove what bodies we could find." Added Marine MP Bob Arieta, "On the third or fourth night, you started smelling the dead bodies. Every night it got worse. They'd take the bodies over to the morgue in Pearl Harbor." John R. Garner, a sailor working with Mobile Hospital #11 at Aiea Hospital, remembered, "Bodies were carried to the Aiea Heights Naval Hospital overlooking Pearl Harbor and kept in meat coolers until identification could be made. Bodies floated to the surface at West Loch for several days after the explosions." As he recalled, most were buried at Redhill near the Army Hospital.[19]

Petty Officer Leo Bednarczyk of LST #124 recalled how he helped collect the bodies after the disaster. "My memories are more vivid of what we did afterwards," Bednarczyk wrote, "because we were in a small boat the next four days picking up what was left in pieces and bodies." A fellow crewman, PhM3/c Ernie Andrus, was away from the ship at the time of the explosion and never knew the part that his shipmate played in the cleanup. "Leo didn't even tell me about his part in tying lines on the dead bodies until a few years ago at a reunion," Andrus admitted.[20]

As it turned out, Bednarczyk was forbidden to talk about the disaster even if he had wanted to. Almost immediately after the disaster, Admiral Nimitz clamped a gag order on the incident. With an invasion in the offing, Nimitz did not want the Japanese to hear that an invasion fleet had run into trouble. If the enemy got word of the disaster, it would not take them long to figure out where the armada was going and strengthen the garrison in the Mariana Islands or set up a gauntlet of submarines between Hawaii and Saipan, or both. As ordered by Admiral Nimitz and his staff, it was against regulations to talk about the disaster with others, including men from your own ship, or to write about it in letters home or elsewhere. In fact, it was a punishable offense to even mention it.

On May 22, one day after the event, Lieutenant Geis of LST #461, which had been at Tare 9 at the beginning of the disaster, posted the following memorandum on the ship's bulletin boards:

From: The Commanding Officer
Subject: Events of 21 May 1944, suppression of
            information concerning
1. All information concerning the events of 21 May 1944 is of vital military significance and should be closely guarded.

2. Therefore, all hands aboard are strictly cautioned against the relation of events of 21 May 1944 or any reference thereto in any mail leaving the vessel.
3. All hands are further directed to refrain from discussion of any happenings of that date with persons other than those who may be authorized to obtain such information.
4. Strict compliance with the above is directed.

On another LST, a similar posting went up which lacked some of the subtleties of the Geis memorandum.

Notice to all hands
1. Yesterday's explosion among LSTs of our group is not to be mentioned in any letters going from this vessel.
2. No mention of "accident," "casualty," "fire," or "explosion" is to appear in any letters.
3. Notice will be posted when and if yesterday's episode can be publicized.
Signed J. W. Murphy
Communications Officer[21]

Whether issued by a commanding officer or a communications officer, the message was the same. There was to be no mention of the West Loch disaster in any way, shape, or form from anybody on any ship, Navy, Marine, Army, Coast Guard, or whatever or from anybody connected with the incident in any way. However, since Admiral Nimitz, in spite of all of his power and prestige, could not stop the sound of the explosions and the dark cloud that had rolled up over West Loch, he had been forced to issue the 25 May press release, stating that "several small vessels" had been destroyed.

Two sailors connected with Lieutenant Geis's LST #461 remembered the censorship. MoMM3/c Dan Tanase was on LST #461 at the time of the disaster and had plenty to talk about. "When the explosions settled and the saved ships were prepared to set sail, the crew was warned never to speak or write to anyone about what happened," wrote Margaret Tanase, Dan's wife. "They also were issued a letter from Fleet Command warning never to write or speak about the event."[22]

Stranger still was the effect on William Wright, Jr., assigned to LST #461. Wright had been away at paymaster school when the disaster occurred and therefore missed the whole thing. Yet when he got back to the ship, he could sense that something had happened. When he asked about it, he got the silent treatment. "Absolutely not one word was said," Wright remembered. "Nobody said a word about it. I knew nothing about it until a long time later. There were orders not to say a word to anybody about it. I didn't even hear anybody talk about it among themselves. I guess they were threatened."[23]

LST #274 had been in the middle of the disaster but had managed to pull out of Tare 8 and save itself. The next day the passengers and crew got word of the censor. Electrician Tidwell of LCT-982 wrote, "I do remember the next day, a bunch of high officers came on board and they asked us to write down everything that happened and what we saw and not to say anything much about it. They were the ones telling us, through the skipper, I guess, they informed him, and he informed us. They were just passing the buck on down."[24]

On the Coast Guard ship LST #23, which had been in Tare 9 almost directly behind LST #353, there was much to talk about, but once again, an order went out to keep quiet. Recalled Bill Montague, "They even put on the bulletin board you are not to discuss anything that happened aboard the ship to anyone."[25]

Roy Sannella, from the tugboat YTB-129, *Osceola*, said, "The last thing we were told was that the disaster was considered a secret and was not to be discussed under penalty of court-martial." Sannella kept his mouth shut for years.[26]

Two Marines, Jim Reed and Jesse Kirkes, were both on LST #43, which had been lost at West Loch. "The Navy didn't want the Japanese to know that this happened," Reed recalled. "We were told not to write home about it. Of course, they were censoring us anyway, and we were told not to talk about it, at any time, to anybody." Confirmed Kirkes, "Back then, everything we wrote back home was censored. We were told not to say anything about it."[27]

Another ship that had been lost was LST #69. There again, the survivors received strict orders. Outspoken Marine Harry Pearce wrote, "Apparently the government filmed the whole damn thing, but the Navy never told anybody. It was a complete cover-up with all various and sundry reasons for not telling. The big reason supposedly for not notifying the world of it was they didn't want the Japanese to know. They didn't want the Japanese to know that we were Marines loaded for combat and that we were shipping out. The government has always had a way of covering its mistakes." Loaded aboard a replacement ship and sent to Saipan, Pearce recalled the orders that came down from above. "We were forbidden to talk about it. I know that anybody that wrote a letter home, that letter never got home because censors would have taken it out."[28]

In spite of the strict censorship, PhM2/c William L. C. Johnson from LST #69 managed to get a letter home to his folks. "It was carried by a crew member to California and mailed to Seattle, Washington," Johnson stated. "It never would have passed the scrutiny of a censor at Pearl Harbor."[29]

However, years later, after researching the disaster for a book, Johnson applauded the censoring. He explained: "The Navy had to keep this under very severe wraps all during the war because anything that we divulged, of course, the Japanese would know it just as fast as we would. So it had to be kept top secret. After all, we were getting ready to invade Saipan, Tinian, and Guam, and you don't want to tell the enemy. So they put this thing under wraps, and in my estimation they did a marvelous job of keeping the Court of Inquiry down to as low a key as they did so you wouldn't have a lot of publicity. We didn't want people to know about it because we had a war to fight."[30]

All of the official information and documents relating to the disaster, including the court of inquiry transcripts and testimonies, were classified as top secret until 1 January 1960.[31] A. Alan Oliver explained the ramifications of such a classification in a magazine article:

In the Navy's divine wisdom, clamping a TOP SECRET status on the tragedy caused much evidence that might have been of importance to be lost because of the interval of time before the incident was declassified and made public in 1960—16 years after its occurrence. Combined with the fact that the larger issue of the successful execution of Operation Forager [the invasion of the Marianas] was only delayed one day by the West Loch fiasco served to ameliorate official interest in the disaster. With 1,051 LSTs on its roster, it might appear that the U.S. Navy considered these ocean-going ferries little better than expendable. . . .

Nevertheless, with the men and ships involved in the tragedy soon dispersed all over the world and the lid of secrecy assuring no further critical analysis by watchdogs or Washington, the events of that long-ago day continue to be shrouded in mystery. . . . Further erasing any evidence of the happening was the intense salvage effort which followed the incident. Within weeks [sic] of the disaster, all of the wrecks save one [LST #480] were removed. Well-applied coats of paint and reconstruction of damaged buildings and piers soon left no visible vestige of the billowing palls of oily black smoke which once rose high over secluded West Loch. That the site was restricted from civilian inspection further served to suppress prying eyes and investigations. These factors, the passage of time and nature's way of healing its blemishes leave the West Loch saga seldom mentioned in history books.[32]

Although Marine Calvin Frawley, who had been aboard LST #179, which was lost from Tare 8, could understand the need for secrecy and censorship at the time, he could not understand the need to classify the material and keep it quiet for so long. "Well, we knew that the story was covered up and had to be," Frawley lamented, "but tragedies like this where boys are lost, these stories should be told because a great deal of them had suffered and died prior to ever seeing the enemy prior to even engaging in war. They were gone, right there at West Loch."[33]

The censorship orders even went out to people who were not aboard the ships during the disaster. Marine MP Bob Arieta, who had used his jeep to shuttle people from the loch to a hospital, remembered that a couple of days later, a big meeting was held. "They said, 'Don't say a word about this.' We were told every day to keep our mouths shut." In covering up the disaster, Arieta felt that the Navy was "right, but yet wrong." He wondered, "What about the moms and dads? People didn't know what had happened to their loved ones."[34]

Unfortunately, the need to cover up the disaster affected the dead almost as much as it did the living. On 7 June 1944, the family of eighteen-year-old Marine PFC Charles M. Stacey received a Western Union telegram from the Marine Corps commandant. The telegram stated that Charles "has been reported missing," which caused consternation for his parents because they knew of no Pacific battles involving their son's unit. The fact that the telegram did not say "missing in action" was even more puzzling.

In early August, when PFC Stacey's parents received another Western Union telegram from the Marine Corps informing them that "private first class Charles M. Stacey USMCR died in explosion which occurred on 21 May 1944," their son's death became even more puzzling. What explosion? How? Where? Who was responsible? Was it an accident? Sabotage? Stacey's parents had a hundred questions that no one could, or would, answer.

To add salt to the wound, the second telegram also included the terse term, "Remains not recovered." The Stacey family had lost their son, and there was no body to bring home to mourn and bury. However, years later, a Stacey family member was visiting Hawaii and stumbled across the gravesite of PFC Charles M. Stacey. His body had been recovered after all and had been quietly buried in a Hawaiian cemetery. Once notified, the Stacey family had the body exhumed and brought home for a decent, loving burial.[35] Questions concerning his demise, however, remained unanswered.

The immediate Navy reaction was to round up all the Marines from the six lost LSTs and quarantine them until it could be determined what, or who, had started the explosions. SGT Jack M. Tagler (Co. L, 6th MarReg, 2nd MarDiv) had been on LST #353 and remembered that although most of the members of his company were off the ship at the time of the disaster, they were soon rounded up and "taken to a stockade area for security reasons for about a week." As Tagler wrote, "I never did find out why [our] company was put in this restricted area and kept apart from everyone else." While Tagler and the other members of his company were in isolation, they learned that their ship had exploded, burned, and sank. "Rumors were rampant at the time of the explosion—spies, saboteurs, workmen's welding torches, carelessness in storing ammunition, and Amtrac's gasoline," he wrote. Eventually, Company L was released and shipped out to Saipan. As Tagler admitted, he never did learn the truth about the disaster or why they had been quarantined.[36]

The Navy crews from the lost vessels were also quarantined. "Well, we really didn't know, you see, what happened to our ship," said RM2/c Art Freer of LST #480. "They of course railed us off and put us in a barracks and didn't tell us anything. I never knew how many people were hurt or anything about anything."

Eventually, when it was determined that the first explosion was not an act of sabotage, they were given a thirty-day survivor's leave. Unfortunately for Freer, trained radiomen were at a premium. "And the radiomen," Freer reported, "they said they need you out here, so all the crew went back to the States except us radiomen, so I was put on the commander of the flotilla ship and sent out to Guam. I made the invasion of Guam and then I got sent back to the States."[37]

In spite of the Navy's strict censorship and veiled threats about reprisals for anyone that even so much as uttered the word *disaster*, word leaked out to the enemy. Marine PFC Joe Drotovick, who was traveling to Saipan aboard LST #42, remembered that "Tokyo Rose broadcasted the tragedy at West Loch, and [said] that an equally disastrous fate would meet the men at wherever they were headed next." In the illegal diary that Alfred E. Erickson was keeping aboard LST #166, he wrote: "Left Pearl and those smoldering LSTs. . . . Tuned in Tokyo Rose and she announced the debacle at Westlock, and our invasion of Saipan. . . . The Japs had pretty good intelligence."[38]

For years, very little, if anything, was known about the disaster outside of West Loch. "No one knew that such a thing occurred," said Coast Guardsman Bill Montague of LST #23. "As a matter of fact, even the Veterans Administration didn't know." Tugboat crewman Roy Sannella, who was given a special banner in 2009 for his life-saving efforts, said, "Always remember this day [May 21, 1944]. Let everyone know what happened on this day, because it was all a secret all these years."[39]

"When I go to these veteran reunions," Marine CPL Jim Reed from LST #43, said, "I tell them, 'I'm not a December 7th survivor of Pearl Harbor, I'm a May 21st survivor.'" To a man, the survivors of the West Loch disaster are an unassuming bunch that have moved on with their lives, yet each one yearns to have the story told and for America, and the world, to know what happened on that terrible Sunday so many years ago. "None of us are seeking glory, nothing like that," Reed said. "I think it bothers a lot of guys, what we went through, and there's been no recognition."[40] Agreed Marine MP Bob Arieta, "It was a second Pearl Harbor. I just want us to be known."

In recent years, the U.S. Navy has held commemorative ceremonies in West Loch, always inviting back veterans of the disaster. In 1994, on the fiftieth anniversary of the event, a memorial plaque was unveiled next to the pier of the ammunition depot, now the Naval Magazine Pearl Harbor, inside an area that is off-limits to civilian personnel. Across the loch, on the southeastern end of Hanaloa Point, sits the visible, beached, rusting remains of half-sunken LST #480, the last ship to explode and catch fire. "When I saw 480's fo'c'sle, that's when I knew I was back," said S2/c Chet Carbaugh, who survived the burning of LST #39 and came back to be a part of the sixtieth anniversary ceremony in May 2004. "It brought tears to my eyes. It's healing. I had to come back for my shipmates and myself." After throwing a rose into West Loch during the ceremony, S1/c Walt Slater of LST #274 said, "I was thinking as I watched that rose in the water how I could still see the faces of my shipmates. I've never forgotten, and I'll never forget."[41]

Chronology

1943

December U.S. commanders decide that the major thrust toward Japan would go through the Central Pacific, using captured islands as bases for the B-29 bombers. The date for the invasion of the Mariana Islands—Saipan and Tinian in the north and Guam in the south—is set for November 1944.

1944

Mid-February With the speedy capture of the Marshall Islands, the invasion date for Saipan is advanced to 15 June.

15-19 May The Saipan invasion fleet and the Second and Fourth Marine Divisions stage invasion rehearsals at Maalaea Bay on Maui and at Kahoolawe Island, Territory of Hawaii. During the night of 14–15 May, in heavy seas, three landing craft are prematurely launched off the decks of their transporting LSTs. Two of the LCTs had been turned into floating gunships, each equipped with eight mortar tubes and ammunition.

20 May The LSTs return to Pearl Harbor after the rehearsal. Most of the LSTs find berths in West Loch and tie up side-by-side. The largest grouping, eight ships, is at Tare 8. There are seven ships at Tare 9 and six at Tare 10. Rearming and refueling begin immediately. Most LSTs carry 80–100 large drums of high-octane aviation fuel on their bow for refueling the amphibious tractors.

21 May VADM Turner decides to remove the mortars and ammunition from the one remaining LCT floating gunship, LCT-963, chained to the deck of LST #353. It has been determined that the other two gunships were launched prematurely because the excess weight caused too great a strain on the retaining chains of the LSTs.

Early morning Civilian workers, including many Japanese Americans, begin adding chains to LCTs strapped to the open top deck of the LSTs. In spite of repeated warnings and No Smoking signs, the men continue to smoke.

0930 African American soldiers from the 29th Chemical Decontamination Company begin removing the mortar ammunition from LCT-963, chained atop LST #353 at Tare 8. Several of the soldiers are seen smoking cigarettes in spite of the No Smoking sign and repeated orders to stop. Numerous wooden crates containing two mortar shells each are carelessly dropped during the removal.

1030 Two crewmen begin welding near the aft section on LST #353.

1400 The civilian workers finish adding chains to LCT-963 and depart from LST #353.

1430 The African American ammunition handlers have finished loading one truck. Another truck is brought up while the loaded truck is carried to shore.

1445 The two crewmen welding on LST #353 finish their work and secure their equipment.

1500 The ammunition handlers take a break while the crates in the new truck are being counted. Some of the men light up a quick cigarette.

1500 A few crewmen are seen smoking on the bow of LST #353, near the 55-gallon drums of high-octane aviation gasoline.

1508 A terrific explosion occurs on the bow of LST #353. Flaming debris and shrapnel are flung in all directions. Windows are shattered in buildings 3,000 feet away. Almost immediately, fires erupt on several vessels moored around LST #353.

1508 Officers and crew on the surrounding ships respond quickly to the immediate threat. While deck crews fight to extinguish the fires on their ships, engine room crews start up the engines.

1511 A second, larger explosion occurs aboard LST #353. More flaming debris is scattered around the loch.

1511 The LSTs at Tare 9, immediately behind LST #353, begin leaving the tare grouping. Some head out to sea down the narrow West Loch channel while others head for a shallow back bay at the southwest corner of West Loch.

1513 LSTs in Tare 10, 1,000 feet behind LST #353, begin to leave the mooring.

1513 LSTs at Tare 5 and Tare 6, approximately 1,700 and 1,500 feet from the explosion, respectively, begin making preparations to leave West Loch.

1520 LCMs with fire pumps are sent from East Loch to West Loch. Fireboats based at Honolulu Harbor, 14 nautical miles away, are dispatched to West Loch.

1520 LST #274 (the third ship at Tare 8) severs the lines to LST #69 (the fourth ship). LST #274 moves forward 200 yards and beaches in Walker Bay. The first and second ships, LSTs #205 and #225, eventually follow. The five outer ships in Tare 8, all burning fiercely, begin a slow drift southward.

1522 The third and most powerful explosion erupts. It is heard 15 miles away and sends flaming debris out 3,000 feet.

1530 LST #69 from Tare 8, wrapped in flames, drifts down beside LST #480, the first ship in Tare 9. LST #480 is snagged on the mooring posts at Tare 9 and cannot get away. LST #480 catches fire, and the flames are soon out of control.

1530 News of the disaster reaches the Intelligence Unit, Naval Air Station. Three officers are immediately dispatched to determine whether or not the initial explosion was an act of sabotage.

1540 The LSTs in Tares 5 and 6 begin to leave after being pelted by debris from the third explosion.

1543 All available waterborne firefighting equipment is sent to West Loch.

1620 The drifting, burning ships threaten the naval ammunition depot on the southern shore of West Loch. A cargo ship, *Joseph B. Francis*, carrying 350 tons of ammunition and being unloaded at the depot, is set on fire by a phosphorous shell thrown out from one of the exploding ships. The fire is quickly extinguished, and the cargo ship starts out down the West Loch channel toward East Loch.

1630 Three PT boats are dispatched from East Loch to West Loch with orders to torpedo and sink the drifting ships that threaten the naval ammunition depot.

1630 Specialized firefighting boats, including several tugboats and the five fireboats from Honolulu Harbor, enter West Loch and begin extinguishing the fires and stopping the movement of the drifting ships.

1640 The three PT boats arrive in West Loch but are ordered to stand down. While the tugboats and fireboats work on the drifting ships, the PT boat crews help in rescue efforts.

1650   LST #353, still carrying LCT-963 on her burning main deck, sinks near Tare 10. LST #39, another drifting and burning ship, comes to a stop nearby. She continues to burn and explode.

1700   Three drifting ships, LSTs #43, #69, and #179, come to a stop 500 feet from the naval ammunition depot. All three continue to burn and explode.

1700   Marine Corps photographers reach West Loch and begin taking still and moving pictures of the disaster.

1705   A sudden explosion in LST #69 sends a huge ball of smoke and flame into the air. It is all caught on film.

1705   The phosphorous shell inside the cargo hold of *Joseph B. Francis* reignites. Fearing a cataclysmic explosion, several ships in East Loch are ordered to evacuate. Within fifteen minutes, however, the fire is extinguished.

2005   A large explosion on LST #39 badly damages the yard net tender *Tamaha*. A large tugboat assists *Tamaha* and pushes LST #39 next to the bank near Tare 10.

2152   LST #39 burst into flames again.

22 May

0130   LST #480, still hung up near Tare 9, begins smoking again.

0510   The Pearl Harbor signal tower reports that fire and smoke are still visible in West Loch.

0715   Sandwiches and coffee are sent to the firefighters in West Loch. The disaster is over. Six LSTs, three LCTs, seventeen amphibious tractors, and eight 155mm howitzers are destroyed. Two other LSTs are too badly damaged to make the trip to Saipan.

1440   A Navy court of inquiry begins an investigation into the circumstances surrounding the disaster in West Loch.

25 May   The surviving LSTs, including several replacement LSTs, leave Hawaii for Saipan. They are only one day behind schedule but make up the time en route.

25 May   Admiral Nimitz issues a press release stating that "several small vessels" have been destroyed in West Loch with "some loss of life."

27 May   The Naval intelligence unit officers determine that the cause of the initial explosion aboard LST #353 was not an act of sabotage.

31 May   Navy salvage crews begin dismantling and demolishing the sunken LSTs. Only LST #480, aground on the southeast shore of Hanaloa Point, will be left intact.

12 June   The Navy court of inquiry releases its findings and determines that the cause of the explosion on LST #353 was a dropped mortar shell during the unloading of LCT-963. The court criticizes the stowage of gasoline in such close proximity to highly explosive ammunition and the nesting of so many LSTs in one berth. The court lists 27 people dead, 100 missing, and 380 injured.

15 June   The invasion of Saipan begins. It is right on schedule.

17 June   The Navy issues a new press release regarding casualties of the West Loch disaster. The overall number, however, remain the same: 27 dead, 100 missing, 380 injured.

29 June   Admiral Nimitz forwards the results of the court of inquiry to the judge advocate general. He attaches a letter stating that he disagrees with the finding of the court as to the cause of the explosion. Nimitz believes the explosion was caused by "gasoline vapor," not a mishandled mortar shell.

18 July   The six lost LSTs, #39, #43, #69, #179, #353, and #480, are stricken from the Navy list of active ships.

24 July   The Navy intelligence unit issues a report listing 27 dead, 74 missing, 377 injured.

1945

17 February   During salvage operations, Navy diver Owen Francis Patrick Hammerberg loses his life while saving the lives of two fellow divers. He is posthumously awarded the Medal of Honor.

1946

27 February   The Navy issues an updated report on the West Loch explosion. The report again claims that the probable cause was the detonation of a dropped mortar shell. The report also reiterated the claim of 127 killed and missing and 380 injured.

1953

Retired ADM Samuel Eliot Morison studies the disaster and claims casualties of 163 killed and missing and 396 injured. The Navy accepts the new figures.

Notes

Chapter 1

1. Dyer, *The Amphibians Came to Conquer*, 892; Rottman, *Saipan & Tinian 1944*, 32.

2. Gilbert, *Marine Tank Battles in the Pacific*, 139; Dunnigan and Nofi, *The Pacific War Encyclopedia*, 398–99; Rottman, *Saipan & Tinian 1944*, 7–8.

3. Anderson, *Western Pacific*, 3, 6.

4. Ibid., 6; Rottman, *Saipan & Tinian 1944*, 7–8; Costello, *The Pacific War, 1941–1945*, 455–57.

5. Rottman, *World War II Pacific Island Guide*, 332–42; Wright, *Tarawa 1943*, 82–83; Hoyt, *Storm over the Gilberts*, 161–65.

6. Rottman, *The Marshall Islands 1944*, 26–29; Costello, *The Pacific War, 1941–1945*, 448–49.

7. Mesko, *Amtracs in Action*, 14; Rottman, *Saipan & Tinian 1944*, 36; Hoffman, *Saipan: The Beginning of the End*, 33; Gilbert, *Marine Tank Battles in the Pacific*, 143.

8. Rottman, *Saipan & Tinian 1944*, 8; Alexander, *Storm Landings*, 65.

9. Rottman, *Saipan & Tinian 1944*, 27, 32; Dyer, *The Amphibians Came to Conquer*, 874.

10. Hoffman, *Saipan: The Beginning of the End*, 27; Rottman, *Saipan & Tinian 1944*, 14–15, 32; Rottman, *Guam 1941 & 1944*, 22; Dyer, *The Amphibians Came to Conquer*, 874.

11. Dyer, *The Amphibians Came to Conquer*, 876.

12. Crowl, *Campaign in the Marianas*, 47; U.S. Marine Corps, "Fourth Marine Division Operations Report Saipan 15 June to 9 July 1944," NA, 16.

13. Hoffman, *Saipan: The Beginning of the End*, 29; Johnston, *Follow Me!* 173; Rottman, *Saipan & Tinian 1944*, 16, 33; Zaloga, *Amtracs: U.S. Amphibious Assault Vehicles*, 11, 16. Joseph H. Alexander (*Storm Landings*, 68) places the number of LVTs used for the invasion of Saipan at 732. Whether the correct number was 719, as noted by Rottman, or 732, as suggested by Alexander, it was the largest concentration of amtracs used to date.

14. Shaw et al., *Central Pacific Drive*, 3:247–48.

15. Johnson, *The West Loch Story*, 12; U.S. Marine Corps, "Fourth Marine Division Operations Report Saipan 15 June to 9 July 1944," NA 15; Rottman, *Saipan & Tinian 1944*, 40.

16. Dyer, *The Amphibians Came to Conquer*, 892–93; Hoffman, *Saipan: The Beginning of the End*, 31; Oliver, "Navy's Hushed-Up Tragedy at West Loch," 27.

17. U.S. Marine Corps, "Fourth Marine Division Operations Report Saipan 15 June to 9 July 1944," 18; Smith, *The Saga of LST 224*, 64.

18. Reminiscences of Pounds, in Smith, *The Saga of LST 224*, 157; Rottman, *U.S. World War II Amphibious Tactics*, 45.

19. Dougherty, *The USS LST 481*, www.ibiblio.org/hyperwar/USN/ships/LST/LST-481-history.html.

20. Smith, *The Saga of LST 224*, 149; Gross, "How to Launch an LCT," http://ww2lct.org/history/stories/launch.htm, accessed May 2009.

21. Tidwell interview.

22. Smith, *The Saga of LST 224*, 150; Gross, "How to Launch an LCT."

23. Slater interview.

24. Dyer, *The Amphibians Came to Conquer*, 893; Johnson, *The West Loch Story*, 13, 15; Hoffman, *Saipan: The Beginning of the End*, 32–33.

25. Testimony of Gubellini in Naval Intelligence Unit, "Destruction of Six LSTs by Explosions and Fire, West Loch, Oahu, T.H., 21 May 1944," dated 24 July 1944, file A17, National Archives [hereafter cited as "Destruction of Six LSTs"], 3.

Chapter 2

1. George, *Too Young to Vote*, 100.

2. Hoffman, *Saipan: The Beginning of the End*, 32.

3. Ballinger quoted in "Maui's World War II Legacy: The Hazards of Training."

4. "Monday, 15 May 1944, 0000–0400 Watch," USN Deck Logs, LST 485, Record Group 24, National Archives (hereafter cited as RG 24, NA).

5. Johnson, *The West Loch Story*, 12.

6. "Confidential Report Dated 21 May 1944, from U.S.S. LST 485 to SECNAV," USN Deck Logs, LST 485, RG 24, NA.

7. "Monday, May 15, 1944, 0000–0400 Watch," USN Deck Logs, LST 71.

8. Ibid., "2000–2400 Watch"; Hoffman, Saipan: The Beginning of the End, 32–33; Johnson, *The West Loch Story*, 12; Koehler, "May 21, 1944, Aboard U.S.S. LST 242"; "Tuesday, May 16, 1944, 0400–0800 Watch," USN Deck Logs, LST 31.

9. "Confidential Report Dated 21 May 1944, from U.S.S. LST 485 to SECNAV"; Hoffman, *Saipan: The Beginning of the End*, 33; "15 May, Mon.," *Warships of World War II: Articles: 1944*.

10. Moore interview.

11. "Monday, May 15, 1944, Various Watches," USN Deck Logs, LST 31; Hoffman, *Saipan: The Beginning of the End*, 32–33.

12. George, *Too Young to Vote*, 101.

13. Tidwell interview.

14. Hoffman, *Saipan: The Beginning of the End*, 33.

15. Koehler, "May 21, 1944, Aboard U.S.S. LST 242"; Slater interview.

16. Dyer, *The Amphibians Came to Conquer*, 893; "Fourth Marine Division Operations Report Saipan 15 June to 9 July 1944," 16–18; "16 May, Mon.," *Warships of World War II: Articles: 1944*; Crowl, *Campaign in the Marianas*, 46.

17. "Fourth Marine Division Operations Report Saipan 15 June to 9 July 1944," 14; Wells, *The Quack Corps*, 101–102.

18. "Tuesday, 16 May '44," USN Deck Logs, LST 39; Wells, *The Quack Corps*, 102; Clements recollection in Johnson, *The West Loch Story*, 98; "Tuesday, 16 May 1944, 1200–1600 Watch," USN Deck Logs, LST 354.

19. "Fourth Marine Division Operations Report Saipan 15 June to 9 July 1944," 15; Johnston, *Follow Me!* 173.

20. "Wednesday, 17 May '44," USN Deck Logs, LST 121.

21. Crowl, *Campaign in the Marianas*, 46.

22. "Fourth Marine Division Operations Report Saipan 15 June to 9 July 1944," 15.

23. Dyer, *The Amphibians Came to Conquer*, 881; Crowl, *Campaign in the Marianas*, 46–47.

24. "Tuesday, 16 May 1944," various watches, USN Deck Logs, LST 34; "Friday, 19 May '44," USN Deck Logs, LST 226; "Friday, 19 May '44, 12 to 16 Watch," USN Deck Logs, LST 275.

25. "Monday, 15 May 1944" and "Tuesday, 16 May 1944," various watches, USN Deck Logs, LST 34.

26. "Tuesday, 16 May 1944, 0800–1200 Watch," USN Deck Logs, LST 275; "Friday, 19 May '44," USN Deck Logs, LST 226.

27. "Friday, 19 May '44," USN Deck Logs, LST 222; "Friday, 19 May '44," USN Deck Logs, LST 129.

28. "Friday, 19 May '44," and "Saturday, 20 May '44," USN Deck Logs, LST 39.

29. "Friday, 19 May '44," "Saturday, 20 May '44," and "Sunday, 21 May '44," USN Deck Logs, LST 222.

Chapter 3

1. Dyer, *The Amphibians Came to Conquer*, 893.

2. "Landing Ship Tank."

3. "Landing Ship, Tank (LST)"; Rottman, *Landing Ship, Tank*, 4–5.

4. "Landing Ship, Tank (LST)"; "Landing Ship Tank"; "Design and Construction," www.insidelst.com/, accessed 28 July 2008; Rottman, *Landing Ship, Tank*, 7–8; Hillman, "50 Yard Line Seats . . . for a Show I Would Rather Have Missed."

5. Rottman, *Landing Ship, Tank*, 9.

6. Ibid., 10; "Schematic," www.insidelst.com/; Smith, *The Saga of LST 224*, 244–45.

7. Dougherty, *The USS LST 481;* "Main Engine Room," and "Reduction Gear & Falk Air Clutch," www.insidelst.com/; Patten, *Another Side of World War II*, 5.

8. Dougherty, *The USS LST 481.*

9. Ibid.; Rottman, *Landing Ship, Tank*, 11; Smith, *The Saga of LST 224*, 244; "Landing Ship Tank"; Hillibush interview.

10. "Tank Deck" and "Steering Gear," www.insidelst.com/; Smith, *The Saga of LST 224*, 244–45; Rottman, *Landing Ship, Tank*, 12, 14.

11. "Tank Deck," www.insidelst.com/; Rottman, *Landing Ship, Tank*, 12.

12. Rottman, *Landing Ship, Tank*, 14; "Aft Crew Quarters and Wing Deck Berthing Compartments," www.insidelst.com; Smith, *The Saga of LST 224*, 144; Patten, *Another Side of World War II*, 5.

13. Rottman, *Landing Ship, Tank*, 12, 13; "Bow Door and Ramp," www.insidelst.com.

14. Panicello, *A Slow Moving Target*, 51; Rottman, *Landing Ship, Tank*, 13; "Landing Ship, Tank (LST)."

15. Panicello, *A Slow Moving Target*, 38; "Main Deck," www.insidelst .com/.

16. Various LST armament specifications, www.navsource.org/archives /10/16/16idx.htm.

17. "Armament," www.insidelst.com/; Rottman, *Landing Ship, Tank,* 26, 27, 28–29, 45; Dougherty, *The USS LST 481.*

18. Rottman, *Landing Ship, Tank,* 14–15. Later models of LSTs were built with a ramp instead of an elevator, which sped up the loading and removal of vehicles from the main deck. However, none of the LSTs involved in the West Loch disaster had ramps.

19. Ibid., 14.

20. "Officer's Country," www.insidelst.com/; Patten, *Another Side of World War II,* 3, 5; Smith, *The Saga of LST 224,* back cover illustration; Rottman, *Landing Ship, Tank,* 15.

21. Rottman, *Landing Ship, Tank,* 15;

22. Panciello, *A Slow Moving Target,* 43

23. "Wheel House," www.insidelst.com/; Rottman, *Landing Ship, Tank,* 15.

24. Dougherty, *The USS LST 481.*

25. "03 Deck" and "Welin Davit," www.insidelst.com/; Rottman, *Landing Ship, Tank,* 16.

26. Smith, *The Saga of LST 224,* 153–54.

27. Dougherty, *The USS LST 481.*

28. Rottman, *Landing Ship, Tank,* 19; Smith, *The Saga of LST 224,* 31.

29. Smith, *The Saga of LST 224,* 31.

30. Rottman, *Landing Ship, Tank,* 9–10, 19; "Landing Ship Tank"; "Landing Ship, Tank (LST)."

Chapter 4

1. Hoffman, *Saipan: The Beginning of the End,* 33; Johnson, *The West Loch Story,* 13, 157.

2. Fischer, "A Brief History of Pearl Harbor prior to World War II"; Wisniewski, *Pearl Harbor and the Arizona Memorial,* 5; Stuckey et al., *Call to Freedom,* 290.

3. Landauer and Landauer, *Pearl,* 198–99; Wisniewski, *Pearl Harbor and the Arizona Memorial,* 6; Fischer, "A Brief History of Pearl Harbor prior to World War II."

4. "List of American Military Reservations and Concrete Gun Batteries: The Harbor Defenses of Pearl Harbor, Hawaii."

5. Strimple interview by Ding, Johnson, and Holyoak, side 2, tape 1. http://oralhistory.rutgers.edu/interviews/strimple_james.html, accessed July 2008.

6. George interview; Arroyo, *Pearl Harbor,* 20–21; "Pearl Harbor and Outlying Islands: U.S. Navy Base Construction in World War II: Island of Oahu"; Slater interview; Tidwell interview.

7. Arroyo, *Pearl Harbor*, 20–21; Landauer and Landauer, *Pearl*, 206, 208, 245.

8. Koehler, "May 21, 1944, Aboard U.S.S. LST 242."

9. Arroyo, *Pearl Harbor*, 20–21; Landauer and Landauer, *Pearl*, 261; "The 76th Seabees of World War II: 76th NCB Cruise Book," http://mysite.verizon.net/vzeo0pwz/76thseabeesworldwar2/id9.html, accessed 5 August 2008, 7; "Pearl Harbor and Outlying Islands."

10. Landauer and Landauer, *Pearl*, 249, 256; "Saturday, 20 May '44, 1600–2000 Watch," USN Deck Logs, LST 226; "Saturday, 20 May 1944, 2000 to 2400 Watch," USN Deck Logs, LST 354.

11. Landauer and Landauer, *Pearl*, 249, 256.

12. "Pearl Harbor and Outlying Islands."

13. Strimple interview by Ding, Johnson, and Holyoak, side 1, tape 2, 17 October 2006. http://oralhistory.rutgers.edu/interviews/strimple_james .html, accessed July 2008.

14. Johnson, *The West Loch Story*, 22; Shuman, "The Pearl Harbor Disaster No One Has Heard Of," 5.

15. Johnson, *The West Loch Story*, 22, 146; "Saturday, 20 May 1944, 2000 to 2400 Watch," USN Deck Logs, LST 354.

16. Funderburg interview.

17. Knebel to author, 14 July 2008; Shuman, "The Other Pearl Harbor Disaster," photographs 34, 35; Johnson, *The West Loch Story*, 18.

18. "Thursday, 18 May '44," USN Deck Logs, LST 272.

19. "Monday, 22 May 1944, 1600–2000 Watch," and "Tuesday, 23 May 1944, 0800–1200 and 1200–1600 Watches," USN Deck Logs, LST 334.

20. "Sunday, 21 May 1944, 0000–0900 Watch," USN Deck Logs, LST 20; "Tank Landing Ship LST-20," *NavSource Online: Amphibious Photo Archive*; "LST-20," *Dictionary of American Naval Fighting Ships*; "Tank Landing Ship LST-343," *NavSource Online: Amphibious Photo Archive*; Time 1534 occurrence, "Chronology of Occurrences of West Loch Fire on 21–22 May 1944," Office of the Judge Advocate General [hereafter cited as OJAG]; "Saturday, 20 May '44," USN Deck Logs, LST 334; "LST-334," *Dictionary of American Naval Fighting Ships*; "History of U.S.S. LST 334."

21. "Thursday, 18 May '44," USN Deck Logs, LST 205; Kaiser interview.

22. "Sunday, 14 May '44," "Monday, 15 May '44," "Tuesday, 16 May '44," and "Thursday, 18 May '44," USN Deck Logs, LST 169.

23. Knebel to author, 14 July 2008; Freer interview.

24. Knebel to author, 14 July 2008.

25. "Sunday, 21 May '44," USN Deck Logs, LST 240; Johnson, *The West Loch Story*, 18.

26. "Sunday, 21 May '44," USN Deck Logs, *Terror*; "Terror," *Dictionary of American Naval Fighting Ships*; Photo # 80-G-276907 "Burning LSTs in West Loch, Pearl Harbor, May 1944," NA.

Chapter 5

1. "Saturday, 20 May '44," USN Deck Logs, LST 23 and LST 224.

2. Testimony of PFC Thomas J. Jacobs, "Destruction of Six LSTs," 9; Mesko, *Amtracs in Action*, 11.

3. "Saturday, 20 May '44, 04–08 Watch," USN Deck Logs, LST 129, LST 42, and LST 43.

4. "Saturday, 20 May '44," USN Deck Logs, LST 205.

5. "Saturday, 20 May '44," USN Deck Logs, LST 274.

6. Leary, Anderson, and Casavant testimonies in "Navy Board of Inquiry Investigating the Causes of the Explosion and Fire at West Loch, Pearl Harbor," Office of the Judge Advocate General [hereafter cited as Navy Board of Inquiry, OJAG], 29, 32, 34; "Friday, 19 May '44, 20–24 Watch," USN Deck Logs, LST 273.

7. "Saturday, 20 May '44," USN Deck Logs, LST 43.

8. "Outline Log for May 1 through 1507, May 21, 1944 and Thereafter through May 31, 1944," USN Deck Logs, LST 179, RG 24, NA; Richeson recollection in Thomas, *Don't Call Me Rosie*, 104; Zuehlke testimony in Navy Board of Inquiry, OJAG, 42–43.

9. "Outline Log for May 1 through 1507"; "Saturday, 20 May '44," USN Deck Logs, LST 205.

10. "Saturday, 20 May '44," USN Deck Logs, LST 23, LST 224, LST 340.

11. "Saturday, 20 May '44," USN Deck Logs, LST 42, LST 244, LST 275.

12. "Saturday, 20 May '44, 0800–1200 Watch," USN Deck Logs, LST 166, LST 244, LST 275; Crankshaw to author, 18 July 2008.

13. "Sunday, 21 May '44," USN Deck Logs, LST 242; Time 1612 Occurrence, "Chronology of Occurrences of West Loch Fire."

14. Saturday, 20 May '44, 8–12 Watch," USN Deck Logs, LST 34, LST 45, LST 121, LST 126, LST 226.

15. Saturday, 20 May '44," USN Deck Logs, LST 129, LST 273, LST 354; Time 1552 occurrence, "Chronology of Occurrences of West Loch Fire."

16. "Saturday, 20 May 1944, 04 to 08 Watch, 08 to 12 Watch, and 12 to 16 Watch," and Sunday, 21 May 1944, 12 to 16 Watch," USN Deck

Logs, *Manley* (APD-1); "Sunday, 21 May 1944, 00–04 Watch," USN Deck Logs, *Stringham* (APD 6); History of high-speed transports USS *Manley* (APD-1), USS *Stringham* (APD-6), USS *Waters* (APD-8), and USS *Overton* (APD-23), all in www.destroyerhistory.org/flushdeck/apd _ships.html.

17. Wells recollection in Johnson, *The West Loch Story*, 123; Wells, *The Quack Corps*, 103–104.

18. Interview of Harry Pearce by Dr. Richard Verrone, 2003, www .vietnam.ttu.edu/oralhistory/interviews/browse/ohp.php [hereafter cited as Pearce interview], accessed June 2008, 55.

19. "Saturday, 20 May '44," USN Deck Logs, LST 23, LST 43, LST 205.

20. "Saturday, 20 May '44, 2000–2400 Watch," USN Deck Logs, LST 226, LST 354.

Chapter 6

1. Gott testimony in Navy Board of Inquiry, OJAG, 48.

2. Pearce interview, 55; Testimony of Feyerabend, "Destruction of Six LSTs," 10; Kalencik recollection in Smith, *The Saga of LST 224*, 140.

3. Slater interview; Tidwell interview.

4. Hillman, "50 Yard Line Seats . . . for a Show I Would Rather Have Missed"; Tidwell interview.

5. Dyer, *The Amphibians Came to Conquer*, 893–94; Jones, *Destiny*, http://cbtsresidents.com/Spectrum/RayJones1.htm, accessed 8 July 2008.

6. Leary recollection in *The Other Tragedy at Pearl Harbor*"; Leary testimony in Navy Board of Inquiry, OJAG, 29.

7. Hillman, "50 Yard Line Seats"; Pearce interview, 55.

8. Hoyt testimony in Navy Board of Inquiry, OJAG, 23; Rhea, *War Is Hell*, 138–40.

9. "Sunday, 21 May '44, 0400–0800 Watch," USN Deck Logs, LST 42, LST 166, LST 244, LST 275.

10. "Sunday, 21 May 1944, 04 to 08 and 08 to 12 Watches," USN Deck Logs, *Manley* (APD-1).

11. "Sunday, 21 May '44, 04–08 and 08–12 Watches," USN Deck Logs, LST 461.

12. "Sunday, 21 May '44, 0800–1200 Watch," USN Deck Logs, LST 127.

13. "Sunday, 21 May '44, 0000–0800 Watch and 0800–2400 Watch," USN Deck Logs, LST 128.

14. "Sunday, 21 May '44," USN Deck Logs, LST 129.

15. "Saturday, 20 May '44," USN Deck Logs, LST 222.

16. "Saturday, 21 May '44, 0000–2400," USN Deck Logs, LST 39; Clements recollection in Johnson, *The West Loch Story*, 97.

17. Frawley recollection in *The Other Tragedy at Pearl Harbor,* History Channel documentary; Hoover recollection in Thomas, *Don't Call Me Rosie*, 109.

18. Shuman, "The Other Pearl Harbor Disaster," 33.

Chapter 7

1. Dyer, *The Amphibians Came to Conquer*, 894.

2. Testimony of Gubellini, "Destruction of Six LSTs," 3.

3. Testimony of Thomas in ibid., 4; comments by Turner et al. in ibid., 5.

4. Testimonies of Carlson and Davis in ibid., 14.

5. Lockwood testimony in Navy Board of Inquiry, OJAG, 17.

6. Testimonies of Marquez and Lebanowski in "Destruction of Six LSTs," 15.

7. Testimony of Marquez in ibid., 15; Sullivan recollection in Johnson, *The West Loch Story*, 27.

8. Thomas testimony in Navy Board of Inquiry, OJAG, 15.

9. Lindsey in ibid. 5; Smith and Cleveland testimonies in Navy Board of Inquiry, OJAG, 46 and 47.

10. Testimony of Thomas in "Destruction of Six LSTs," 10; testimony of Knox in ibid., 11.

11. Testimony of Scriva in ibid., 12; Morrissey testimony in Navy Board of Inquiry, OJAG, 48–49.

12. "LST Deck Plan," enclosure C in "Destruction of Six LSTs"; testimony of Kane in ibid., 6; Thomas testimony in Navy Board of Inquiry, OJAG, 15.

13. Testimonies of Kuscavage and Stovall in "Destruction of Six LSTs," 13, 14.

14. Testimony of Thomas in ibid., 4; Thomas and Lockwood testimonies in Navy Board of Inquiry, OJAG, 15 and 16.

15. Sullivan recollection in Johnson, *The West Loch Story*, 28; Smith and Cleveland testimonies in Navy Board of Inquiry, OJAG, 46 and 47.

16. Testimonies of Cross and Knox in "Destruction of Six LSTs," 11.

17. Testimony of Zuehlke in ibid., 31.

18. Sutcliffe recollection in ibid., 116.

19. Slater interview; Tidwell interview.

20. Wells, *The Quack Corps*, 104.

21. Testimony of Smith and Cleveland in Navy Board of Inquiry, OJAG, 46, 47.

22. Testimony of Smith in ibid., 45–46.

23. Testimony of Nichols in ibid., 35; testimony of Thomas, Nichols, and Connor in "Destruction of Six LSTs," 4, 6, 13.

24. Testimonies of Urich and Kane in "Destruction of Six LSTs," 5, 14.

25. Testimony of Gillian and Austin in ibid., 13–14.

26. "Preliminary Survey," in ibid., 1; Time 1508 Occurrence, "Chronology of Occurrences of West Loch Fire"; Shuman, "The Other Pearl Harbor Disaster," 33.

Chapter 8

1. "Destruction of Six LSTs," 1.

2. "Sunday, 21 May 1944, 12–16 Watch," USN Deck Logs, LST 273.

3. "Sunday, 21 May 1944," USN Deck Logs, LST 354.

4. Time 1508 occurrence, "Chronology of Occurrences of West Loch Fire"; "Sunday, 21 May 1944, 12 to 16 Watch," USN Deck Logs, LST 124.

5. Testimony of Martin and Hindman, both in "Destruction of Six LSTs," 5, 9.

6. Testimony of Kane in ibid., 5–6.

7. Testimony of Urich in ibid., 5.

8. Testimonies of Connor and Nichols in ibid., 6.

9. Testimony of Garcia in ibid., 7.

10. Testimony of Crerar in ibid., 6.

11. U.S. Navy, "Report of Explosion at West Loch, Pearl Harbor, T.H., 21 May 1944," 27 February 1946, file #326, NA, 2.

12. Carbaugh recollection in Wright, "West Loch Remembered"; Boch recollection in Johnson, *The West Loch Story*, 143.

13. Mincey statement in Ryan and Mincey, *USS* Terror: *War Cruise of USS* Terror, *Her Officers and Men, 1942–1947*, 16; Arieta statement in Hill, "Veteran Recalls Forgotten WWII Disaster."

14. Clements recollection in Johnson, *The West Loch Story*, 98.

15. "Destruction of Six LSTs," 16.

16. Lockwood testimony in Navy Board of Inquiry, OJAG, 17.

17. Morrissey testimony in ibid., 41.

18. Johnson interview.

19. Drake interview.

20. U.S. Navy, "Report of Explosion at West Loch," 2.

21. "Destruction of Six LSTs," 7.

22. Testimony of Kane in ibid., 6.

23. Testimony of Nichols in ibid., 6; Nichols testimony in Navy Board of Inquiry, OJAG, 25–26.

24. Testimony of Bonne in "Destruction of Six LSTs," 9.

25. Testimony of Weinberger in ibid., 8.

26. Testimony of Tumblson in ibid., 9–10.

27. Testimony of Garcia in ibid., 7.

28. Testimony of Zito in ibid., 10.

29. Johnson interview.

30. Ellis recollection in Berry, *Semper Fi, Mac*, 207.

31. Pearce interview, 56.

32. Claven recollection in Johnson, *The West Loch Story*, 96.

33. George, *Too Young to Vote*, 99.

34. "Destruction of Six LSTs," 7.

35. George, *Too Young to Vote*, 100.

36. Testimony of Thomas in "Destruction of Six LSTs," 4.

37. Carlson, "More Info on West Loch," 11.

Chapter 9

1. Boulware, Tagler, Boch, and Gourley reminiscences in Johnson, *The West Loch Story*, 127, 134, 142, 147; Graf statement in Goldberg, *D-Day in the Pacific: The Battle of Saipan*, 48; Sannella, *My Nine Lives*, 10; Kinney autobiography in Barger, *Large Slow Target: A History of the LST*, 156.

2. Testimony of Caldwell in Sample, "West Loch's Lost Tale"; Clevelend testimony in Navy Board of Inquiry, OJAG, 47–48.

3. Testimonies of Connor and Nichols in "Destruction of Six LSTs," 6; Nichols testimony in Navy Board of Inquiry, OJAG, 25–26.

4. Testimony of Thomas in "Destruction of Six LSTs," 4; Thomas testimony in Navy Board of Inquiry, OJAG, 13–14.

5. Testimony of Urich and Kane in "Destruction of Six LSTs," 5–6.

6. Thompson recollection in ibid., 136.

7. Ibid., 136–37.

8. Dearborn reminiscence in Johnson, *The West Loch Story*, 102–103.

9. Morrissey testimony in Navy Board of Inquiry, OJAG, 48–51.

10. Sheppard testimony in ibid., 51–52.

11. Harmer recollection in Thomas, *Don't Call Me Rosie*, 105; Frawley recollection in *The Other Tragedy at Pearl Harbor*.

12. Richeson statement in Thomas, *Don't Call Me Rosie*, 104.

13. "Sunday, 21 May 1944, 0000–2400 Watch," USN Deck Logs, LST 39.

14. Carbaugh recollection in Wright, "West Loch Remembered."

15. "Sunday, 21 May '44, 00–24 Watch," USN Deck Logs, LST 43.

16. Zuehlke testimony in Navy Board of Inquiry, OJAG, 41–42.

17. Kirkes statement in Flick, "Second Tragedy at Pearl Harbor Is Little Known"; Reed recollection in *The Other Tragedy at Pearl Harbor.*

18. Wachter recollection in Johnson, *The West Loch Story,* 155.

19. Interview of unknown sailor from LST #69 at an LST reunion, date and interviewer unknown.

20. Pearce interview, 56.

21. Claven recollection in Johnson, *The West Loch Story,* 96–97.

22. Johnson reminiscence in ibid., 158–59; Johnson, "The Other Pearl Harbor Disaster," 7; Arbuckle citation in *United States Coast Guard Book of Valor,* www.uscg.mil/History/awards/Book_of_Valor_WWII.asp, accessed June 2009.

23. Casavant testimony in Navy Board of Inquiry, OJAG, 44.

24. Anderson and Gott testimonies in ibid., 41, 47.

25. Gott testimony in ibid., 39, 48.

26. Angelich testimony in ibid., 43–44.

27. "Sunday, 21 May 1944, 12–16 Watch," USN Deck Logs, LST 274.

28. Tidwell interview; Slater interview.

29. Sutcliffe reminiscence in Johnson, *The West Loch Story,* 116–17.

30. Broadwell interview.

31. Birch interview.

32. "Sunday, 21 May 1944, 12–16 Watch," USN Deck Logs, LST 225.

33. Cobb reminiscence in Johnson, *The West Loch Story,* 99.

34. Kaiser interview.

35. Hoyt testimony in Navy Board of Inquiry, OJAG, 21, 24–25.

36. Ibid., 18–19.

37. "Sunday, 21 May 1944, 1200 Watch," USN Deck Logs, LST 205.

Chapter 10

1. "Sunday, 21 May 1944, 12–16 Watch," USN Deck Logs, LST 222.

2. "Sunday, 21 May 1944, 12–16 Watch," USN Deck Logs, LST 461.

3. Futterman, "Jack S. Futterman, Oral History," 15–16.

4. Cavalier interview.

5. Tanase letter to author, July 2008; Fritts interview.

6. "Sunday, 21 May 1944, 0900–1600 Watch," USN Deck Logs, LST 23.

7. Unknown author's reminiscence in "The Voyage of the '23': Part 2."

8. "Sunday, 21 May 1944, 12–16 Watch," USN Deck Logs, LST 340.

9. Cooper reminiscence in Petty, *Saipan*, 105.

10. Tesori reminiscence in Johnson, *The West Loch Story*, 154.

11. "Sunday, 21 May 1944, 12 to 16 Watch," USN Deck Logs, LST 224.

12. Farrow reminiscence in Smith, *The Saga of LST 224*, 165.

13. Gregory reminiscence in ibid., 188.

14. Schofield and Gregory reminiscences in ibid., 179, 188; "Sunday, 21 May 1944, 12 to 16 Watch," USN Deck Logs, LST 224.

15. Williams reminiscence in Smith, *The Saga of LST 224*, 112.

16. Harter reminiscence in ibid., 136–37.

17. "Sunday, 21 May 1944, 12–16 Watch," USN Deck Logs, LST 240.

18. Gooley reminiscence in Johnson, *The West Loch Story*, 146.

19. Sacco, "LST 480."

20. Knebel to author, July 2008.

21. "Sunday, 21 May 1944, 1200–1600 Watch," USN Deck Logs, LST 127.

22. Tabin letter to Paul (?), 10 March 2002, from Hillibush, August 2008.

23. "Sunday, 21 May 1944, 1200–1600 Watch," USN Deck Logs, LST 166.

24. Erickson, diary, entry for 21 May 1944.

25. MacNealy, *Life History of Richard MacNealy*, unpublished, 2008; MacNealy interview.

26. Maxam reminiscence in Johnson, *The West Loch Story*, 130.

27. "Sunday, 21 May 1944, 1200–1600 Watch," USN Deck Logs, LST 244.

28. Johnson reminiscence in Johnson, *The West Loch Story*, 149.

29. "Sunday, 21 May 1944, 12 to 20 Watch," USN Deck Logs, LST 275.

30. "Sunday, 21 May 1944, 1200–1600 Watch," USN Deck Logs, LST 42.

31. Warren, "The 'Second' Pearl Harbor," 35.

32. Drotovick reminiscence in Johnson, *The West Loch Story*, 104.

33. Fahnestock reminiscence in ibid., 105.

Chapter 11

1. "Sunday, 21 May 1944, 12 to 16 Watch," USN Deck Logs, USS *Overton*, APD 23.

2. "Excerpts from the Quartermaster's Log," USS *Overton*, APD 23.

3. "Excerpts from the Log of the U.S.S. *Waters* (APD 8) of May 21, 1944," RG 24, NA; "USS *Waters* (DD-115)" http://en.wikipedia.org /wiki/USS_Waters_(DD-115), accessed August 2008.

4. "Sunday, 21 May 1944, 12 to 16 Watch," USN Deck Logs, USS *Overton*, APD 23.

5. Folstad account in *The Four Stack APDs*, 104.

6. "Sunday, 21 May 1944, 12–16 Watch," USN Deck Logs, LST 273.

7. Gourlay recollection in Johnson, *The West Loch Story*, 146–47.

8. "Sunday, 21 May 1944, 0900–1800 Watch," USN Deck Logs, LST 169.

9. Cook reminiscence in Johnson, *The West Loch Story*, 144.

10. "Wednesday, 24 May 1944, 1200–1600 Watch," USN Deck Logs, LST 272; Danio reminiscence in Johnson, *The West Loch Story*, 157.

11. "Sunday, 21 May 1944, 0900–1600 Watch," USN Deck Logs, LST 20; Bloomfield, Church, Hammond, and Tezanos citations in *United States Coast Guard Book of Valor*; Time 1534 Occurrence, "Chronology of Occurrences of West Loch Fire."

12. "Sunday, 21 May 1944, 1200–1600 Watch," USN Deck Logs, LST 334.

13. "Sunday, 21 May 1944, 12–16 Watch," USN Deck Logs, LST 34.

14. "Sunday, 21 May 1944, 12–16 Watch," USN Deck Logs, LST 45.

15. "Sunday, 21 May 1944, 12–16 Watch," USN Deck Logs, LST 121.

16. "Sunday, 21 May 1944, 12 to 16 Watch," USN Deck Logs, LST 126.

17. Hillman, "50 Yard Line Seats."

18. Lux, "Captain Donald Lux, LST 35-126, West Loch, May 21, 1944"; Lux to Dale Moore and Bernard Hillman, 24 January 2001.

19. "Sunday, 21 May 1944, 1200–1600 Watch," USN Deck Logs, LST 242; Kennedy to Commanding Officer, "Fire in West Loch, May 21, 1944—Report on," 24 May 1944.

20. "Sunday, 21 May 1944, 1200–1600 Watch," USN Deck Logs, LST 242.

21. Moore interview.

22. Goodman, "The Second Pearl Harbor."

23. "Sunday, 21 May 1944, 12–16 Watch," USN Deck Logs, LST 129.

24. "Sunday, 21 May 1944, 0800–2400 Watch," USN Deck Logs, LST 128.

25. Craven, "Another Sunday in Pearl Harbor, May 21, 1944," 2.

26. "Sunday, 21 May 1944, 12–16 Watch," USN Deck Logs, USS *Terror*.

27. Beeghly statement in Kakesako, "Survivors Recall West Loch."

28. Shuman, "The Other Pearl Harbor Disaster," 33, 35.

29. Time 1510 Occurrence, "Chronology of Occurrences of West Loch Fire."

30. Arieta statements in Hill, "Veteran Recalls Forgotten WWII Disaster."

31. Wells, *The Quack Corps*, 104.

32. Boulware reminiscence in Johnson, *The West Loch Story*, 127–28.

33. Spence, "76th Seabees of World War II."

34. Meehan reminiscence in *The Four Stack APDs*, 37.

35. Bernal recollection in *The Other Tragedy at Pearl Harbor*; Bernal statement in Kakesako, "Survivors Recall West Loch."

36. Sannella, *My Nine Lives*, 10; Sannella statement in Kakesako, "Survivors Recall West Loch."

37. Clark, "Dispatch 3: Hawaii, A Young Man Discovers the Navy."

38. Thomey, *Immortal Images*, 91–95; Harrold Weinberger filmography in www.imdb.com/name/nm0918166/, accessed May 2009; Weinberger reminiscence in Johnson, *The West Loch Story*, 120–21.

39. Jones recollection in Johnson, *The West Loch Story*, 160.

Chapter 12

1. U.S. Navy, "Report of Explosion at West Loch," 1.

2. Lockwood testimony in Navy Board of Inquiry, OJAG, 16.

3. Thomas testimony in ibid., 14, 15.

4. "Sunday, 21 May 1944, 000–2400 Watch," USN Deck Logs, LST 39.

5. Alsaker reminiscence in Johnson, *The West Loch Story*, 94.

6. Ernest Lefner, "James Robert Maloney," *UAlbany Veterans Project*, www.albany.edu/alumni/VETERANS/archives/individuals/maloney.htm, accessed May 2009.

7. Carbaugh recollection in Wright, "West Loch Remembered."

8. Thomas testimony in Navy Board of Inquiry, OJAG, 14.

9. Carbaugh recollection in Wright, "West Loch Remembered."

10. Clements recollection in Johnson, *The West Loch Story*, 98.

11. Thompson recollection in Johnson, *The West Loch Story*, 137.

12. Harmer recollection in Thomas, *Don't Call Me Rosie*, 105.

13. Frawley recollection in *The Other Tragedy at Pearl Harbor*; Frawley statement in McNeeley, "Remembering the Disaster at West Loch."

14. Seehode recollection in Johnson, *The West Loch Story*, 132.

15. Zuehlke testimony in Navy Board of Inquiry, OJAG, 42–43.

16. Gott testimony in ibid., 38.

17. Dinwiddie testimony in ibid., 35.

18. Hedges reminiscence in Johnson, *The West Loch Story*, 106–107.

19. Pearce interview, 56.

20. Angelich testimony in Navy Board of Inquiry, OJAG, 35.

21. Silva testimony in ibid., 32–33.

22. "Sunday, 21 May 1944, 12–16 Watch," USN Deck Logs, LST 274.

23. Tidwell interview.

24. Slater interview.

25. Hoyt testimony in Navy Board of Inquiry, OJAG, 19.

26. Kaiser interview.

27. "Sunday, 21 May 1944, 12–16 Watch," USN Deck Logs, LST 225.

28. Hoyt testimony in Navy Board of Inquiry, OJAG, 22.

29. "Sunday, 21 May 1944, 1200 Watch," USN Deck Logs, LST 205.

30. Kirkes statement in Flick, "Second Tragedy at Pearl Harbor Is Little Known"; Reed recollection in *The Other Tragedy at Pearl Harbor*.

31. "Sunday, 21 May 1944, 12–16 Watch," USN Deck Logs, LST 225.

Chapter 13

1. "Sunday, 21 May 1944, 12–16 Watch," USN Deck Logs, LST 222.

2. "Sunday, 21 May 1944, 12–16 Watch," USN Deck Logs, LST 461.

3. Cavalier interview; "Sunday, 21 May 1944, 12–16 Watch," USN Deck Logs, LST 461.

4. Montague recollection in *The Other Tragedy at Pearl Harbor*; Montague statements in McNeeley, "Remembering the Disaster at West Loch."

5. Sortevik reminiscence in "The Voyage of the '23': Part 2."

6. "Sunday, 21 May 1944, 12–16 Watch," USN Deck Logs, LST 340; Cooper reminiscence in Petty, *Saipan*, 105; Tesori reminiscence in Johnson, *The West Loch Story*, 154.

7. Cooper reminiscence in Johnson, *The West Loch Story*, 101; Cooper reminiscence in Petty, *Saipan*, 105.

8. Hoffman reminiscence in Smith, *The Saga of LST 224*, 198.

9. Harter letter of commendation in ibid., 139.

10. Harter reminiscences in ibid., 125, 136.

11. Kalencik statement in ibid., 140.

12. Schofield reminiscence in ibid., 179.

13. Simpson reminiscence in Johnson, *The West Loch Story*, 115–16.

14. "Sunday, 21 May 1944, 12–16 Watch," USN Deck Logs, LST 240.

15. Freer interview.

16. Knebel to author, July 2008.

17. MacNealy interview.

18. Erickson, diary, entry for 21 May 1944.

19. "Sunday, 21 May 1944, 1200–1600 Watch," USN Deck Logs, LST 166.

20. "Sunday, 21 May 1944, 1200–1600 Watch," USN Deck Logs, LST 127.

21. Hillibush letter to author, August 2008.

22. "Sunday, 21 May 1944, 1200–1600 Watch," USN Deck Logs, LST 244.

23. Rupprath, "West Loch Disaster," 24.

24. "Sunday, 21 May 1944, 1200–1600 Watch," USN Deck Logs, LST 244.

25. Johnson reminiscence in Johnson, *The West Loch Story*, 149.

26. "Sunday, 21 May 1944, 12 to 20 Watch," USN Deck Logs, LST 275.

27. Warren, "The 'Second' Pearl Harbor," 35.

28. "Sunday, 21 May 1944, 0800–2400 Watch," USN Deck Logs, LST 128.

Chapter 14

1. "Sunday, 21 May 1944, 12–16 Watch," USN Deck Logs, USS *Overton*, APD 23.

2. "Sunday, 21 May 1944, 12–16 Watch," USN Deck Logs, LST 273.

3. Gourlay reminiscence in Johnson, *The West Loch Story*, 147–48.

4. "Sunday, 21 May 1944, 0900–1800 Watch," USN Deck Logs, LST 169.

5. "Sunday, 21 May 1944, 0900–1800 Watch," USN Deck Logs, LST 272; Cook reminiscence in Johnson, *The West Loch Story*, 144.

6. "Sunday, 21 May 1944, 0900–1600 Watch," USN Deck Logs, LST 20; Time 1534 Occurrence, "Chronology of Occurrences of West Loch Fire."

7. "Sunday, 21 May 1944, 1200–1600 Watch," USN Deck Logs, LST 334.

8. "Sunday, 21 May 1944, 12–16 Watch," USN Deck Logs, LST 45.

9. Moses recollection in Johnson, *The West Loch Story*, 150.

10. "Sunday, 21 May 1944, 12–16 Watch," USN Deck Logs, LST 121.

11. "Sunday, 21 May 1944, 12 to 16 Watch," USN Deck Logs, LST 126.

12. Hillman, "50 Yard Line Seats."

13. Lux to Dale Moore and Bernard Hillman, 24 January 2001; Lux, "Captain Donald Lux, LST 35-126, West Loch, May 21, 1944."

14. "Sunday, 21 May 1944, 1200–1600 Watch," USN Deck Logs, LST 242.

15. Moore interview.

16. Koehler, "May 21, 1944, Aboard U.S.S. LST 242."

17. "Sunday, 21 May 1944, 1200–1600 Watch," USN Deck Logs, LST 354.

18. Yeomanjoe reminiscence from www.pearlharborattacked.com/cgi-bin/IKONBOARDNEW312a/ikonboard.cgi?act=ST;f=35;t=6;&#top, accessed May 2009.

19. "Sunday, 21 May 1944, 12–16 Watch," USN Deck Logs, USS *Terror*.

20. Goodman, "The Second Pearl Harbor."

Chapter 15

1. Time 1519 and 1520 Occurrence, in "Chronology of Occurrences of West Loch Fire."

2. Time 1520, 1523, 1527, and 1529 Occurrence, in ibid.

3. Sannella, *My Nine Lives*, 10.

4. Bernal statement in TheHawaiiChannel, "Navy Recognizes 'Other' Pearl Harbor Tragedy"; Bernal interview in KITV broadcast, 21 May 2009, www.kitv.com/news/19532348/detail.html, accessed 15 June 2009; Bernal statement in McNeeley, "Remembering the Disaster at West Loch."

5. Bernal recollection in *The Other Tragedy at Pearl Harbor*.

6. Bloomfield, Church, Hammond, and Tezanos citations in *United States Coast Guard Book of Valor*.

7. "Sunday, 21 May 1944, 1600–2400 Watch," USN Deck Logs, LST 20.

8. Johnson reminiscence in Johnson, *The West Loch Story*, 159; Johnson, "The Other Pearl Harbor Disaster," 7.

9. Hillman, "50 Yard Line Seats."

10. Wells, *The Quack Corps*, 107–108.

11. Arieta statements in Hill, "Veteran Recalls Forgotten WWII Disaster."

12. Spence, "76th Seabees of World War II."
13. Boulware reminiscence in Johnson, *The West Loch Story*, 127.
14. Weinberger in ibid., 121.
15. "Destruction of Six LSTs," 1.
16. Dyer, *The Amphibians Came to Conquer*, 894.
17. Alexander, *Storm Landings*, 69n.

Chapter 16

1. "Destruction of Six LSTs," 1; Shuman, "The Other Pearl Harbor Disaster," 34.
2. Shuman, "The Other Pearl Harbor Disaster," 36; Shuman, "The Pearl Harbor Disaster No One Has Heard Of," 19; Boulware reminiscence in Johnson, *The West Loch Story*, 127–28.
3. "Sunday, 21 May 1944, 000–2400 Watch," USN Deck Logs, LST 39.
4. Sheppard testimony in Navy Board of Inquiry, OJAG, 52.
5. "Sunday, 21 May 1944, 00–24 Watch," USN Deck Logs, LST 43.
6. Zuehlke testimony in Navy Board of Inquiry, OJAG, 43–45.
7. Anderson testimony in ibid., 32.
8. Silva testimony in ibid., 33.
9. Gott testimony in ibid., 29–30, 39–40.
10. "Sunday, 21 May 1944, 12–16 Watch," USN Deck Logs, LST 274.
11. Broadwell interview.
12. Ellis statement in Berry, *Semper Fi, Mac*, 207.
13. Slater interview.
14. Broadwell interview.
15. Birch interview.
16. "Sunday, 21 May 1944, 12–16 Watch," USN Deck Logs, LST 225.
17. Hovis reminiscence in Johnson, *The West Loch Story*, 107.
18. "Sunday, 21 May 1944, 1200 Watch," USN Deck Logs, LST 205.
19. Pearce interview, 57.
20. Slater interview.
21. Hoyt testimony in Navy Board of Inquiry, OJAG, 21.

Chapter 17

1. Futterman, "Jack S. Futterman, Oral History, 15–16.
2. "Sunday, 21 May 1944, 12–16 Watch," USN Deck Logs, LST 461.

3. "Sunday, 21 May 1944, 0900–1600 and 1600–2400 Watches," USN Deck Logs, LST 23; Time 1542, 1555, 1558, and 1603 Occurrences, "Chronology of Occurrences of West Loch Fire."

4. "Sunday, 21 May 1944, 12–16 Watch" and "Tuesday, 23 May 1944 00–04 Watch," USN Deck Logs, LST 340; 1530 Occurrence, "Chronology of Occurrences of West Loch Fire."

5. "Sunday, 21 May 1944, 12 to 16 and 16 to 20 Watches," USN Deck Logs, LST 224.

6. "Sunday, 21 May 1944, 12–16 and 16–20 Watches," and attachment entitled, "USS LST 240, 21 May 1944, Survivors aboard this vessel this date," USN Deck Logs, LST 240.

7. Freer interview.

8. Knebel to author, July 2008.

9. Hoyt testimony in Navy Board of Inquiry, OJAG, 24–25; Shuman, "The Other Pearl Harbor Disaster," 35.

10. Sacco, "LST 480."

11. Knebel to author, July 2008.

12. Sacco, "LST 480"; Kierl autobiography in Barger, *Large Slow Target: A History of the LST*, 156.

13. Hill, "Veteran Recalls Forgotten WWII Disaster"; Paulus statement in Alexander, *Storm Landings*, 69n.

14. Erickson, diary, entry for 21 May 1944.

Chapter 18

1. Photo #80-G-276913, "Burning LSTs in West Loch, Pearl Harbor, May 1944," NA; "Destruction of Six LSTs," 2.

2. Pearce interview, 58; Freer interview.

3. Slater interview.

4. Reed recollection in *The Other Tragedy at Pearl Harbor*.

5. Swallow reminiscence in Johnson, *The West Loch Story*, 119; "Vet Recalls 'Second Pearl Harbor.'"

6. Wachter reminiscence in Johnson, *The West Loch Story*, 155.

7. Ellis statement in Berry, *Semper Fi, Mac*, 207.

8. Pearce interview, 58–59.

9. Tidwell interview.

10. Knebel to author, July 2008.

11. Slater interview.

12. Claven reminiscence in Johnson, *The West Loch Story*, 97.

13. Cobb reminiscence in ibid., 100.

14. Thompson reminiscence in ibid., 139.

15. Well, *The Quack Corps*, 108–109.

16. Arieta statements in Hill, "Veteran Recalls Forgotten WWII Disaster."

17. Pearce interview.

18. Knebel to author, July 2008.

19. Goldberg, *D-Day in the Pacific*, 49.

20. Hillman, "50 Yard Line Seats."

21. Bernal recollection in *The Other Tragedy at Pearl Harbor*"; Bernal statement in Sample, "Deadly 1944 Pearl Harbor Disaster Remembered"; Bernal statements in Kakesako, "Survivors Recall West Loch."

Chapter 19

1. Time 1543 Occurrence, "Chronology of Occurrences of West Loch Fire."

2. Time 1610 Occurrence, "Chronology of Occurrences of West Loch Fire"; "Sunday, 21 May 1944, 1200–1600 and 1600–2000 Watches," USN Deck Logs, LST 272; Lux, "Captain Donald Lux, LST 35-126, West Loch, May 21, 1944."

3. "Sunday, 21 May 1944, 1600–2400 Watch," USN Deck Logs, LST 23; Sortevik reminiscence in "The Voyage of the '23': Part 2." LST #23 rescued survivors from the following ships: LST #39, 2; LST #166, 1; LST #179, 1; LST #340, 7; LST #353, 1. Also, one person belonging to the 534th Amphibious Tractor Battalion was taken aboard.

4. Time 1549 and 1551 Occurrences, "Chronology of Occurrences of West Loch Fire."

5. "Sunday, 21 May 1944, 1200–1600 and 1600–1800 Watches," USN Deck Logs, LST 242; Time 1612, 1617, and 1630 Occurrences, "Chronology of Occurrences of West Loch Fire."

6. Time 1616, 1617, 1618, and 1625 Occurrences in ibid.

7. Time 1630 Occurrence in ibid.

8. George interview.

9. Shuman, "The Other Pearl Harbor Disaster," 35; Photo #80-G-276913, "Burning LSTs in West Loch, Pearl Harbor, May 1944," NA.

10. Shuman, "The Other Pearl Harbor Disaster," 34–35; Photo #80-G-276945 "USS LST-480 Burning in Pearl Harbor, 23 May 1944," NA; Time 1650 Occurrence, "Chronology of Occurrences of West Loch Fire."

11. Shuman, "The Other Pearl Harbor Disaster," 34.

12. Ibid., 34–35.

13. Ibid., 36; Bohlmann reminiscence in Johnson, *The West Loch Story*, 143; U.S. Navy, "Report of Explosion at West Loch," 1–2.

14. Time 1702, 1705, 1707, 1710, 1711, 1720, 1722, 1730, 1731, 1810, and 1914 Occurrences, "Chronology of Occurrences of West Loch Fire."

15. "Sunday, 21 May 1944, 16–18 Watch," USN Deck Logs, *Terror.*

16. Tabin letter to Paul (?), 10 March 2002, from Hillibush, August 2008; "Sunday, 21 May 1944, 1600–2000 Watch," USN Deck Logs, LST 127.

17. "Sunday, 21 May 1944, 1200–1600 Watch," USN Deck Logs, LST 244.

18. Johnson reminiscence in Johnson, *The West Loch Story*, 149; Crankshaw to author, July 2008.

19. Time 1640, 1645, and 1653 Occurrences, "Chronology of Occurrences of West Loch Fire."

20. Clark, "Dispatch 3: Hawaii, A Young Man Discovers the Navy."

21. Time 1610, 1630, 1637, and 1640 Occurrences, "Chronology of Occurrences of West Loch Fire." The USN fireboats sent to West Loch were X1426, X1428, X1640, and S1425, along with the U.S. Coast Guard fireboat #58728.

22. Schiering reminiscence in Johnson, *The West Loch Story*, 153.

23. Sannella, *My Nine Lives*, 10; Sannella reminiscence in James, "Special Banner to Fly This Flag Day."

24. Jones reminiscence in Johnson, *The West Loch Story*, 160–61; Livingston and Noack, Jr., citation in *United States Coast Guard Book of Valor.*

25. Dyer, *The Amphibians Came to Conquer*, 894–95.

26. Jones reminiscence in Johnson, *The West Loch Story*, 160–61.

27. Hoyt testimony in Navy Board of Inquiry, OJAG, 21.

28. Hovis reminiscence in Johnson, *The West Loch Story*, 107.

29. "Sunday, 21 May 1944, 1200 Watch," USN Deck Logs, LST 205.

30. "Sunday, 21 May 1944, 16–20 Watch," USN Deck Logs, LST 274; "Sunday, 21 May 1944, 1200 Watch," USN Deck Logs, LST 205; "Sunday, 21 May 1944, 16–18 Watch," USN Deck Logs, LST 225; "U.S. Coast Guard USS LST-205," www.uscg.mil/hq/g-cp/history/WEB CUTTERS/LST_205.pdf, accessed May 2008.

31. "Sunday, 21 May 1944, 12 to 16 and 16 to 20 Watches," USN Deck Logs, USS *Overton*, APD 23; "Excerpts from the Quartermaster's Log."

32. "Excerpts from the Log of the U.S.S. *Waters* (APD 8) of May 21, 1944"; "Sunday, 21 May 1944, 16 to 20 Watch," USN Deck Logs, USS *Waters*, APD 8; "USS *Waters* (DD-115)" http://en.wikipedia.org/wiki/USS_Waters_(DD-115), accessed August 2008.

33. Folstad account in *The Four Stack APDs*, 104; "Sunday, 21 May 1944, 12–16 Watch," USN Deck Logs, *Stringham* (APD 6).

34. "Sunday, 21 May 1944, 12 to 16 Watch," USN Deck Logs, LST 224.

35. Williams and Harter reminiscences in Smith, *The Saga of LST 224*, 112, 137.

36. Scale map prepared by Howard E. Shuman in Shuman, "The Other Pearl Harbor Disaster," 35.

Chapter 20

1. Simpson reminiscence in Johnson, *The West Loch Story*, 115.

2. Weinberger reminiscence in ibid., 121–22.

3. Schiering reminiscence in ibid., 153.

4. Shuman, "The Other Pearl Harbor Disaster," 35; Photo #80-G-276913 "Burning LSTs in West Loch, Pearl Harbor, May 1944," NA.

5. Shuman, "The Other Pearl Harbor Disaster," 35–36.

6. History of USS *Valve* in "*Valve.*"

7. Hillman, "50 Yard Line Seats."

8. Shuman, "The Other Pearl Harbor Disaster," 34; Time 1940 and 2005 Occurrences, "Chronology of Occurrences of West Loch Fire"; "Excerpts from the Log of the U.S.S. *Waters* (APD 8) of May 21, 1944."

9. Jones reminiscence in Johnson, *The West Loch Story*, 161–62.

10. Wells, *The Quack Corps*, 110.

11. Time 1955, 2003, and 2006 Occurrences, "Chronology of Occurrences of West Loch Fire."

12. Time 2035 Occurrences in ibid.; Shuman, "The Other Pearl Harbor Disaster," 36.

13. Time 2105, 2112, 2125, 2146, and 2154 Occurrences, "Chronology of Occurrences of West Loch Fire."

14. Time 2152, 2230, and 2334 Occurrences in ibid.

15. Time 2227, 0129, 0335, 0510, and 0715 Occurrences in ibid.

Chapter 21

1. Destruction of Six LSTs," 1–2.

2. Ibid., 2–3.

3. Ibid. 3.

4. Ibid., 16.

5. Matthews reminiscence in Goldberg, *D-Day in the Pacific*, 48; Matthews autobiography in "G-Company, 23rd Regiment, Fourth Marine Division," in *Wendell Nightengale, Navarro County, Texas.*

6. "The Voyage of the '23': Part Two."

7. "Monday, 22 May 1944, 1600–1800 Watch," USN Deck Logs, LST 169; "Monday, 22 May 1944, 16–20 Watch," USN Deck Logs, LST 240; "Monday, 22 May 1944, 1600–2000 Watch," USN Deck Logs, LST 272; "Monday, 22 May 1944, 16–18 Watch," USN Deck Logs, LST 461.

8. "Monday, 22 May 1944, 16–20 Watch," USN Deck Logs, LST 45; "Monday, 22 May 1944, 16 to 20 Watch," USN Deck Logs, LST 126.

9. Lux, "Captain Donald Lux, LST 35-126, West Loch, May 21, 1944"; Moses reminiscence in Johnson, *The West Loch Story*, 150–52.

10. Jones reminiscence in Johnson, *The West Loch Story*, 162–63.

11. "Monday, 22 May 1944, 12–16 and 16–20 Watches," USN Deck Logs, LST 129.

12. "Monday, 22 May 1944, 0800, 1600, and 2000 Watches," USN Deck Logs, LST 205.

13. "Sunday, 21 May 1944, 16–20 and 20–24 Watches" and "Monday, 22 May 1944, 4–8, 12–16, and 16–20 Watches," USN Deck Logs, LST 274.

14. "Monday, 22 May 1944, 20–24 Watch," USN Deck Logs, LST 225; Compiled list of Northern Attack Force in Dyer, *The Amphibians Came to Conquer*, 881.

15. Cobb reminiscence in Johnson, *The West Loch Story*, 100.

16. Hovis reminiscence in ibid., 108.

17. "Monday, 22 May 1944, 04–08 and 08–12 Watches," USN Deck Logs, LST 340.

18. "Monday, 22 May 1944, 1200 to 1600 Watch," USN Deck Logs, LST 127; Hoyt testimony in Navy Board of Inquiry, OJAG, 22.

19. "Tuesday, 23 May 1944, 8 to 12 and 12 to 16 Watches," USN Deck Logs, *Overton* (APD 23); Horn statement in Sample, "Deadly 1944 Pearl Harbor Disaster Remembered."

20. Lunney reminiscence in Johnson, *The West Loch Story*, 108–109.

21. Weinberger reminiscence in ibid., 122.

Chapter 22

1. Weinberger reminiscence in Johnson, *The West Loch Story*, 122–23.

2. "Vice Adm. Shafroth Dies; Hero in 2 World Wars"; "Adm. Shafroth Dies at 80"; "Adm. Shafroth Arrives Here and Mum Is the Word."

3. Johnson, *The West Loch Story*, 23–63; Nimitz, letter to Commanding General, U.S. Army Forces, Central Pacific Area on subject, "Court of Inquiry; Forwarding copy of record of proceedings," 12 June 1944, file A17, NA; Shuman, "The Pearl Harbor Disaster No One Has Heard Of," 23.

4. Weinberger reminiscence in Johnson, *The West Loch Story*, 123.

5. CINCPAC press release no. 414, 25 May 1944, NA.

6. Rupprath, "West Loch Disaster," 24.

7. CINCPAC press release no. 443, 14 June 1944, NA.

8. Shuman, "The Pearl Harbor Disaster No One Has Heard Of," 23.

9. Citation for 21 May, Sun, in "Hyperwar: The Official Chronology of the U.S. Navy in World War II, Chapter VI: 1944," www.ibiblio.org/hyperwar/USN/USN-Chron/USN-Chron-1944.html, accessed May 2008.

10. "Tuesday, 23 May 1944, 0 to 4, 4 to 8, and 8 to 12 Watches," USN Deck Logs, LST 19; Nasmyth, "A Journey to War: One Coast Guardsman's World War II Experience Serving Aboard the USS LST-19."

11. Hillibush statement in Thomas, *Don't Call Me Rosie*, 110.

12. Futterman, "Jack S. Futterman, Oral History, Part III—Wartime Experience."

13. Dyer, *The Amphibians Came to Conquer*, 895.

14. Hoffman, *Saipan: The Beginning of the End*, 34.

15. Tidwell interview.

16. Slater interview.

17. MacNealey, *Life Story of Richard MacNealey*.

18. Farrow reminiscence in Smith, *The Saga of LST 224*, 165.

19. Citation for 21 May, Sun, in "Hyperwar: The Official Chronology of the U.S. Navy in World War II, Chapter VI: 1944," www.ibiblio.org/hyperwar/USN/USN-Chron/USN-Chron-1944.html, accessed May 2008.

20. Pearce interview.

21. Hoffman, *Saipan: The Beginning of the End*, 34n108.

22. Pearce interview.

23. Owens, "It's Hard to Dig with No Shovels," in "The Loch Ness Monster: West Loch Story," *Follow Me*, January/February 2002, www.2marine.com/FollowPDFs/Follow01_17-32.pdf, accessed 4 May 2008.

24. Pearce interview.

25. Shuman, "The Pearl Harbor Disaster No One Has Heard Of," 24; Oliver, "Navy's Hushed-Up Tragedy at West Loch."

26. Shuman, "The Pearl Harbor Disaster No One Has Heard Of," 24; Shuman, "The Other Pearl Harbor Disaster," 36.

27. King commentary in Dyer, *The Amphibians Came to Conquer*, 895.

28. Phillips, letter to Fourteenth Naval District et al., "LST Bow Loading and Mooring Berths and Anchorages in the Hawaiian Area," 13 July 1944, NA, 1.

29. Ibid., 2.

30. Bureau of Ships, letter to Chief of Naval Operations, "Court of Inquiry—Explosion at West Loch, Pearl Harbor, T.H.—Deaths of and Injuries to U.S. Naval Personnel—Convened by CINCPAC 22 May 1944," 5 December 1944, NA, 2–3.

31. Sample, "Deadly 1944 Pearl Harbor Disaster Remembered"; Department of the Navy—Naval Historical Center, "Port Chicago Naval Magazine Explosion, 1944," www.history.navy.mil/faqs/faq80-1.htm, accessed August 2009.

Chapter 23

1. Shuman, "The Pearl Harbor Disaster No One Has Heard Of," 14–17; Department of the Navy, "LST-39," "LST-43," "LST-69," "LST-179," "LST-353," and "LST-480," all in *Dictionary of American Naval Fighting Ships.*

2. History of USS *Valve* in *"Valve."*

3. History of USS *Vent* in "USS *Vent* (ARS-29)."

4. McNaught reminiscence in "Ray McNaught, Diver 1/c."

5. Department of the Navy, "LST-39," *Dictionary of American Naval Fighting Ships*; "YF-1079 ex USS LST 39 (1943–1944)," *NavSource Online: Amphibious Photo Archive.*

6. Greenwell oral presentation at Ohio LST Association Reunion, 7 December 2000.

7. Hammerberg citation in *The Congressional Medal of Honor*, 336.

8. LST #267, "Saturday, 21 July 1945 Log Entry."

9. Wright comments from Stone, "The LSTs of Pearl Harbor, Part 2"; Department of the Navy, "LST-179," *Dictionary of American Naval Fighting Ships.*

10. Department of the Navy, "LST-43," *Dictionary of American Naval Fighting Ships.*

Chapter 24

1. "Destruction of Six LSTs," 2.

2. Morison, *History of United States Naval Operations in World War II*, 8:171.

3. Kakesako, "Disaster's Toll Still Debated, but Dead Are Not Forgotten."

4. Ibid.; Kakesako, "36 Killed in Blast to Be Recognized."

5. Warren, "The 'Second' Pearl Harbor."

6. Kierl autobiography in Barger, *Large Slow Target: A History of the LST*, 156; Drotovick and Johnson reminiscences in Johnson, *The West Loch Story*, 104, 160.

7. Slater interview.

8. Sutcliffe reminiscence in Johnson, *The West Loch Story*, 118.

9. Ellis statement in Berry, *Semper Fi, Mac*, 207.

10. Tidwell interview.

11. George interview.

12. Hovis reminiscence in Johnson, *The West Loch Story*, 108.

13. U.S. Marine Corps, "Fourth Marine Division Operations Report Saipan 15 June to 9 July 1944," NA, 18.

14. Hoffman, *Saipan: The Beginning of the End*, 34; Johnston, "Follow Me!" 174.

15. Groshong statement in "Les Groshong, Sergeant, USMC."

16. Knebel to author, July 2008.

17. MacNealy, *Life History of Richard MacNealy*.

18. Schofield reminiscence in Smith, *The Saga of LST 224*, 179.

19. Yeomanjoe reminiscence from www.pearlharborattacked.com/cgi -bin/IKONBOARDNEW312a/ikonboard.cgi?act=ST;f=35;t=6;&#top, accessed May 2009; Sannella reminiscence in James, "Special Banner to Fly This Flag Day"; Hill, "Veteran Recalls Forgotten WWII Disaster"; Garner reminiscence in Johnson, *The West Loch Story*, 145.

20. Bednarczyk interview; Andrus, letter to author, July 2008.

21. Censorship memorandum from *The Other Tragedy at Pearl Harbor*.

22. Tanase to author, July 2008.

23. Wright interview.

24. Tidwell interview.

25. Montague recollection in *The Other Tragedy at Pearl Harbor*.

26. Sannella, *My Nine Lives*, 10.

27. Reed recollection in *The Other Tragedy at Pearl Harbor*; Kirkes statement in Flick, "Second Tragedy at Pearl Harbor Is Little Known."

28. Pearce interview.

29. Johnson reminiscence in Johnson, *The West Loch Story*, 160.

30. Johnson interview.

31. Shuman, "The Other Pearl Harbor Disaster," 36.

32. Oliver, "Navy's Hushed-Up Tragedy at West Loch," 37.

33. Frawley recollection in *The Other Tragedy at Pearl Harbor*.

34. Arieta statements in Hill, "Veteran Recalls Forgotten WWII Disaster."

35. Telegrams from Vandergrift to Stacey family dated 7 June and 4 August 1944, in *The Other Tragedy at Pearl Harbor*.

36. Tagler reminiscence in Johnson, *The West Loch Story*, 134.

37. Freer interview.

38. Drotovick reminiscence in Johnson, *The West Loch Story*, 104; Erickson, diary, entry for 25 May 1944.

39. Montague statement in McNeeley, "Remembering the Disaster at West Loch"; Sannella reminiscence in James, "Special Banner to Fly This Flag Day."

40. Reed recollection in *The Other Tragedy at Pearl Harbor.*

41. Carbaugh statement in Wright, "West Loch Remembered"; Slater interview.

Bibliography

Government Documents

Bureau of Ships. Letter to Chief of Naval Operations, "Court of Inquiry—Explosion at West Loch, Pearl Harbor, T.H.—Deaths of and Injuries to U.S. Naval Personnel—Convened by CINCPAC 22 May 1944." 5 December 1944. National Archives.

"Chronology of Occurrences of West Loch Fire on 21–22 May 1944." Office of the Judge Advocate General.

"Confidential Report Dated 21 May 1944, from U.S.S. LST 485 to SECNAV." USN Deck Logs, LST 485, RG 24, National Archives.

"Excerpts from the Log of the U.S.S. *Waters* (APD 8) of May 21, 1944." RG 24, National Archives.

"Excerpts from the Quartermaster's Log," USS *Overton*, APD 23. RG 24, National Archives.

Naval Intelligence Unit. "Destruction of Six LSTs by Explosions and Fire, West Loch, Oahu, T.H., 21 May 1944." 24 July 1944. File A17, National Archives.

"Navy Board of Inquiry Investigating the Causes of the Explosion and Fire at West Loch, Pearl Harbor." Office of the Judge Advocate General.

Nimitz, Adm. Chester A. Letter to Commanding General, U.S. Army Forces, Central Pacific Area on subject, "Court of Inquiry; Forwarding copy of record of proceedings," June 12, 1944, file A17, National Archives.

"Outline Log for May 1 through 1507, May 21, 1944 and Thereafter through May 31, 1944," USN Deck Logs, USS LST 179, RG 24, National Archives.

Phillips, W. B. Letter to Fourteenth Naval District et al. "LST Bow Loading and Mooring Berths and Anchorages in the Hawaiian Area." 13 July 194. National Archives.

U.S. Marine Corps, "Fourth Marine Division Operations Report Saipan, 15 June to 9 July 1944," National Archives.

U.S. Navy. "Report of Explosion at West Loch, Pearl Harbor, T.H., 21 May 1944," 27 February 1946, file #326, National Archives.

USN Deck Logs, LSTs 19, 20, 23, 31, 34, 39, 42, 43, 45, 71, 121, 124, 126, 127, 128, 129, 166, 169, 205, 222, 224, 225, 226, 240, 244, 246, 272, 273, 274, 275, 334, 340, 354, 461, 484, 485, *Manley, Overton, Stringam, Terror, Waters*, RG 24, National Archives.

Correspondence and Interviews

Andrus, Ernie. Electronic letter to author, July 17, 2008.

Bednarczyk, Leo. Interview by author, August 5, 2008.

———. Interview by Paul Zarbock, University of North Carolina at Wilmington, May 22, 2002, Transcript no. 270, http://capefearww2.uncwil.edu/voices/leo_bednarczyk270.html, accessed May 2009.

Broadwell, Bob. Interview by author, July 1, 2008.

Cavalier, Vincent. Interview by author, July 9, 2008.

Crankshaw, Milo F. Letter to author. July 18, 2008.

Craven, Frank. Letter to author, August 30, 2008.

Drake, Carlton. Interview by author, August 30, 2008.

Freer, Arthur T. Interview by author, July 9, 2008.

Fritts, Dr. Harry. Interview by author, July 8, 2008.

Funderburg, Lonnie. Interview by author, July 30 and August 3, 2008.

Futterman, Jack S. "Jack S. Futterman, Oral History, Part III—Wartime Experience." Social Security Administration: Oral History Interview, www.ssa.gov/history/jfpart3.html, accessed April 2001.

Hillibush, Francis T. Letter to author, August 18, 2008.

Johnson, William L. C. Interview at LST Reunion, date and interviewer unknown.

Kaiser, Ford. Interview by author, July 1, 2008.

Kennedy, J. P. Letter to the Commanding Officer [LT J. W. Winney, LST #242], "Fire in West Loch, May 21, 1944—Report on," 24 May 1944, from Dale Moore.

Knebel, Harold J. Letter to author. July 14, 2008.

Lux, Don. Letter to Dale Moore and Bernard Hillman, January 24, 2001.

MacNealy, Richard. Interview by author, August 3, 2008.

Moore, Dale. Interview by author, July 29, 2008.

Pearce, Harry. Interview by Dr. Richard Verrone, session 2 of 3, December 10, 2003. www.vietnam.ttu.edu/oralhistory/interviews/browse/ohp.php, accessed June 2008.

Slater, Walter. Interview by author. August 11, 2008.

Strimple, James Hoyt. Interview by Jessica Ding, William Johnson, and Sandra Stewart Holyoak, side 2, tape 1 and side 1, tape 2, October 17, 2006. http://oralhistory.rutgers.edu/Interviews/strimple_james.html, accessed July 2008.

Tabin, Seymore. Letter to Paul (?), March 10, 2002. Received from Francis T. Hillibush, August 2008.

Tanase, Margret. Letter to author, July 2, 2008.

Tidwell, Kenneth. Interview by author, August 11, 2008.

Wright, William J., Jr. Interview by author, July 8, 2008.

Unpublished and Web Sources

Clark, Bill. "Dispatch 3: Hawaii, A Young Man Discovers the Navy." www.the-athenaeum.net/dispatches/stories/hawaii.html, accessed June 23, 2008.

Cooney, Lisa. "Francis T. Hillibush." www.republicanherald.com, accessed June 2008.

Craven, Frank. "Another Sunday in Pearl Harbor, May 21, 1944." Memoirs, n.d. Supplied by Craven to author, August 30, 2008.

Department of the Navy. "LST-20," "LST-39," "LST-43," "LST-69," "LST-179," "LST-353," and "LST-480." *Dictionary of American Naval Fighting Ships.* www.history.navy.mil/danfs/19/lst-20.htm, accessed May 2008.

Dougherty, John H. *The USS LST 481.* www.ibiblio.org/hyperwar/USN/ships/LST/LST-481-history.html, accessed August 4, 2008.

Erickson, Alfred E. Wartime diary: 1944 to 1946. U.S. Coast Guard Museum, New London, CT.

Fischer, John. "A Brief History of Pearl Harbor prior to World War II." http://gohawaii.about.com/cs/pearlharbor/a/Lest_We_Forget1.htm?p=1, accessed July 30, 2008.

"Fourth Marine Division Operations Report Saipan 15 June to 9 July 1944." www.american-divisions.com/doc.asp?documentid=113&pagenumber=1, accessed July 23, 2008.

"The Fuel System." www.chl.chalmers.se/mrk/cdrom_ROC/smcp/fuel system.pps, accessed July 28, 2008.

"G-Company, 23rd Regiment, Fourth Marine Division." In *Wendell Nightengale, Navarro County, Texas*. www.txgenweb6.org/txnavarro /biographies/n/nightengale_wendell.htm, accessed May 2009.

Geis, C. P. "Memorandum to Ship's Company," 22 May 1944. Courtesy of Margaret Tanase.

Greenwell, Paul. Oral presentation at Ohio LST Association Reunion, December 7, 2000.

Groshong, Les. "Les Groshong, Sergeant, USMC." Thu July 19, 2007 4:08 pm posting, www.gruntsmilitary.com/forum/viewtopic.php?t= 8557, accessed July 2008.

Hillman, Bernard M. "50 Yard Line Seats . . . for a Show I Would Rather Have Missed." www.emmitsburg.net/archive_list/articles/history /ww2/stories/west_lock.htm, accessed May 21, 2008.

History of high-speed transports *USS Manley* (APD-1), *USS Stringham* (APD-6), *USS Waters* (APD-8), and *USS Overton* (APD-23). www .destroyerhistory.org/flushdeck/apd_ships.html, accessed August 6, 2008.

"History of U.S.S. LST 334." http://home.st.net.au/~dunn/usnavy /usslst-334.htm, accessed July 2008.

"Landing Ship, Tank (LST)." www.globalsecurity.org/military/systems /ship/lst.htm, accessed July 27, 2008.

"Landing Ship Tank." http://home.comcast.net/~usslst173/lst173htm files/LST173_Basic_LST_Info.htm, accessed July 23, 2008.

"List of American Military Reservations and Concrete Gun Batteries: The Harbor Defenses of Pearl Harbor, Hawaii." www.cdsg.org/maps pdf/HDHI1921.pdf, accessed August 3, 2008.

LST #267. "Saturday, 21 July 1945 Log Entry." http://usslst267.com /ships_log.htm, accessed May 2009.

MacNealy, Richard. "Life History of Richard MacNealy." Manuscript, 2008.

"Maui's World War II Legacy: The Hazards of Training," National Oceanic and Atmospheric Administration, National Marine Sanctuaries. http://sanctuaries.noaa.gov/maritime/expeditions/maui/hazards .html, accessed March 2013.

Miscellaneous LST information. www.insidelst.com/, accessed July 28, 2008.

Nasmyth, Walter. "A Journey to War: One Coast Guardsman's World War II Experience Serving Aboard the USS LST-19." www.uscg .mil/history/WEBCUTTERS/LST_19_Nasmyth_Memoir.html, accessed July 2008.

NavSource Online: Amphibious Photo Archive. www.navsource.org /archives, accessed July 2008.

The Other Tragedy at Pearl Harbor. History Channel documentary, DVD, Cat. no. AAE-72425, 2001.

"Owen Francis Patrick Hammerberg." www.goldengatewing.org/prop talk/speaker.cfm?ID=19, accessed June 2009.

Owens, Donald. "It's Hard to Dig with No Shovels," in "The Loch Ness Monster: West Loch Story," *Follow Me,* January/February 2002, www.2marine.com/FollowPDFs/Follow01_17-32.pdf, accessed May 4, 2008.

Paull, Bill. "Camp Tarawa Hilo, Hawi, Kohala, December 1943–June 1944." www.microworks.net/pacific/personal/bill_paull5.htm, accessed August 2008.

"Pearl Harbor and Outlying Islands: U.S. Navy Base Construction in World War II: Island of Oahu." www.history.navy.mil/library/online /constructpearlww2.htm#Oahu, accessed August 2008.

Rath, J. Arthur. "Secret at West Loch." http://starbulletin.com/2007 /05/20/editorial/special.html, accessed May 2008.

"Ray McNaught, Diver 1/c." www.goldengatewing.org/proptalk/speaker .cfm?ID=19, accessed June 2009.

Ryan, Allie, and David Mincey. *USS* Terror: *War Cruise of USS* Terror, *Her Officers and Men, 1942–1947.* www.ringleib.com/terror/Ryan -BookUSSTerror.pdf, accessed July 12, 2008.

Sample, Herbert A. "Deadly 1944 Pearl Harbor Disaster Remembered." www.armytimes.com/news/2009/05/ap_west_loch_disaster _052109/, accessed May 2009.

———. "West Loch's Lost Tale." www.starbulletin.com/news/20090520 _West_Lochs_lost_tale.html, accessed June 2009.

Shuman, Howard E. "The Pearl Harbor Disaster No One Has Heard Of." Manuscript. Naval Historical Center.

Spence, Harry D. "76th Seabees of World War II: Recollections of Harry Spence, EM3c." http://mysite.verizon.net/vzeo0pwz/76thseabees worldwar2/id19.html, accessed May 2009.

Stone, Spessard. "The LSTs of Pearl Harbor, Part 2." http://free pages.genealogy.rootsweb.ancestry.com/~crackerbarrel/LST.html, accessed May 2009.

"USS *Pyro,* Report of Pearl Harbor Attack." Naval Historical Center. www.history.navy.mil/docs/wwii/pearl/ph72.htm, accessed August 3, 2008.

"USS *Vent* (ARS-29)." *Academic Dictionaries and Encyclopedias.* http:// dic.academic.ru/dic.nsf/enwiki/7134635,http://dic.academic.ru/dic .nsf/enwiki/7134635, accessed May 2009.

"*Valve.*" *Dictionary of American Naval Fighting Ships.* www.history.navy .mil/danfs/v1/valve.htm, accessed May 2009.

Various LST Armament Specifications. www.navsource.org/archives/10 /16/16idx.htm, accessed July 2008.

"Vet Recalls 'Second Pearl Harbor.'" http://kansaspost70.us/ww2 _Lamb-JA_02.html, accessed April 2009.

Warships of World War II: Articles: 1944. www.warshipsww2.eu/givetbl .php?language=E&hist=USN_1944_5E, accessed July 20, 2008.

Journal and Newspaper Articles

"Adm. Shafroth Arrives Here and Mum Is the Word," *Rocky Mountain News,* March 29, 1944.

"Adm. Shafroth Dies at 80." *Washington Post,* September 3, 1967.

Carlson, Jim. "More Info on West Loch." *Follow Me,* May/June 2003.

Cianflone, Eugene M. "The West Loch Disaster." *LST Scuttlebutt,* July /August 1997.

Colbert, JO2 Corwin. "Survivor Returns to West Loch Disaster Site." *Hawaii Navy News,* November 23, 2005.

Davidson, Donald. "More Open Letters." *LST Scuttlebutt,* July/August 1999.

Flick, David, "Second Tragedy at Pearl Harbor Is Little Known." *Seattle Times,* May 21, 1997.

Goodman, H. D. "The Second Pearl Harbor." *LST Scuttlebutt,* n.d.

Hill, Angela. "Veteran Recalls Forgotten WWII Disaster." *Oakland Tribune,* May 21, 2004.

James, Mike. "Special Banner to Fly This Flag Day." *LST Scuttlebutt,* November/December 2009, 14.

Johnson, William L. C. "The Other Pearl Harbor Disaster." *Naval History,* Fall 1988.

Kakesako, Gregg K. "Disaster's Toll Still Debated, but Dead Are Not Forgotten." *Honolulu Star Bulletin,* May 22, 2009.

———. "Survivors Recall West Loch." *Honolulu Star Bulletin,* May 22, 2009.

———. "36 Killed in Blast to Be Recognized." *Honolulu Star Bulletin,* August 6, 2006.

Koehler, Karl F. "May 21, 1944, Aboard U.S.S. LST 242." *LST Scuttlebutt,* n.d.

"The Loch Ness Monster: West Loch Story." *Follow Me,* January/February 2002.

Lux, Donald. "Captain Donald Lux, LST 35-126, West Loch, May 21, 1944." *LST Scuttlebutt,* August 1984.

McNeeley, PH2 Chad. "Remembering the Disaster at West Loch." *Hawaii Navy News,* May 18, 2001, A-4.

Oliver, A. Alan. "Navy's Hushed-Up Tragedy at West Loch," *Sea Classics* 38, no. 11 (November 2005).

Rupprath, Bernard A. "West Loch Disaster." *LST Scuttlebutt*, May/June 2004.

Sacco, Art. "LST 480." *LST Scuttlebutt*, January/February 2004, 45.

Shuman, Howard. "The Other Pearl Harbor Disaster." *Naval History*, Summer 1988.

"Vice Adm. Shafroth Dies; Hero in 2 World Wars." *Washington Star*, September 3, 1967.

"The Voyage of the '23': Part 2." *LST Scuttlebutt*, November/December 2003, 22.

Warren, Bill. "The 'Second' Pearl Harbor." *LST Scuttlebutt*, January/February 1994.

Wright, JO2 Devin. "West Loch Remembered." *Hawaii Navy News*, May 28, 2004.

Zajic, Ray. "It Was a Welder's Torch." *Follow Me*, November/December 2002.

Books

Alexander, Joseph H. *Storm Landings: Epic Amphibious Battles in the Central Pacific*. Annapolis, MD: Naval Institute Press, 1997.

Anderson, Charles R. *Western Pacific: The U.S. Army Campaigns of World War II*. Washington: Government Printing Office, 1994.

Arroyo, Ernest. *Pearl Harbor*. New York: Metro Books, 2001.

Barger, Melvin D. *Large Slow Target: A History of the LST*. Toledo: U.S. LST Association. 1986.

Chapin, John C. *Breaking the Outer Ring: Marine Landings in the Marshall Islands*. Washington: Marine Corps Historical Center. 1994.

The Coast Guard at War, vol. 7, *Lost Cutters*. Washington: Historical Section, Public Information Division, U.S. Coast Guard Headquarters, 1947.

The Congressional Medal of Honor: The Names, the Deeds. Chico, CA: Sharp & Dunnigan, 1988.

Costello, John. *The Pacific War, 1941-1945*. New York: Quill, 1982.

Crowl, Philip A. *Campaign in the Marianas*. Washington: Center of Military History, U.S. Army, 1993.

Dunnigan, James F., and Albert A. Nofi. *The Pacific War Encyclopedia*. New York: Checkmark Books, 1998.

Dyer, George C. *The Amphibians Came to Conquer: The Story of Admiral Richmond Kelly Turner*. Vol. 2. Washington: Government Printing Office, 1991.

The Four Stack APDs. Paducah, Ky.: Turner, 2003.

George, Robert L. *Too Young to Vote*. Bend, OR: Maverick, 2001.

Gilbert, Oscar E. *Marine Tank Battles in the Pacific*. Conshohocken, PA: Combined, 2001.

Hammel, Eric, and John E. Lane. *76 Hours: The Invasion of Tarawa*. Pacific, CA: Pacifica Press, 1985.

Hoffman, Carl W. *Saipan: The Beginning of the End*. Washington: Battery Press, 1987.

Hoyt, Edwin P. *Storm over the Gilberts: War in the Central Pacific, 1943*. New York: Van Nostrand Reinhold, 1978.

Johnson, William L. C. *The West Loch Story: Hawaii's Second Greatest Disaster in Terms of Casualties*. Seattle: Westloch, 1986.

Johnston, Richard W. *Follow Me! The Story of the Second Marine Division in World War II*. New York: Random House, 1948.

Landauer, Lyndall, and Don Landauer. *Pearl: The History of the United States Navy in Pearl Harbor*. Lake Tahoe, CA: Flying Cloud Press, 2002.

Mesko, Jim. *Amtracs in Action*. Carrollton, TX: Squadron/Signal, 1993.

Morison, Samuel Eliot. *History of United States Naval Operations in World War II*, vol. 8, *New Guinea and the Marianas*. Urbana: University of Illinois Press, 2001.

Panicello, Joseph Francis. *A Slow Moving Target: The LST of World War II*. 1st Books.com, 2001.

Patten, Juliana Fern, ed. *Another Side of World War II: A Coast Guard Lieutenant in the South Pacific*. Shippensburg, PA: Burd Street Press, 2005.

Petty, Bruce M. *Saipan: Oral Histories of the Pacific War*. Jefferson, NC: McFarland, 2009.

Rhea, Milton A. *War Is Hell*. Victoria, BC: Trafford, 2004.

Rottman, Gordon L. *Guam 1941 & 1944: Loss and Reconquest*. Oxford: Osprey, 2004.

———. *Landing Ship, Tank (LST) 1942–2002*. Oxford: Osprey, 2005.

———. *The Marshall Islands 1944: Operation Flintlock, the Capture of Kwajalein and Eniwetok*. Oxford: Osprey, 2004.

———. *Saipan & Tinian 1944: Piercing the Japanese Empire*. Oxford: Osprey, 2004.

———. *U.S. World War II Amphibious Tactics: Army & Marine Corps, Pacific Theater*. Oxford: Osprey, 2004

———. *World War II Pacific Island Guide: A Geo-Military Study*. Westport, CT: Greenwood Press, 2002.

Salecker, Gene Eric. *Rolling Thunder against the Rising Sun: The Combat History of U.S. Army Tank Battalions in the Pacific in World War II.* Mechanicsburg, PA: Stackpole Books, 2008.

Sannella, Roy. *My Nine Lives: An Autobiography of Roy Sannella.* iUniverse.

Shaw, Henry I., Jr., Bernard C. Nalty, and Edwin T. Turnbladh. *Central Pacific Drive: History of U.S. Marine Corps Operations in World War II.* Vol. 3. Washington: Government Printing Office, 1966.

Smith, Carl V. *The Saga of LST 224.* Jackson, TN: Main Street, 2004.

Stuckey, Sterling, et al. *Call to Freedom: 1865 to the Present.* Austin, TX: Holt, Rinehart and Winston, 2003.

Thomas, Kathleen. *Don't Call Me Rosie: The Women Who Welded the LSTs and the Men Who Sailed on Them.* Tigard, OR: Thomas/Wright, 2004.

Thomey, Tedd. *Immortal Images.* Annapolis, MD: Naval Institute Press, 2008.

United States Coast Guard Book of Valor: A Fact Book of Medals and Decorations Awarded to Coast Guardsmen for Valor during World War II. Washington: Public Relations Division, U.S. Coast Guard, May 1945. www.uscg.mil/History/awards/Book_of_Valor_WWII.asp, accessed June 2009.

Wells, Arthur W. *The Quack Corps.* Chico, CA: Dolart, 1992.

Wisniewski, Richard A. *Pearl Harbor and the* Arizona *Memorial: A Pictorial History.* Honolulu: Pacific Basin Enterprise, 1986.

Wright, Derrick. *Tarawa 1943: The Turning of the Tide.* Oxford: Osprey, 2000.

Zaloga, Steven. *Amtracs: U.S. Amphibious Assault Vehicles.* Oxford: Osprey, 1990.

Index